OLIVER WENDELL HOLMES, JR.

Soldier, Scholar, Judge

TWAYNE'S TWENTIETH-CENTURY AMERICAN BIOGRAPHY SERIES

John Milton Cooper, Jr., General Editor

OLIVER WENDELL HOLMES, JR.

Soldier, Scholar, Judge

Gary J. Aichele

TWAYNE PUBLISHERS • BOSTON
A Division of G. K. Hall & Co.

Copyright 1989 by Gary J. Aichele
All rights reserved
Published by Twayne Publishers
A Division of G. K. Hall & Co.
70 Lincoln Street, Boston, Massachusetts 02111

Twayne's Twentieth-Century
American Biography Series No. 11

Designed by Marne B. Sultz
Produced by Gabrielle B. McDonald
Copyediting supervised by Barbara Sutton
Typeset in 11/13 Goudy by Compset, Inc.

Printed on permanent/durable acid-free paper
and bound in the United States of America

First Printing, 1989

Library of Congress Cataloging-in-Publication Data

Aichele, Gary Jan.
Oliver Wendell Holmes, Jr.—soldier, scholar, judge / Gary J.
Aichele.
p.   cm.—(Twayne's twentieth-century American biography
series ; no. 11)
Bibliography: p.
Includes index.
ISBN 0-8057-7766-0.   ISBN 0-8057-7784-9 (pbk.)
1. Holmes, Oliver Wendell, 1841–1935.   2. Judges—United States—
Biography.   I. Title.   II. Series.
KF8745.H6A62 1989
347.73'2634—dc19
[B]
[347.3073534]
[B]
                                                      88-24750
                                                      CIP

For Wendy

CONTENTS

INTRODUCTION

Thirty years ago, a noted legal scholar commented that Justice Oliver Wendell Holmes, Jr., was "in greater danger than ever of becoming a legend, or more accurately, the subject of several diverse and contradictory legends."[1] This observation remains a fair one. "The Yankee who strayed from Olympus" only to become "the devil's disciple" has more recently been chastised as a friend of late nineteenth-century laissez-faire capitalism in its most virulent form.[2] A new study of Holmes's jurisprudence, however, rejects the argument that his legal theory was primarily "a shield for capitalist interests" in favor of an interpretation that views him as an American "legal positivist" in the English tradition of Jeremy Bentham and John Austin. This study also disputes the assertion that Holmes's legal theory is flawed by certain irreconcilable inconsistencies and internal contradictions.[3] Thus, the "rise and fall" of Justice Holmes's reputation continues unabated, and the significance of his contribution to American jurisprudence remains a subject of scholarly debate.[4]

Whatever the final judgment of the scholars, Holmes's popular reputation remains secure. One of the most celebrated judges in the nation's history, Holmes is the only jurist whose name is commonly associated with that of America's most famous judge, Chief Justice John Marshall. Described by one intellectual historian as "the very perfection and flowering of the New England aristocracy," Holmes is nevertheless esteemed by most Americans as the most democratic of judges.[5] Regardless of whether such a reputation is based more on myth than on reality, it is clear that Holmes's intellectual power, command of language, and association in the public mind with progressive ideas distinguish him as "an especially noteworthy representative of American civilization."[6]

Nevertheless, it is difficult to study the life and work of Oliver Wendell Holmes, Jr., for very long without becoming uncomfortably aware of the enigmatic nature of this seminal figure in American legal history. As at least one observer has noted, Holmes increasingly withdrew behind a carefully constructed "public mask," an official personality that permitted him to "step out

ix

of life."[7] Thus, Holmes's personal detachment and isolation provides at least a partial explanation for his historical inscrutability. Another factor, however, that may account for the difficulty in understanding this complex individual is the unusually paradoxical nature of his impact on American history and society. Agreeing that "the significance of his genius would evaporate in any analysis of specific decisions," one biographer concluded that "the apotheosis of Holmes defeats understanding." He offered the following evidence in support of his judgment:

> Primarily interested in the common law, as a judge Holmes greatly influenced only constitutional law. Remarkably dogmatic, Holmes exemplifies "humility." Fatalistic, mistrustful of reason, and obsessed with the ubiquity of force, Holmes is nevertheless classified with John Dewey. Generally indifferent to civil liberties interests, Holmes is regarded as their champion. Unconcerned with contemporary realities, Holmes inspires a school of legal "realists." Uninvolved with the life of his society, Holmes affected it profoundly.[8]

Such a summary suggests that any synthetic analysis or interpretive study of Holmes's life and work will be hard pressed to explain adequately seemingly unexplainable mysteries.

It is important to note that much of the difficulty in ever really "knowing" Holmes is traceable to the subject himself. Writing of his reaction to the only biographical work published during his lifetime, Holmes commented: "You speak of my biography. I have not read it, but should think it was harmless. I had nothing to do with it . . . [and] I have done my best to destroy illuminating documents."[9] There is little question that the reason biographical resources—diaries, letters, and other primary materials—are far richer for the period of Holmes's life prior to his marriage results directly from Holmes's later efforts to maintain his privacy behind a carefully constructed public facade. Holmes purposefully destroyed all the papers within his control that might have threatened to expose his personal life to scrutiny.[10] Thus, despite every effort, the Holmes described in the pages that follow remains to some extent only a shadow, a portrait of a man drawn largely from sketches he himself chose to disclose.

Finally, in this case as in any other, the biographer, distanced in time from his subject and dependent upon such historical materials as may be available, cannot be trusted to tell the whole truth even if he is careful to tell nothing but the truth. As Justice Holmes once remarked, "men carry their signatures upon their persons, although they may not always be visible at the first glance."[11] The signature of "Oliver Wendell Holmes, Jr.," I hope, will emerge more clearly as a result of this study of his person. Such hope should be tempered, however, with a dose of Dr. Holmes's wisdom: "I should like to see any man's biography with corrections and emendations by his ghost. We don't know each other's secrets quite so well as we flatter ourselves we do. We don't always know our own secrets as well as we might."[12] In the end, the figure that emerges will be seen from the perspective of the present age, and not in the light of his own. Each reader will find in these pages his or her own Holmes, and whether that man is a hero or not will depend more upon the reader's judgment than upon historical evidence.

1

FATHERS AND SONS

Seldom does a son's reputation overshadow that of a famous father. But when one hears the name Oliver Wendell Holmes today, it is invariably the son rather than the father who comes to mind. Born in 1809 in Cambridge, Massachusetts, the elder Holmes was one of the most conspicuous Americans of his generation. A prominent member of the faculty of the Harvard Medical School, he was as well known for his poetry as for his medical genius. Like Benjamin Franklin before him, Dr. Holmes's scientific and literary achievements made him famous on both sides of the Atlantic. Few men achieve such fame in a lifetime; fewer still have been so completely forgotten. In the final analysis, Dr. Holmes's place in history has been secured as a result not of his own distinction but of his having been the father of an even more famous son.

Dr. Holmes was aware of the extent to which "each generation strangles and devours its predecessor."[1] He himself had confronted his own father, the Reverend Abiel Holmes, with "those *enfant terrible* questions" and had found him wanting in his answers.[2] Perhaps as a result of his own considerable struggle to assert his identity as the son of a prominent father, Dr. Holmes was particularly sensitive to the potential challenge posed by his firstborn and namesake.

Great men, no less than ordinary ones, are shaped by their time and place in history. To understand who Oliver Wendell Holmes, Jr., was, it is first necessary to discover who he understood himself to be. Born in Boston, Massachusetts, on 8 March, Wendell—as the boy was known to his family and friends—grew to maturity in a community proud of its Puritan roots and confident of its intellectual and cultural superiority. Related to many of the first families of the city, the young Holmes was surrounded by an unusually secure and sophisticated family environment, and enjoyed all the benefits comfortable financial circumstances and favorable social position could bestow. Fate had favored him with everything a boy in Boston could have wanted—a respected family, a fine home, a circle of close comrades, and the best education available in America. But life in these surroundings did something more; it stamped him indelibly with the mark of his Puritan inheritance. In order to enjoy such privileges, one was first required to demonstrate that one deserved them.

Writing to his mother on 9 March 1841, Dr. Holmes noted proudly that "a nice little gentleman" had come to the house the evening before; in a letter written to his sister the same day, he added that "the little individual" might "hereafter be addressed as—Holmes, Esq., The Hon.—Holmes, M.C., or His Excellency,—Holmes, President." Perhaps the most revealing reference to the birth of his first child—a son— was the one included in a letter to an old school chum: "I believe you learned, when you were here, that there was a second edition of your old acquaintance, an o.w.h."[3]

The infant was christened Oliver Wendell on Sunday, 25 April 1841, in King's Chapel, the citadel of Boston Unitarianism. From that day on, the boy would have to come to terms with being a "Jr." and Dr. Holmes with being a father. The significance of those tiny initials— "o.w.h."—soon became apparent, as Dr. Holmes exhibited difficulty accepting his son as anything but his "little boy."[4] Unusually critical of everything the boy did, the father called constant attention to shortcomings others could barely perceive. Whether as a result of his own vanity or a genuine desire to make his son great, an intense rivalry would in time develop between the two, a struggle of such emotional intensity that it dwarfed all others.

If Dr. Holmes seemed intent on undermining his son's self-confidence at every turn, his wife, Amelia Lee Jackson Holmes, did her best to support and encourage her firstborn. The daughter of Judge Charles Jackson, a distinguished Boston attorney and associate justice of the Supreme Judicial Court of Massachusetts, she was undoubtedly familiar

2

with habits and attitudes of famous men. Understanding the burdens her child might have to bear as the son of a famous man, Mrs. Holmes tried to lessen Wendell's sense of vulnerability and inadequacy. Perhaps sensing some potential greatness in this child of hers, as distinguished from her husband's son, she nurtured the boy with her love and strengthened him with her resolve. From his mother, Wendell received his first book; at her feet, he received his first lessons. Perhaps most important, it was through her eyes that he first learned to see the world.[5]

Although Wendell never bothered much with his family's genealogy, he was consciously raised a patrician. There was no way he could escape the constant reminder of who he was; his name proclaimed to all that he was an Oliver, a Wendell, and a Holmes, and throughout his long and distinguished life, he would struggle to prove that he was their worthy heir. Holmeses had helped found several early Massachusetts towns and had served with distinction as leaders of colonial New England. His great-grandfather, Capt. David Holmes, fought in the French and Indian War and served as a surgeon and officer in the American Revolution. Captain Holmes's wife, Temperance Bishop Holmes, enjoyed a reputation of her own, something rather uncommon for women of the period. A remarkable woman, she delighted in learning, and was as likely to quote from Virgil or Milton as from Genesis or Isaiah. When her husband died in 1779 at the age of fifty-seven, she became the head of a household that included seven sons and two daughters, the youngest a three-year-old son named Liberty.[6]

Abiel Holmes, Captain Holmes's second son and Wendell's grandfather, was fifteen when his father died. At his mother's urging, he entered Yale College, which at that time was a bastion of Calvinist orthodoxy. He graduated in 1783 and quickly earned the respect of the church hierarchy as a rising young minister of the Congregational faith. In 1790, he married Mary Stiles, the daughter of the Reverend Ezra Stiles, president of Yale College. The marriage, which undoubtedly helped advanced Abiel's career and social standing, was cut tragically short; Mary Stiles Holmes died in 1795, leaving her young husband a childless widower.[7]

Abiel Holmes was an unusually devout Calvinist, who accepted the Puritan judgment that accomplishment was a religious duty, and ambition an inescapable moral obligation. As a minister of the faith, he took seriously the responsibilities that accompanied priestly stewardship. Following his wife's death, he accepted a call to minister to a Congregational colony in Georgia. Preaching the gospel and exhorting his flock to follow strictly the law of God, he delivered a message that was well received by a struggling community anxious to do good and thus receive the full measure of God's blessing. Not surprisingly, Reverend Holmes's reputation as a young leader in the church continued to grow as his mission prospered.[8]

Perhaps as a reward for the success of his southern mission, Reverend Holmes was called to become the pastor of the First Congregational Church of Cambridge, Massachusetts. Distinguished by its great spire and graceful belfry, the meetinghouse was an imposing structure. The sanctuary, lit by rows of tall clear windows and filled with square white pews, served a congregation that counted among its members the leading families of the community. A young Congregational minister with ambition could have wished for no better parish or spoken from any more important pulpit.

In addition to his regular duties and responsibilities as a pastor, Abiel Holmes was a passionate antiquarian and scholar. An avid writer, he composed such diverse works as a history of the Mohegan Indians, a biography of his father-in-law, and a book of poetic verse. His evenings alone in the Old Manse adjoining the meetinghouse were devoted to tireless work on a monumental project—the *Annals of America*—a detailed chronicle of American history. As a result of these interests, an active friendship quickly developed between the young pastor and Judge Oliver Wendell, a founder and enthusiastic member of the Massachusetts Historical Society and one of Boston's most influential public men. Although Reverend Holmes enjoyed a position of considerable respect within the community as the spiritual and intellectual leader of his congregation, his prominence was something quite different from the prestige and social standing that resulted from simply being a Wendell.[9]

Few families in Massachusetts were more renowned than the Wendells. Among the first settlers in the region, Evert Jensen Wendell had made a home in the upper Hudson River valley by 1640, having come to America from East Freisland, Holland, to settle in the Dutch colony of New Amsterdam. Judge Wendell's father, Col. Jacob Wendell, founded a prosperous trading company, and married Sarah Oliver, the daughter of Dr. James Oliver, a respected member of the Boston establishment, and a descendant of Anne Bradstreet. Through this marriage, the Wendells joined the true aristocracy of New England. Anne Bradstreet had arrived in the Massachusetts Bay Colony in 1630 with John Winthrop's group of Puritan settlers. Her father, Thomas Dudley, succeeded Winthrop as governor of the colony and was one of the founders

4

and original trustees of Harvard College. Her husband, Simon Bradstreet, also served as governor of the colony. Participants together in a
great calling, the Bradstreets labored diligently to establish God's king-
dom on earth, a "holy city set on a hill" which would serve as a model
for others to emulate. Anne Bradstreet's first book of verse, *The Tenth
Muse Lately Sprung Up in America*, was published in London in 1650,
establishing her reputation as one of America's first authors. Her true
reputation, however, was established by the example she set as a dutiful
Puritan wife and mother.[10]

Anne Bradstreet's granddaughter, Mercy Bradstreet, was Sarah
Oliver's mother; a true daughter of the Puritan aristocracy, Sarah
brought added prestige and honor to the Wendell family through her
marriage to Col. Jacob Wendell. Their son, Oliver Wendell, was born
in 1734. Following his graduation from Harvard College in 1751, he
joined his father in running the family's commercial empire. By this
time, Colonel Wendell had become one of the wealthiest men in New
England. Oliver Wendell soon took his place among the leading men of
Boston, first as a representative to the colonial assembly, and as a dele-
gate to the Continental Congresses of 1775 and 1776, and later as a
probate judge. A leading patriot and supporter of the American Revolution, the judge could count among his close friends such men as John
Hancock, Joseph Warren, and Samuel Adams.

Like his father before him, Oliver Wendell married the daughter of
another prominent Boston family, Mary Jackson; the couple had a
daughter, whom they named Sarah after the judge's mother. As a child,
she was unusually quick, and as she grew older, she acquired a charming
grace which suited perfectly a young woman surrounded by inherited
riches. Whether as a result of her social position or her own sense of
discrimination, Sarah was unmarried at thirty-one when she met her
father's new friend, the Reverend Abiel Holmes. Although long considered a spinster by her family and friends, Sarah soon attracted the attention of the thirty-six-year-old widower; the couple married in March
1801.[11]

Abiel Holmes's marriage changed his life in many ways. Although
his own mother and grandmother possessed a certain grace, they were
gravely serious and full of stern Calvinist purpose. Raised by his family
to seek self-improvement rather than self-gratification, Abiel Holmes at
times found it difficult to reconcile his newfound happiness with the rigid
requirements of his religious faith. He loved his wife passionately, and
yet was troubled that such love might be a sin. Sally, as Mrs. Abiel

Holmes was known, was more confident that the Lord loved a cheerful heart and did everything she could to brighten her husband's dour habits. She transformed the severe and sparse furnishings of the Old Manse into a warm and inviting home reflecting her own more refined and sophisticated tastes. Chippendale furniture, oil paintings in gilded frames, silver bearing the patina of age, and fine china from her father's Boston mansion soon filled the parsonage.

To the surprise of many of Reverend Holmes's parishioners, the couple's first child was born within a year of their marriage. The young daughter was named Mary Jackson for Mrs. Holmes's mother. After years of silence, the sounds of new life filled the old house. Another daughter, Ann Susan, arrived a year later. In 1805, a third daughter, Sarah Lathrop, was born, and the parsonage reverberated with the comings and goings of the growing family. In the same year, Reverend Holmes published his *American Annals* in two stout volumes. The work received immediate critical acclaim; President Thomas Jefferson was sufficiently impressed to commence an active correspondence with the author, and Edinburgh University in Scotland awarded Abiel Holmes an honorary degree.[12]

In 1807, Judge Wendell decided to sell his mansion on Oliver Street. Although one of the finest houses in Boston, it was no longer convenient as the judge had begun to spend more and more of his time with his daughter's family in Cambridge. This being his primary consideration in his decision to relocate across the Charles River to Cambridge, he determined to purchase a large home known as the Gambrel House, and invited his daughter and son-in-law to live with him there. In addition to its favorable location immediately adjacent to Harvard College, the house was close to the First Congregational meetinghouse. Rich in history, the house had served as General Ward's headquarters during the Battle of Bunker Hill, and General Washington had been a frequent guest. It was doubtful that there was any finer house in the entire village. The plan suited everyone; the new house was much more commodious and comfortable than the Old Manse, and perhaps more important, it would be theirs rather than the parish's. Now if Sally Holmes wanted to make some changes, she would not first have to consult with church elders.[13]

On 29 August 1809, Reverend Holmes noted the following in the daily journal he kept: "= son b."[14] With this brief inscription, Holmes commemorated the birth of his first son, whom he and his wife named Oliver Wendell in honor of her father. Three years later, another son,

John, was born. As a child, young Oliver Wendell was very much like his mother. Small and slight in stature, he was an unusually quick learner. Raised in an active family of older sisters and a younger brother, he received at least his share of his parents' love and affection. The children spent much of their early years with their grandfather. Judge Wendell took them to market and to the courthouse; holding his hand, they traveled to Boston to see the Common and the great tall-masted ships along the Long Wharf. Farmers in their fields and gentlemen wearing silk hats would stop to greet the judge and his young charges. Gentle rather than stern, the old man seemed to know everyone; there could have been no better person to introduce inquisitive young minds to the wonders of the world.

After attending a local dames school and William Biglow's Port School in Cambridgeport, Oliver Wendell was sent to Phillips Academy in Andover, Massachusetts, for a year. Despite his mother's reservations, Reverend Holmes hoped that a year at the recognized stronghold of orthodox Calvinism would temper his son's growing enthusiasm for the way of the world. Writing to the boy shortly after the new year in 1825, Reverend Holmes expressed his earnest hope that he would devote "his time and talents" so as to attain "those virtues and graces which will make all time pleasant and profitable." He also pointed out to his son that as his "opportunity for such improvement" was "very much greater" than that of most other boys, he would "expect the more accordingly."[15] Like so many young men before and since, Oliver Wendell heard often the perennial admonition of parent to child: be diligent, be punctual, be prudent; observe the rules; and most important, avoid bad company.

After completing his studies at Phillips Academy in the spring of 1825, Holmes entered Harvard College in the fall. Like many of his mother's relations before him, he took his place at Harvard, a place assured by his family's social position. He lived at home in the Gambrel House that had once belonged to a Harvard professor, moving in his senior year to a room in Stoughton Hall. A member of the Hasty Pudding Club and a Knight of the Square Table, a club that later merged with the Porcellian Club, the young man enjoyed the company of his peers and evidenced on more than one occasion an interest in wine and song. He mentioned in a letter to a friend from Phillips Academy that he wouldn't be content until he won "the undisputed mastery of a petticoat." Elected class poet and invited to join Phi Beta Kappa, Holmes stood seventeenth out of fifty-nine when he took his degree with the class of '29.[16]

During Holmes's senior year at Harvard, a serious dispute arose within his father's parish. It had become clear that the traditional doctrine of the Congregational church, which was the bedrock upon which Abiel Holmes had constructed his personal faith and his professional ministry, was under serious attack from a new faith known as Unitarianism. It was not simply a question of theology; rather, the old Puritan morality was being challenged by a new worldliness that encouraged the believer to love life more and fear God less. The new individualism characteristic of the successful self-made Yankee merchant was simply inconsistent with a religious tradition that taught that "in Adam's fall, so sinned we all."[17]

Reverend Holmes could not understand the distance that had grown between his own traditional faith and the new faith of many of his parishioners. He refused to join the Unitarian movement and urged his flock to remain faithful to the teachings of their youth. His congregation became more and more intolerant of their pastor's old-fashioned habits, and in time, a deep schism developed within the parish. Finally, a majority of the congregation voted to call a younger man as their new minister. Having served more than thirty years in the pulpit of the First Congregational Church, Reverend Holmes could not believe that he had been let go; together with a group of loyal followers, he fought his removal in court, but lost. Never doubting that the judgment of the Lord was close at hand, Abiel Holmes built a new church in Cambridge and continued to minister unto the faithful. As he told his old parishioners in his last sermon at the First Church, if he had seemed to disregard their "wishes or tastes," it was because he was more "desirous to save them than to please them."[18]

For several months following his graduation from Harvard College, Oliver Wendell Holmes read law in his grandfather's library. He also attended lectures at the new Dane School of Law at Harvard. Disillusioned and depressed at his lack of progress, he wrote a friend that he was "sick at heart" with the law and everything connected with it: "I know not what the temple of the law may be to those who have entered it, but to me it seems very cold and cheerless about the threshold."[19] In the fall of 1830, the discouraged young law student took a room in a boardinghouse at 2 Central Street in Boston. The distance from his family's home was more a symbolic gesture of independence than an actual one; both financially and emotionally, Holmes remained his father's dependent.

In September 1830, Reverend Holmes became extremely agitated by an article in the newspaper which suggested that the Navy Department had finally decided to scrap the most famous ship of the American Revolution, the frigate *Constitution*. Although the ship lay rotting beside a Boston wharf, Reverend Holmes's sense of history and patriotism would not permit him to rest until something was done to reverse the government's decision. He proposed to his son that someone should write a letter to the editor of the paper. Impressed by his father's emotional appeal, Holmes sat down and quickly penned not a letter but a poem. Characteristically, when he had finished, he took it to his father for his approval. Upon reading what his son had intended as only a rough draft, Reverend Holmes was moved to tears. Published the next day in Boston's *Daily Advertiser* over the modest signature "H," the poem was an immediate success. Entitled "Old Ironsides," the lines spoke with both majesty and power:

> Ay, tear her tattered ensign down!
>   Long has it waved on high,
> And many an eye has danced to see
>   That banner in the sky; . . .
>
> Oh better that her shattered hulk
>   Should sink beneath the wave;
> Her thunders shook the mighty deep,
>   And there should be her grave;
> Nail to the mast her holy flag,
>   Set every threadbare sail,
> And give her to the God of storms,
>   The lightning and the gale![20]

The public's response to the poem's appeal was overwhelming. The government rescinded its order, the children of America restored the old ship with their pennies, and Oliver Wendell Holmes was nationally famous at the age of twenty-one.

Rather surprised by his unexpected celebrity, and certain that anything that had come so easily could not last long, Holmes was at least liberated from the persistent doubts about his future that had troubled him since graduation. Writing to a friend, he announced his resolve to change his field of study: "I do not know what you will say, but I cannot help it. . . . I know I might have made an indifferent lawyer—I think I will make a tolerable physician. I do not like the one and do like the other."[21] Holmes enrolled in a private medical school in Boston and quickly came under the instruction of its principal teacher, Dr. James Jackson, one of Boston's most prominent physicians. Holmes also attended lectures at the Harvard Medical School and began to work in the local hospitals. Deeply affected by the grim realities of sickness, suffering, and death, the young poet grew increasingly serious about his new course of study. His new dedication and the sense of urgency that characterized his work surprised even those closest to him. It appeared that the young man had finally found his true calling.[22]

While Holmes was applying himself in earnest to his medical studies, his younger brother, John, graduated from Harvard College and entered the law school. Although he never chose to compete with his older brother for first honors in the family, he quietly completed his legal studies, took his degree, and joined a long line of ancestors as a member of the bar.

In January 1833, Holmes completed his studies with Dr. Jackson and, upon his advice, determined to go to Europe to continue his medical training. Although there was some question as to whether Reverend Holmes would be prepared to finance such a plan, there was no question that the best medical education available at the time was to be found in Paris. Dr. Jackson was sending his own son there to study with the eminent French physician, Dr. Pierre Charles Alexander Louis, at the Ecole de Medicine in Paris. Perhaps not wanting to be compared unfavorably to a more generous father, Reverend Holmes agreed to underwrite the enterprise, and in March, the young medical student set sail from New York City for Paris.[23]

Upon his arrival, he set himself to his task with considerable enthusiasm. His dutiful letters home reflected a new sense of genuine liberation and growing independence. "Merely to have breathed a concentrated scientific atmosphere like that of Paris," he wrote, "must have an effect on anyone who has lived where stupidity is tolerated, where mediocrity is applauded, and where excellence is deified." He continued in the same letter that he had learned three principles since his arrival in Paris: "not to take authority where I can have facts; not to guess where I can know; and not to think a man must take physic because he is sick."[24] Such letters home made it painfully clear to his parents that their son would never again accept the moral authority of his father's faith.

During the summer of 1834, Holmes proposed to his parents that he join other Bostonians studying in Paris on what was commonly referred to as the Grand Tour, extensive travels planned to occupy the better part of the summer. Lacking the necessary funds, he wrote his parents a letter that attempted to justify an expense not directly related to his medical studies:

> What better can be done with money than putting the means of instruction—the certain powers of superiority, if not of success—into the hands of one's children? Besides, economy, in one sense, is too expensive for a student. . . . Once and for all I say that you may trust me, and I beg you to remember that being in Europe for my good, I am here for yours. . . . To conclude, a boy is worth his manure as much as a potato patch, and I have said all this because I find it costs rather more to do things than to talk about them.[25]

The appeal was successful, and the money was forwarded. Holmes visited England and Scotland during the summer of 1834 and traveled through southern France to Italy the following summer. His letters suggest an attitude more characteristic of a bon vivant than the son of a Congregational divine: "every New England deacon ought to see one Derby Day to learn what sort of world this is he lives in—man is a sporting animal as well as a praying animal." In another letter, Holmes inquired of his parents, "Have you any news. . . . How flourish the red and white roses of orthodoxy and heterodoxy?"[26] So much for the irreverence of youth.

Holmes sailed from Havre, France, for home in November 1835. He arrived in New York City forty-three days after his departure from Europe and returned to Boston shortly thereafter; he had been away some thirty months. He had employed his time with diligence, and had taken his pleasures moderately, and thus approached his reunion with his father with confidence, knowing he could justify his parents' considerable investment. If he was at all reluctant to return, it was because he was less confident that his training in Europe would prove sufficient to place him "at once at the head of the younger part" of his profession.[27] Preoccupied with his own personal growth, Holmes was unprepared when he was welcomed home by a father who had grown old in his absence. Remembering a strong-willed patriarch, Holmes found instead a gentle, white-haired man who carried candy in his pockets for children he encountered. Perhaps recalling that his grandfather, Judge Wendell, had done the same thing in his old age, Dr. Holmes would in time perpetuate the custom himself.[28]

In 1836, Holmes completed his Harvard dissertation on "Acute

Pericarditis," and received his medical degree. He became a member of the Massachusetts Medical Society and continued his research. Soon thereafter, he presented a paper on "Intermittent Fever in New England" which was awarded the prestigious Boylston Prize at Harvard. With this measure of success, he established himself in a rented room in Boston and at the age of twenty-seven commenced his practice of medicine. With few patients to distract him, he continued his scientific study, finding it more to his liking than taking care of sick people. Late in the year, his first volume of published poems appeared in Boston, and many wondered whether the young Dr. Holmes was not perhaps a better poet than physician.[29]

Despite these notable successes, 1836 had been a difficult year for Holmes. It was also becoming increasingly evident that Reverend Holmes's health was declining. In May 1837, the old man finally suffered a crippling stroke, and he died a month later. Following their father's death, John Holmes assumed the responsibility of looking after their mother, thereby freeing his older brother of the obligation. Dr. Holmes, as he was now called, resumed his medical career with increased intensity. Before the end of the year, he won two additional Boylston Prizes for his work on neuralgia and quickly published his award-winning research in a volume that established his professional reputation on both sides of the Atlantic. Significantly, Holmes dedicated the volume to Dr. Louis.[30]

Another event occurred in 1837 that would have a lasting effect upon the young doctor. In August, Ralph Waldo Emerson presented a lecture at Harvard entitled "The American Scholar." Six years Holmes's senior, Emerson had been elected class poet for his year. A student of William Ellery Channing at the Harvard Divinity School, the young Unitarian minister clearly reflected a new current in the tides of religious doctrine. Here at last was someone who shared Holmes's frustration with the past and was prepared to articulate a different course for the future. Emerson's language was equally impressive: "Our day of dependence, our long apprenticeship to the learning of other lands, draws to a close. . . . We will walk on our own feet; we will work with our own hands; we will speak our own minds."[31] The speech was an intellectual declaration of independence hurled at the stultifying moral orthodoxy of New England's Puritan heritage, and it marked the beginning of a new age of American learning. Bright young Harvard men from every discipline rallied around Emerson, who became their chief proof of the excellence of native American intelligence. Among these gifted and talented Harvard men, Dr. Holmes took his rightful place as the most distinguished young practitioner of medical science in Boston. On the eve of his thirtieth birthday, he could find satisfaction in having achieved that which he had so desperately sought.

Despite these achievements, however, Holmes was becoming increasingly concerned about his lack of success in making a living. His poems and research might make him famous and earn him the respect of his peers, but it certainly was not going to make him rich. His early prominence had been purchased at the cost of a prolonged dependence upon his family's financial resources; finding a stable source of financial independence now became Holmes's chief goal. In 1838, Dr. Holmes and three other young doctors established a private medical school on Tremont Street, and Holmes began to cultivate a closer association with the faculty of the Harvard Medical School. In addition, he accepted an offer from Dartmouth College in Hanover, New Hampshire, to become professor of anatomy. The title was an important consideration, but the promise of a salary decided the issue. Working at Dartmouth primarily during the summer months, he had the opportunity to work on his teaching skills and add to his academic credentials.[32]

At last secure in the knowledge that he could support himself, Dr. Holmes finally turned his attention to a subject that had been too long deferred—the matter of finding a wife. Like his father before him, by the time Dr. Holmes began courting in earnest, he was over thirty and firmly established as an important member of Boston society. Although politically he defended the principle of equality, socially he stood for aristocracy. He was naturally attracted to those who like himself had enjoyed the benefits of inherited wealth and a good family name. Following his father's example, Holmes found himself particularly interested in the daughter of one of Boston's most prominent lawyers, Judge Charles Jackson, a former justice of the state's high court. Amelia Lee Jackson, related to Holmes on his mother's side, was in fact a great deal like his mother. Diminutive and charming, she was the product of an excellent home. Always attentive to the young doctor's interests, she had known Oliver Wendell Holmes all her life. Her father's fine home on Bedford Street must have reminded Holmes of his grandfather's mansion on Oliver Street, as the extensive gardens and comfortable libraries were much alike. Like his mother's family, Amelia's relatives were part of Boston's merchant aristocracy. Proud of their Puritan roots, they nevertheless devoted their energies to making their way in this world rather than worrying about their place in the next. Ironically, in the court fight over the property of Abiel Holmes's First Congregational Church in Cambridge, Justice Jackson had sided with the parishioners against their pastor. Even though Dr. Holmes, through his close association with Ralph Waldo Emerson, had joined the opposition, he was nevertheless a "son of orthodoxy"; Amelia Jackson, in contrast, was clearly a "daughter of heresy."[33]

Dr. Oliver Wendell Holmes married Amelia Lee Jackson in King's Chapel on 15 June 1840. Between them, the couple was related to virtually every significant family in Boston—the Olivers and the Wendells, the Dudleys and the Quincys, the Jacksons and the Cabots. Returning from a summer holiday, the Holmeses moved into a three-story brick townhouse—No. 8 Montgomery Place—which Judge Jackson had given to the young couple as a wedding present. Conveniently located near Tremont Street just off the Boston Common, the house was pleasantly situated in a quiet dead-end court. Equally important, the home provided ample space for a growing family.

Amelia Holmes proved an ideal wife for Dr. Holmes, a helpmate whose abilities seemed arranged by providence to supply his particular needs—"in a word, she took care of him, and gave him everyday the fullest and freest chance to be always at his best. . . . She contributed immensely to his success."[34] Eight months and twenty-eight days after their marriage, the couple's first child, Oliver Wendell Holmes, Jr., was born; within a few years, a daughter and another son would follow. Together, the young family grew and prospered. The family lived at 8 Montgomery Place until the summer of 1857, when they moved to a new house at 21 Charles Street; in 1870, the family moved for a final time to a new home Dr. Holmes had built on Beacon Street. Like most of the families that composed Boston society of the time, their lives were free of any hint of scandal. Faithful husbands and faithful wives worked together to bring up children who in time would take their places as parents of similar households. Such families found their principal strength in remarkable women who were loved as wives and revered as mothers. If not the material of romantic novels, these relationships certainly reflected a story of quiet and sincere devotion.[35]

If his family life was a calm haven, twice during 1842 and 1843, Dr. Holmes found himself at the center of a storm of professional controversy. The source in each case was a paper Dr. Holmes presented to his colleagues in the Boston medical community. The first, "Homeopathy and Its Kindred Delusions," condemned Dr. Samuel Hahnemann and his followers for practicing a "pseudo-science"; the second, "The Contagiousness of Puerperal Fever," relied on extensive empirical findings to assert that the deadly pestilence which was killing newborn children and their mothers was a contagious infection that physicians attending at childbirth were helping to spread. The response of many of his colleagues was unexpected; they attacked him as an irresponsible and arrogant young doctor. It was unacceptable that he had attacked another physician in public, and unforgivable that he had suggested that doctors were contributing to the spread of the disease rather than its cure. Several years later, two prominent Philadelphia physicians—Dr. Hugh Hodge of the University of Pennsylvania and Dr. Charles Meigs of the Jefferson Medical College—denounced Holmes in the harshest terms. Despite the continuing debate, his research on puerperal fever nevertheless catapulted Holmes to the forefront of his profession. He was appointed Parkman Professor of Anatomy and Physiology at the Harvard Medical School in 1847; apparently, science and not respect for tradition was more important in the minds of the Harvard faculty. An immensely popular professor and lecturer affectionately referred to as "Uncle Oliver" by generations of Harvard students, Dr. Holmes retained his chair for thirty-five years and served as dean of the medical school from 1847 to 1853.[36]

As he had planned, his academic employment provided him with the financial stability essential to support his other activities. Nevertheless, he was perpetually short of money. In 1852, he joined the Lyceum lecture circuit and soon became a well-known missionary of Boston's view of civilization. Traveling from Maine to western New York State, he presented more than seventy lectures in a single year. Holmes was an unusually able and witty speaker, and his lectures drew large and appreciative audiences; along with increased revenues came a growing national prominence. In 1853, largely as a result of the success of his Lyceum lectures, the Lowell Institute invited Dr. Holmes to present the prestigious Lowell Lectures for that year. Holmes chose as his subject the major English poets of the nineteenth century—Wordsworth, Moore, Keats, and Shelley. As expected, the lectures were a success and confirmed Holmes in the public's mind as the very embodiment of American culture.[37]

In 1855, Holmes and a group of his closest friends founded the Saturday Club, an association of the best minds of Boston and Cambridge who gathered on the last Saturday of each month to dine at the Parker House in Boston. No comparable group in American history comes readily to mind. Rather than men distinguished by great wealth, the members of the Saturday Club sought each other's company to share ideas and enjoy the stimulation that results from the clash of powerful minds. The fourteen original members of the group were all old friends of Emerson's, who had regularly gathered to dine with him whenever he came to Boston from his home in Cambridge. Within a year of its founding, however, the club had expanded to include virtually every major intellectual figure in Boston. In addition to Emerson and Holmes, the group included Richard Dana, Louis Agassiz, Benjamin Peirce, James Russell Lowell, Henry Wadsworth Longfellow, John L. Motley, John Greenleaf Whittier, Nathaniel Hawthorne, and Charles Eliot Norton. Collectively referred to as the "flowering of New England" by the historian Van Wyck Brooks, these men seemed to attain their fullest maturity as thinkers, writers, and scientists at approximately the same time and in close proximity to one another.[38] Holmes revealed his own view of his circle of friends in one of his books: "the good and true and intelligent men whom we see, all around us, laborious, self-denying, hopeful and helpful."[39] Enjoying the company of such men more than any other, Holmes was solidly allied to the patrician elements of Boston society by the most intimate ties of life.

In 1857, Holmes cofounded with James Russell Lowell the *Atlantic Monthly,* a literary magazine dedicated to literature, art, and politics. Associated with Emersonian ideals and political reform, the magazine was edited by Lowell and served as a public forum for the ideas of the Saturday Club. Holmes was a regular contributor to the publication; in particular, his "Breakfast-Table" sketches proved especially popular with the readership. Subsequently collected and published in a series of books, the first and most significant of which was entitled *The Autocrat of the Breakfast-Table,* the sketches provided Holmes with a perfect vehicle for his pithy prescriptions and established him even more firmly as a national arbiter on a wide range of social issues. Like Dr. Franklin's *Poor Richard's Almanac,* this series found a permanent place in American culture and added measurably to Dr. Holmes's financial security.[40]

Several years later, Dr. Holmes published a novel of a different kind altogether. *The Professor's Story,* subsequently republished under the title *Elsie Venner,* was as strikingly unsuccessful as his previous books had been popular. Published in 1861, the book presented a scientific approach to the subject of human psychology. Anticipating ideas that Sigmund Freud would develop forty years later, Holmes may have written the work as an extended response to Hawthorne's consideration of the same subject ten years earlier in his novel *The Scarlet Letter.* Like Hawthorne's book,

Holmes's contained a heroine who was plagued by evil. But unlike Hawthorne, Holmes suggested that the source of such evil was not moral depravity, more commonly known as sin, but rather, hereditary weakness. His heroine, Elsie Venner, could not be held accountable for her faults because her fate was determined even before her birth; bitten by a snake while she was carrying her child, Elsie's mother had passed the venom through her body to the unborn infant. Significantly, Charles Darwin's revolutionary *Origins of the Species* was published just two years earlier in 1859. Dr. Holmes's novel left little doubt in a Calvinist's mind that he found Darwin's theories of evolution and natural selection more persuasive than the biblical account of Adam's fall. Consistent with this view, Holmes also seemed to suggest that intelligence too was hereditary. Referring to a type he called the "Boston Brahmin," Holmes described a class of men whose only birthright was "an aptitude for learning": a "harmless, inoffensive, untitled aristocracy" of scholars, who "break out every generation or two in some learned labor which calls them up after they seem to have died out."[41] In full revolt against his Calvinist heritage, Holmes appeared prepared to displace God and Holy Scripture, and to put in their place a Boston Brahmin armed with a subscription to the *Atlantic Monthly.* Regarded as an incredibly arrogant heretic, even by many of Boston's Unitarian clergy, Holmes encountered a storm of protest against himself and his novel.[42]

The most public of men, Dr. Holmes had little time to devote exclusively to his children; what time they spent with their father was usually in the company of others. The boys, Wendell and Edward, grew up in the midst of a vast extended family which included the most celebrated men of Boston. That Oliver Wendell Holmes, Jr., felt closer to Emerson, "Uncle Waldo," than to his own father is suggested by his comment that Emerson was the only "firebrand" of his youth that continued to burn "as brightly as ever."[43] Emerson was quiet and patient; Dr. Holmes was always talking and in a hurry. Emerson seemed to possess a deeper and truer sense of reality than the "Autocrat." As Wendell grew older, his father found it difficult to acknowledge his son as anything but "a boy." The growing tension between the two was obvious to those close to the family. William James, a particularly close friend of Wendell's, observed in a note sent after dining at the Holmeses in 1873 that "no love is lost between W. *pere* and W. *fils.*" Dr. Holmes had himself asked James's father whether his sons "despised him." Although the elder James replied that he had no reason to believe that they did, it was clear to those who knew Dr. Holmes well that he believed himself despised by at least one of his sons.[44]

As time went on, it became increasingly difficult for the son to understand how his father could possess such a celebrated scientific mind and yet live a life devoted to tradition, rigidly committed to a hundred little habits prescribed by social convention. Repulsed by the apparent contradiction, and frustrated by his father's rather self-righteous observance of religious customs, Wendell increasingly sought the solitude of his own thoughts. It was impossible to discuss such things with "the Governor," as Wendell invariably referred to his father. Dr. Holmes was always too witty, too sure, too correct. Yet his son could never fully accept either his advice or his example. In a revealing letter written many years after his father's death, Oliver Wendell Holmes, Jr., wrote the following about Dr. Holmes:

> He had the most penetrating mind of all that lot. After his early medical work which was really big (the puerperal fever business) I think he contented himself too much with sporadic aperçus. . . . If he had had the patience to concentrate all his energy on a single subject, which perhaps is saying if he had been a different man, he would have been less popular, but he might have produced a great work.[45]

Aware of the obligations of his pedigree and confronted by the overwhelming presence of his father, Holmes determined from an early age to become precisely that "different man."

2

THE YOUNG BRAHMIN

The Boston of Holmes's youth was a city considerably different than it is today. To an outsider, it might have seemed little more than a provincial capital, but to those who lived there, it was the "hub" of the universe around which the entire world revolved.[1] Experiencing its greatest period of artistic and intellectual achievement in the years prior to the Civil War, the city could boast a collection of distinguished authors, scholars, and statesmen unequaled in the country. In a city with a population of less than 100,000 residents, a few men like Charles Sumner, Ralph Waldo Emerson, Henry Wadsworth Longfellow, Nathaniel Hawthorne, and James Russell Lowell made a considerable difference. In a single generation, a remarkably talented and accomplished group of men established Boston as an "American Athens" and raised to a new level their city's reputation as the nation's leading center of learning. Dr. Holmes was very much a part of this group. As a poet, publicist, scientist, and scholar, he was in many ways the very embodiment of the "Boston spirit."[2] It is not surprising that he would expect his children someday to take their place in his world and that they were educated accordingly.

Wendell, Jr.—or "Wendy," as his family called him—learned his earliest lessons at his mother's knee, as did all young children of his time. When he was two, he was joined by a sister, Amelia; three years later a brother, Edward Jackson, completed the family circle. Mrs. Holmes was a strong woman devoted to her family and its well-being. Her central concern was with her children's development—"what they are, and what they will be."[3] Although Mrs. Holmes was loving and generous with all her children, a special relationship existed between her and her firstborn. Perhaps sensing the vulnerability of her eldest child to his unusually critical father, she provided Wendell with the security and encouragement of her affection and nurtured the young boy's growth.

Growing up in the Holmes's household was something of a challenge for children. Led by their father's example, the youngsters soon came to play an active role in a "family of talkers." Known for the high quality of their conversation, the family engaged in discussions usually dominated by Dr. Holmes, who tended to talk "book talk not talk talk."[4] The children accused each other of ending every sentence with a "but" so as to hold the floor until they could think of something else to say. At meals, the child who provided the most engaging conversation, or a particularly clever remark, was frequently rewarded with "an extra spoon of marmalade."[5] Not surprisingly, Wendell's first school conduct report included the comment: "Talks too much."[6]

For the first sixteen years of Wendell's life, the family lived at 8 Montgomery Place, just off Tremont Street opposite the Old Granary Burying Ground. Surrounded by the first families of Boston throughout his life, Holmes was raised among an already well-established aristocracy. His claim to a place in such a society was doubly secure; previously noted, his father was descended from a distinguished line of the Puritan elect, and his mother's family counted among its number many of the city's most prosperous Yankee merchants. Surrounded by Cabots, Eliots, Bigelows, Lees, Lodges, and Lowells, the young patrician had little contact with the less privileged children of Boston.

Like other young boys of the Brahmin caste, Wendell attended a local dames school until his father enrolled him as a pupil of Mr. T. Russell Sullivan, who taught school in the basement of the Park Street Church. A pleasant man whose grandfather had been a governor of Massachusetts and whose great-uncle had served as a general in the Revolutionary War, Mr. Sullivan had begun his career as a Unitarian minister in Keene, New Hampshire. Abandoning the ministry in 1835, he commenced teaching children of Boston's upper class in studies heavily laced with scriptural passages and moral instruction.[7]

In 1851, Wendell was ten years old and ready to begin in earnest his preparation for college. Dr. Holmes considered sending his son to the Boston Latin School on Bedford Street. It had the enviable reputation of ensuring its graduates a place at Harvard College, Wendell's inevitable destination. Upon a closer examination of the school, however, Dr. Holmes concluded that the new headmaster's approach to education left much to be desired. In addition, the school's finest teacher, Epes Sargent Dixwell, was leaving to begin his own school on Boylston Place just west of the Boston Common. A Harvard graduate in the class of '27, Dixwell had read law in Dr. Holmes's father-in-law's office and had impressed Judge Jackson. After practicing law for three years, he had joined the faculty of the Boston Latin School and distinguished himself as its headmaster. Regarded by many as the most eminent classical scholar in Boston, Dixwell had married a daughter of the famous navigator and author, Nathaniel Bowditch, whose son had studied medicine with Dr. Holmes in Paris. Dixwell and his family lived on Garden Street in Cambridge and were well known by John Holmes, Dr. Holmes's brother. Dixwell was leaving the Boston Latin School because the city fathers had adopted an ordinance requiring members of the school's teaching staff to reside in Boston. Rather than move his home from Cambridge, Dixwell decided to open his own school.[8]

A member of Dixwell's first class of students, Wendell arrived for his first day in September 1851 armed with a letter of introduction from Mr. Sullivan to Mr. Dixwell:

Dear Sir:

O. W. Holmes, Jr., the bearer, whom (like his cousin J. T. Morse) I take delight in calling my young friend, has been for four years under my charge as a pupil. He has been uniformly docile, thoughtful, amiable, and affectionate. Young as he is, his habits of application are confirmed, while his proficiency in all the English branches, and his love of study are remarkable for his age.

Yours respectfully,
T. R. Sullivan

Sullivan had been impressed by what he considered Holmes's inherited talent, and he was confident that his young student would not disappoint his new teacher.[9]

Dixwell was a tall, spare man who dressed rather eccentrically. Nicknamed "Dicky" by his admiring young pupils, he had a gentlemanly manner and an infectious love of learning. The purpose of Dixwell's instruction was always clear; his students were being prepared to assume positions of responsibility in the community. It was taken for granted that they would attend Harvard College as generations of their fathers had before them. Anxious to rid his students of any "slovenliness of mind," Dixwell was equally eager to inculcate in his charges the morals and manners befitting sons of Boston's patrician class.

With entrance to Harvard College as their goal, teacher and students labored together to master those subjects covered by Harvard's entrance exams—Latin, Greek, ancient history, and mathematics. In addition, Dixwell included instruction in English, French, and German. Modern history was also taught, but not emphasized so heavily, as it was not included on the entrance examination. Dixwell's students received a classical education from a distinguished scholar of the classics, and generally did very well on their college tests. Perhaps more important, they received a broad and generous view of civilization from a man who taught as much by example as by precept.[10]

As a student, Wendell made no particular mark as a scholar. Not surprisingly, the young Holmes liked to read; he was particularly fond of the novels of Sir Walter Scott, whose heroes provided welcome relief from the study of Latin and Greek. *Ivanhoe* was the young boy's favorite, with dashing knights and mysterious women standing in stark contrast to the rather dull and proper activities of Boston.[11] Together with his cousin and closest childhood chum, John T. Morse, Holmes did his best to make his way through his early years of schooling. Although "Fatty" Morse was one year "Leany" Holmes's senior, they were nearly inseparable during their years together, first at Mr. Sullivan's Park Street School, and later at Mr. Dixwell's. Together, they shared the experiences and excitement of boyhood, forming a bond that would last all their lives. More like brothers than cousins, the two confided in each other their most secret fears and dreams, and together, they developed from boys to young men. On one particular occasion, Holmes sought moral instruction from his older friend. In reply to the question of whether it could ever be right to tell a lie, Morse properly replied, "Of course not." Pointing to the path along which they were walking, Holmes continued by suggesting a hypothetical situation. "Suppose a man came running along here with terror in his eyes and panting from breath and hid in the thicket . . . and the pursuers came along and asked us if we had seen him? Which would be better, to give the man away or to tell a lie?" After giving the matter some thought, his companion admitted that perhaps it might be better to lie under such circumstances. Even as a young boy,

Holmes had reached the conclusion that the right answer might not always be the best answer.[12]

Although Wendell disliked football and cricket, he loved to skate and enjoyed sledding on the Boston Common. More than once, such activities exposed him and his schoolmates to "attacks" by boys from the South End. Known to Holmes and his friends as "muckers" or "toughs," these boys were mostly the sons of Irish immigrants. Through snowball fights and other youthful skirmishes, Holmes encountered for the first time the sons of Boston's less fortunate families, many of whom he would not meet again until his service in the Civil War.[13]

From 1849 to 1856, Wendell and his family spent their summers in the Berkshire Mountains. Called Canoe Meadows, the home was located two miles south of Pittsfield, Massachusetts, on the Lenox road. Dr. Holmes had inherited 280 acres of land overlooking the Housatonic River from his mother, the residue of a section of land six miles square that his great-grandfather, Col. Jacob Wendell, had purchased from the Province of Massachusetts in 1738. When Mrs. Holmes received a two-thousand-dollar inheritance from her family, the couple decided to build a country retreat. A "snug little place" with a wide front porch with a view of the river and the mountains, the house and barn cost twice that amount to construct. Surrounded by rolling meadows and granite-strewn fields, Canoe Meadows provided a safe and peaceful environment for the young family. While the children swam in the swimming hole and picked blueberries, Dr. Holmes visited with Nathaniel Hawthorne and Henry Wadsworth Longfellow, both of whom had summer homes nearby. During those summers, Wendell learned to fish and shoot; he also developed a special appreciation for the beauty of nature, which he attempted to express through pencil and ink sketches. This interest in drawing would become stronger during his college years, and his appreciation for fine engravings would last a lifetime.[14]

By the time Wendell was thirteen, he was already as tall as his father, who by all accounts was a very short man. A strong, healthy, and handsome boy, Wendell was nevertheless very self-conscious about his appearance. He avoided most sports and spent much of his time alone with his books and drawings. More reserved and self-contained than the other members of his family, he found a special friend and adviser in his Uncle John, who was so unlike his father. A bachelor who lived with his mother, Uncle John seemed to understand what the young boy was thinking, making conversation between them unnecessary. Wendell looked forward to the days the family spent in Cambridge, visiting Grandmother and Uncle John. He would often go to see his teacher, Mr. Dixwell; together they would take walks along the river, discussing whatever happened to be on the young boy's mind. It was upon these two men that Wendell depended for the love and support his father seemed peculiarly unable to provide, and together, they guided the boy's inquisitive mind, assuring him through their affection that he was going to be a fine young man.[15]

The time Wendell did spend alone with his father was infrequent and generally difficult for both of them. Perhaps because they were too much alike, the father wanted always to be right, and the son chafed at always being wrong. Undoubtedly, Dr. Holmes loved his son, but his straight-laced New England manners and nearly constant criticism contributed significantly to his son's discontent. Despite their difficulties, the two enjoyed spending Saturday afternoons together on the Charles River. Dr. Holmes was an avid rowing enthusiast, and the family boathouse contained a small fleet including a skiff, a dory, and a shell. Although the son's interest in rowing never equaled the father's, the time Wendell spent with his father on the river was very important for a boy who often felt that he was competing with the entire world for his father's attention and approval.[16]

Years later, Oliver Wendell Holmes, Jr., recalled that "the Boston of my youth was still half-Puritan Boston," a city "with no statues, few pictures, little music outside the churches and no Christmas." Loneliness and melancholy were his frequent companions, and the "shadows of damnation" kept the boy from experiencing many of the pleasures of youth. Holmes eagerly anticipated a future that would liberate him from a "weary time" lived in "barren surroundings."[17] But in addition to these rather gray thoughts, there were also happier memories of time spent away from Boston, of summers at Canoe Meadows and holidays on Cape Cod. "What we love most and revere generally," Holmes once observed, "is determined in early associations. I love granite rocks and bayberry bushes, no doubt because with them were my earliest joys that reach back through the past eternity of my life."[18] Despite what Holmes remembered as the bleakness of his adolescence, his character was irrevocably shaped by the "early associations" of his youth. His family, his teachers, and his friends provided a constant reminder of who he was and what was expected of him. To be equal to that responsibility, and never to be found wanting, became the boy's greatest challenge and fear.

In the fall of 1857, Wendell entered Harvard College as a freshman.

That he should have found his way to Harvard was not surprising. His great-grandfather, Judge Wendell, had been a fellow of the Corporation, and a great-uncle, Jonathan Jackson, had been treasurer. Judge Jackson, his grandfather, was an overseer of the Corporation, and Josiah Quincy, a cousin, was president of the college. His father had graduated from Harvard in 1829 and, in 1847, had joined the faculty of the medical school as professor of anatomy and physiology.[19]

The transition from Mr. Dixwell's school to the college was not a difficult one. His grandmother's gambrel-roofed house was visible across an open field, and the close proximity of his lodgings at Mr. Danforth's to his Uncle John provided an important source of reassurance to a young man living away from home for the first time. He was also closer to the Dixwells' home on Garden Street and continued his association with the family while in college. Mr. Dixwell still took an active interest in his young friend, and Wendell increasingly came to view the Dixwells as his second family.[20]

Moreover, during the summer of 1857, Dr. Holmes had moved his family from the house at 8 Montgomery Place to a new home he had built across the common at 21 Charles Street on a site overlooking the Charles River. Even though Wendell and his brother, Neddy, both had rooms on the third floor, the move from the home of his childhood marked the end of an important period in Holmes's life. The boy was quickly becoming his own man, and 21 Charles Street would hereafter be referred to as his father's home rather than his own.[21]

Harvard College, the bastion of Boston's Brahmins, was at mid-century an institution solidly committed to the rigorous indoctrination of its students in the orthodoxy of New England's Puritan past. Receiving a college education was viewed by the faculty as primarily a matter of "organized self-control."[22] Refuting "the stream of licentious and infidel speculations" pouring in "like a flood" from Europe was the faculty's chief challenge and preoccupation.[23] A community of eminent clergymen and respectable scholars, members of the faculty "attended to their duties with commendable assiduity, and drudged along in a dreary, humdrum sort of way."[24] Although it was asserted by supporters of the college that it "helped men of lofty natures to make good their faculties," it was also said that Harvard "taught little, and that little ill."[25]

Despite the presence of a distinguished faculty, teaching at the college had changed remarkably little over the years. In many ways, Harvard was more like a boarding school for the sons of the New England elite than a center of learning. Considerable attention was devoted to enforcing a strict set of ancient rules designed to mold behavior. Employing an elaborate "scale of merit," the faculty attempted to measure moral failings as well as academic achievement. As an institution that considered its primary objective the education of young men in the philosophy and practice of Christianity, even small infractions of the rules were a matter of grave concern. Students could earn points for recitation, written exercises, and final examinations, but they could lose them for sleeping in chapel, shouting out windows, smoking in the yard, or swearing in class.[26]

There were professors, however, who were more concerned with the substance of education than with its form. But even men like Louis Agassiz, who taught the new science of zoology, and Asa Gray, who taught natural history, continued to rely heavily on traditional methods of instruction. Lectures were given with little change year after year; if the truth never changed, why should the lectures? Students learned the principles through rote memorization, never challenging the faculty and rarely asking any questions. Called to educate ministers of the gospel and convince young gentlemen of the virtues of a Christian education, the faculty at Harvard College seldom challenged the conventional wisdom or threatened traditional understanding.[27]

Most of these men were well known to Wendell when he arrived at Harvard; many were either personal friends of his father's or family acquaintances. But rather than exploit this familiarity, Holmes chose to distance himself from the college crowd by taking a room off campus at Mr. Danforth's on Linden Street. Close to the college yard, the room suited his preference for quiet and removed him from the "constant war" between the faculty and students. Thus attaining a measure of anonymity, the young man faced the challenge of making it on his own name rather than on his father's. Dr. Holmes's position and reputation could introduce his son to the intellectual aristocracy of the college, but it was clear that his son would have to "make good his own place."[28]

Although reserved and something of a spectator during his first year at Harvard, Wendell soon formed friendships that would last throughout the years. In addition to John Morse, who had entered Harvard the previous year, many of Holmes's classmates from Mr. Dixwell's had made the trip to Cambridge with him. Among them was Henry Bowditch, a Dixwell relation whom Wendell had gotten to know and like. Most of the young men at Harvard were from New England. There were several boys from the South, however, like William Henry Fitzhugh Lee, the son of Robert E. Lee and the grandson of "Lighthorse" Harry Lee, and others from throughout the country. One of these, Norwood P. Hallowell, the son of a distinguished Philadelphia Quaker family, soon became one of Wendell's closest friends.[29]

Wendell Holmes entered his sophomore year with an undistinguished but better than average academic record. He had suffered the mild disgrace of being punished with fourteen other students for creating a disturbance in the yard following freshmen examinations, but despite the loss of thirty-two points for this misconduct, had managed to accumulate 4,933 points, and stood twenty-second among ninety-six students.[30] During his second year at college, things did not go as well, and he dropped to thirtieth among eighty-four students.[31] In December of 1858, however, the *Harvard Magazine* published an anonymous article entitled "Books." The first of Holmes's contributions to the magazine, the piece displayed considerable disdain for those who preferred the life of events over that of ideas.

The article suggested that students at Harvard who had "somewhat higher aspirations than the mass of their companions" had turned to books for inspiration, as they had found the society of their peers unsatisfying. Expressing considerable frustration with the orthodoxy that governed education at Harvard, the author exclaimed that "a hundred years ago we burnt men's bodies for not agreeing with our religious tenets; we still burn their souls." Going even further, he inquired, "Do Men own other men by God's law?" Perhaps the most telling lines were the ones that follow:

> Can we help going to our rooms and crying that we might not think? And we whistle or beat on the piano, and some—God help 'em!— smoke and drink to drive it away, and others find their resting-place in some creed which defines all their possibilities, and says, thus far shall we think, and no further.[32]

Perhaps as a reward for what his classmates must have recognized as his handiwork, Wendell was chosen to write the class poem for the sophomore class banquet in the spring of 1859. Accepting the challenge, Holmes composed an ode to youth and brotherhood reflecting an altogether different sentiment:

> Babies in life, we shall play with its roses,
> Boys, see their opening; men watch their decay;

But the beauty departing a higher discloses,
And we find the fruit just as the flower drops away.

Then drink to our mother, our bountiful mother,
For we shall all love her, wherever we go;
Both for her motherhood, and for our brotherhood,
We shall all love her wherever we go.[33]

Such words suggest that at least as a second-year college student, Holmes experienced both the emotions of an angry young man and the satisfaction of establishing his own identity.

In 1859, Wendell Holmes returned to Harvard as a junior and soon began what would be his best year at college. His reading had increased dramatically over the summer, as his interest in philosophy commenced in earnest. Works by Plato, Comte, Fichte, and Spenser were among the books Holmes began to absorb.[34] At Christmas, Wendell received a copy of Plato's *Works* and a copy of Homer's *Iliad* as gifts from his sister, Amelia, and brother, Edward.[35] Starting on Plato, he became discouraged and sought help in interpreting the Greek philosopher from Uncle Waldo. Holmes undoubtedly hoped to find the answers to his questions from Emerson; instead, the philosopher set his eager young pupil "on fire" with a challenge befitting Socrates: "Hold him at arms length [and] say to yourself: 'Plato, you have pleased the world for two thousand years—let us see if you can please me.'"[36] Thus cautioned by the sage of Concord, Holmes reread Plato with a new discernment. The extent of his involvement with his reading was evidenced by an article he wrote as a means of understanding better Plato's writing. When completed, he rushed to show it to his mentor. After reading it, Emerson returned it with the comment, "When you strike at a king, you must kill him." Disappointed but not disheartened, Holmes went to work rethinking his analysis.[37]

In addition to his developing interest in literary study, Holmes was also increasingly active in less scholarly pursuits. Toward the close of his sophomore year, he had joined the Christian Union, a considerably more liberal student organization than the orthodox Christian Brethren. Like political parties, these two groups reflected the competing views of the students at Harvard during Holmes's day. Undergraduates were faced with a choice of being considered either a "prig" or a "snob," with membership in the Christian Brethren suggesting the first, and membership in the Christian Union the latter. Despite Holmes's membership, he attempted a compromise between being either a bookish snob or a moralistic prig. A comrade in arms with men in both camps, Holmes enthusiastically participated in the fraternity of numerous organizations; among these were the Hasty Pudding Club, the Porcellian Club, and Alpha Delta Phi.[38]

At the end of his junior year, Holmes had risen to thirteenth place in his class and had been invited like his father before him to accept membership in the distinguished honorary society, Phi Beta Kappa.[39] During the summer of 1860, Holmes rewrote his essay on Plato, and when he returned to Harvard in the fall, he submitted it to the *University Quarterly*, a collegiate journal known for its demanding standards. In October, the article was published, and in addition, he received the annual prize of twenty dollars for submitting the best undergraduate essay of 1860.[40]

As a senior, Holmes was asked to become an editor of the *Harvard Magazine*, a publication containing primarily articles and notes from undergraduates. In the October issue, Holmes published an article entitled "Notes on Albert Dürer" which reflected his intense interest in drawing and the engraver's art. Most likely another product of his active summer of writing, the essay was characterized by one art historian as "a magnificent piece of precocious writing."[41] Holmes's principal argument challenged in a fundamental way Harvard's conventional wisdom: "Art does not finally depend for inspiration on religious form. The ideal spirit may be influenced by circumstances, but it is a great gift of humanity, not of a sect; it inspired the philosopher, Plato, the artist among thinkers, as well as the Christian Dürer, a thinker among artists."[42] Like his article on Plato, his essay on Dürer suggested the extent to which the "accumulation of new material" might result in the "correction or annulling" of previously settled beliefs.[43] Taken together, Holmes's articles on Plato and Dürer revealed his attempt to discover a "noble philosophy," one that might properly teach him his duty to "himself, his neighbor, and his God."[44]

The unorthodox nature of Holmes's quest did not go unnoticed by his peers; the December issue of the *Harvard Magazine* contained a highly critical review of Holmes's essay on Albert Dürer. Written by an indignant classmate destined to become an Episcopal minister, the review accused Holmes of being an Emerson disciple, and of endorsing a "dreamy, transcendent, artistic religion" antithetical to true Christian reason and piety. Holmes, one of the three senior editors of the paper, allowed the review to be published without comment, apparently willing to permit a member of the Christian Brethren to have his say.[45]

A more serious challenge to the circulation of Holmes's views and those of his fellow editors involved an unsigned article commenting upon the resignation of a member of the faculty. Written by Wendell Phillips Garrison, the piece was arguably disrespectful in both tone and language. Given the faculty's general distaste for the liberal philosophy expounded by the student magazine, it was not surprising that the faculty pressured the president of the college to threaten that if such intolerable behavior continued, publication of the periodical would be discontinued.[46]

Nor was this Holmes's only problem with the faculty. During his senior year, he was twice "publicly admonished" for his "repeated and gross indecorum" during class. Specifically, he had disturbed recitation in Professor Bowen's religion class. An outspoken opponent of Emerson, Dr. Bowen took every opportunity to denounce in his classes Emerson's "glowing but vague conception of virtue" which Bowen believed Emerson intended to take "the place of religion as a guide of life." A staunch supporter of the Christian Brethren, Dr. Bowen urged his students to accept the reality that morality could not "find anywhere a sure and permanent support except in a recognition of its dictates as the command of God." Given Holmes's association with Emerson, and his stark statement in his essay on Dürer that man was bound by a moral duty that would be "no less binding had the Bible never been written," his antagonism toward Professor Bowen might have been expected. But his willingness to challenge openly the instruction of a member of the faculty indicated more than his disagreement with the subject matter; it reflected the increasing rebellion of a young mind which no longer accepted the authority of the conventional wisdom.[47]

As the American nation passed from a precarious unity to the brink of Civil War during the early months of 1861, Wendell Holmes widened his personal breach with Harvard College and the traditional moral values it represented. As one state after another seceded from the Union, Boston's State Street continued to hum with southern trade. Closely aligned with Boston's commercial aristocracy, the Harvard faculty was politically conservative, and not particularly opposed to slavery. Although philosophically committed to the ideal of individual freedom, most professors were more concerned with the protection of private property. They generally supported the legal position of southern slave owners that they were entitled to hold their property without interference. In the debate over Abolition, only Emerson, Sumner, and Lowell had spoken out unambiguously against the "peculiar institution" of slavery;

the majority of Harvard's learned men had chosen to remain silent on the issue.[48]

During his college years, Holmes himself had become "a pretty convinced abolitionist."[49] As he would later recall, he was so deeply moved by the Abolition cause that a Negro minstrel show shocked him, and "the morality of Pickwick" seemed "painfully blunt."[50] Undoubtedly, Holmes's sympathetic attitude was at least partially influenced by childhood experiences. In April 1851, a fugitive slave by the name of Thomas Sims was captured and imprisoned in the Boston courthouse located only a short distance from Dr. Holmes's home on Montgomery Place. Public opinion was fiercely divided concerning whether or not slavery should be tolerated in such a civilized place as Boston. The question was eventually decided in court; the judge ordered that Sims be returned to his lawful owner, and under heavy guard, the black man was escorted down the Long Wharf to a ship bound for Savannah. Law and order were preserved, but many Bostonians argued that justice had not been done.[51] Three years later, another fugitive slave, Anthony Burns, was captured and placed in the Boston courthouse. On this occasion, however, the distinguished Boston attorney Richard Dana offered to defend the imprisoned man. While the case was pending, a group of radical abolitionists known as the Vigilance Committee attempted to free Burns from jail. Led by two of Holmes's relatives—Wendell Phillips and Edmund Quincy—an angry group of abolitionists met at Faneuil Hall to plan the rescue. They were soon confronted by an equal number who opposed their plan, and a riot broke out. Shots were fired, and several men were wounded. One of these, T. W. Higginson, sought the aid of Dr. Holmes at his home, and while having his head wound bandaged, he recounted the events of the evening to the doctor's wide-eyed son.[52]

Despite the active involvement of Holmes's cousins in the affair, his father remained completely outside the Abolition movement. Along with many other prominent men of the Brahmin class, Dr. Holmes saw no way that "the compact made by their fathers" could be kept and slavery abolished. If the Constitution of 1787 and the nation it brought into being were to be preserved, the institution of slavery would have to be tolerated.[53] Dr. Holmes's hesitancy to condemn those who owned slaves may also have been influenced by the fact that one of his own forebears—Dorothy Quincy Jackson—had owned slaves. Although the elder Holmes personally considered slavery "dreadful business," he defended its existence as the cost of avoiding "the catastrophe of disunion."[54]

31

Oliver Wendell Holmes, Jr., however, had come to a different conclusion on the issue. Throughout his senior year at Harvard, he had
become increasingly convinced that slavery was wrong and that it should
be abolished by force of arms if necessary. In January 1861, shortly after
the election of Abraham Lincoln as president of the United States, the
Massachusetts Anti-Slavery Society planned its annual meeting at the
Tremont Temple in Boston. City officials knew that such a meeting
would likely provoke violence and made it clear to the organizers that
the safety of those attending the meeting could not be guaranteed.
Among those scheduled to speak were Boston's most outspoken abolitionists—Ralph Waldo Emerson, Wendell Phillips, James Freeman
Clarke, and Edmund Quincy. With the exception of Emerson, these men
were generally viewed with contempt by Boston's leading families. Wendell Phillips, in particular, was looked upon as an extremely dangerous
demagogue. The son of the first mayor of Boston, Phillips had forfeited
his place among the city's elite through his militant and unrestrained
support of Abolition. Excluded from homes of refined and prosperous
Bostonians where he had once been welcome, he further alienated himself from his former friends by associating with others who shared his
extreme political views.[55]

One of these associates was Richard Price Hallowell, the elder
brother of Holmes's classmate and close friend, Norwood Penrose Hallowell. A Philadelphia Quaker turned Boston merchant, Hallowell was
at the center of the Boston abolitionist movement. When he learned
that Phillips's life had been threatened, he took it upon himself to organize a private bodyguard of young men loyal to the cause. Holmes was
one of the "little band" who "intended to see Wendell Phillips through
if there was a row after the meeting of the Anti-Slavery Society."[56] Although the mayor of Boston closed the Tremont Temple after the society's morning session when it appeared that a serious clash might occur,
the threat against the abolitionists was very real, as was Holmes's willingness to stand against it. More than a college lark, or the simple commitment of a friend to a friend, his action reflected his loyalty to Emerson
and those who shared his principles. Although the actual threat was
made against the unpopular Phillips, the mob's message to the abolitionists was clear; it would decide who could speak and be heard in Boston
and who could not. The fact that Emerson and his associates refused to
be silenced by such intimidation impressed Holmes and helped him reach
the conclusion that his place was with those defending the right of
the unpopular minority to be heard. As if to make his decision clear

to the world, Holmes's name soon appeared among a list of supporters of the abolitionist cause published in the *Liberator;* although his actual financial contribution was only twenty-five cents, it was sufficient to make a public gesture of where he stood on the issue of slavery and free speech.[57]

Holmes's behavior reflected the strivings of an adolescent college student to become independent. Rather than merely becoming a rebel against his father and his father's world, Holmes struggled to become his own man—to think his own thoughts and live his own life. His sense of urgency in becoming a man may have been intensified in February 1861 as a result of the death of his close friend Francis Lowell Gardner. A fellow roommate at Mr. Danforth's, Gardner and several other young men—including Holmes—had gone on a shooting trip to Cotuit on Cape Cod. In a tragic accident, Gardner was killed. Holmes and his classmates were deeply affected by this unexpected loss. In a eulogy written for the Porcellian Club, Holmes exalted the "manly qualities" that had won Gardner "the love of his companions" and earned him the respect of all who knew him. A "truly chivalrous gentleman," this "beloved brother and friend" had brought honor "to his college, his class, and his club." There was little doubt that Holmes hoped to measure up to the same standard.[58]

As public debate over slavery intensified, the governor of Massachusetts, John Andrew, began to prepare for war in earnest. While proper Bostonians scoffed, Andrew sent agents to Europe to procure necessary military supplies. As one after another state slipped out of the Union, Boston's merchants continued to concern themselves with the economic impact of secession on their businesses. On 9 April 1861, President Lincoln attempted to assert Union control over Fort Sumter in Charleston Harbor, South Carolina. Against the advice of his principal counselors, he ordered that military provisions be sent to the fort immediately. South Carolina, the first of the southern states to secede from the Union, retaliated by shelling the fort, which surrendered on 14 April 1861. Within a few days, Lincoln had appealed to the governors of the northern states to raise a force of seventy-five thousand militiamen to suppress the southern rebellion.[59]

In response to Lincoln's urgent plea, Governor Andrew placed at the president's immediate disposal five Massachusetts infantry regiments, one battalion of riflemen, and one artillery battalion. On 19 April, the Sixth Massachusetts Regiment reached Baltimore, Maryland, on its way south to protect the federal capital at Washington, D.C.; as the soldiers marched through the streets, they were stoned and fired upon by Confederate sympathizers. Four men were killed, and forty-one wounded. With these deaths, debate over slavery ended in Boston.[60]

While the nation prepared for war, the Harvard faculty prepared for graduation. The professors met on 22 April to review the class standing of the members of the class of 1861. The following day, President Cornelius Felton sent Dr. Holmes a distressing letter; he informed Holmes that although his son was "an excellent young man," his conduct of late had become the subject of frequent complaint. Specifically, the boy had incurred the wrath of the faculty by breaking a freshman's window, a most grievous offense usually punished by expulsion from the college. As those responsible for the offense had voluntarily confessed their misdeed and made an appropriate apology, the faculty had voted on a "public admonition" and a fine of ten dollars. President Felton observed that the incident seemed to be the result of "some influence" to which Holmes "had not heretofore yielded."[61]

Much to the faculty's surprise, Dr. Holmes personally informed President Felton that it was his son's intention to enlist in the army and that he was already on his way to Fort Independence. In fact, Holmes had decided several days earlier to join his classmates, Penrose Hallowell and Henry Abbott, in the Fourth Battalion of the New England Guard. On the twenty-fifth, he reported to the Boston Armory, and was sent to Fort Independence on Castle Island in Boston Harbor for drill instruction and garrison duty. Reveille at the fort was at sunrise, and the young recruits drilled on the parade ground for six hours every day. Responsibilities included guard duty and other routine tasks. Surrounded by his old friends and acquaintances, Holmes learned the basic skills of soldiering. On 25 May, his tour of duty at the fort ended; the battalion boarded a steamer, and sailed from Castle Island across the harbor to the Long Wharf. Received with enthusiastic acclamation, the battalion marched to the parade ground on Boston Common to the sound of a military band.[62]

In response to Dr. Holmes's notification of his son's decision, Dr. Felton had conveyed to the boy's father the faculty's concern that Holmes had neither informed the college of his plans nor returned to take his final exams. He had, in short, abandoned "his duties at the College without saying a word to any of the College authorities"; as a consequence, the faculty had voted to allow him to take his degree, but without rank or any honors at graduation.[63] Dr. Holmes was outraged at this intentional slight. In language befitting his mood, he challenged the faculty's decision: "He left College suddenly, no doubt, but if he did not stop to kiss his Alma Mater, neither did many other volunteers stop to kiss their mothers, wives, and sweethearts. . . . For his promptitude in offering his services, he is not only deprived of . . . honors, but is consigned to the inglorious half of the Class."[64] Dr. Holmes's letter concluded by noting that it seemed particularly harsh that his son should be punished for so promptly answering his nation's call to arms. The letter thus questioned at least indirectly the college's lack of enthusiasm for the war. It is interesting to note that whereas thirty-two of the thirty-five faculty members of the College of William and Mary, a distinguished southern college, enlisted in the Confederate Army, only one member of the Harvard faculty offered his services to the Union Army during the war. George Adam Schmitt, a German refugee who had taught Holmes German in his junior year, became an officer in the Twentieth Massachusetts Regiment. Although many Harvard alumni would join this unit—including Holmes—no other member of the faculty left the college for the front during the Civil War.[65]

Compelled by conscience and his sense of himself, Holmes had joined "the Christian Crusade of the 19th Century" expecting to be sent south as a private as soon as his training at Fort Independence was completed. Although aware of the likely consequences of his abrupt departure from Harvard, he was prepared to forfeit his college degree if necessary to join what he considered a fight "in the cause of the whole civilized world."[66] If his professors at Harvard couldn't understand his actions, their reactions only served to confirm Holmes's suspicion that these old men had little of real value to teach him. It soon became clear, however, that the Fourth Battalion would not be sent south, and Holmes would not be leaving Boston as soon as he had hoped. By the end of May, Governor Andrew was calling for the formation of new regiments and was anxious to recruit as many men with military experience as possible as officers. With little more than a month's training, Holmes sought the assistance of one of his mother's cousins, Colonel Henry Lee, who was serving as Governor Andrew's aide. With his help, Holmes hoped to secure a commission as a junior officer in one of Andrew's new Massachusetts regiments.[67]

While his petition to the governor was pending, Holmes was notified by the Harvard faculty that he would be allowed to graduate with his class if he returned to take his final examinations. Moreover, if Holmes passed his exams, he would suffer no other penalty than the loss of points for accumulated absences from mandatory recitations and chapel. Holmes and Hallowell returned to Harvard and successfully completed the faculty's requirements for graduation. On 21 June, they participated in their Class Day exercises—Holmes had been elected by his classmates as class poet like his father before him, and Hallowell had been elected class orator. Before family and friends in the First Church meetinghouse in Cambridge, Oliver Wendell Holmes, Jr., urged his classmates from his grandfather's old pulpit to "be brave, for now the thunder rolls."[68]

Shortly before graduation, Holmes wrote an autobiographical sketch for his class album. He mentioned in his piece for the yearbook that members of his family were in the habit of acquiring a college education, and added that he hoped to study law if he survived the war, "at least as a starting point."[69] On 10 July, as Holmes was walking home from the Boston Athenaeum with a copy of Hobbes's *Leviathan* under his arm, he passed the state house and learned that Governor Andrew had signed his commission as a first lieutenant in the Twentieth Massachusetts volunteers—the new "Harvard Regiment." He returned the book to the library and rushed home to prepare to enter his three-year enlistment in the Union Army.[70]

The final months of Holmes's college career had been a time of testing for the young man, a time when both his convictions and his doubts had begun to take their final shape. Accustomed as a boy to distrusting his own judgment, Holmes had finally begun to trust his intuition instead of the instruction of others. Rather than shrinking from physical hardship, he accepted willingly the "very hard, very cold, very vacant" glare that the war cast over Boston. Like his Puritan ancestors before him, Holmes seemed to find in this harsh reality the very "heart of his being."[71] Deeming it his duty to fight, he was determined that his "manly qualities" should not be found wanting.

3

CALL TO ARMS

Impatient with college life and anxious to become a man, Wendell Holmes had enlisted in the Fourth Battalion at Fort Independence. Resolved to join in the fight, he had used his family's influence to gain a commission in a regular Massachusetts regiment when it became clear that the Fourth Battalion would not be sent south. During the second week in July 1861, the eager recruit learned that Governor Andrew had finally acceded to the recommendations of Holmes's supporters. Commissioned a first lieutenant in the newly formed Twentieth Regiment, Massachusetts Volunteers, the young junior officer was ordered to Pittsfield, Massachusetts, to recruit additional enlisted men from the regiment. Among old friends and surrounded by scenes from his childhood summers, Holmes began his military career.[1]

Holmes was not alone in his enthusiasm for the war. Of the eighty-one men in his class at Harvard, sixty-two joined the army—fifty-seven for the Union and five for the Confederacy.[2] Military service would change all of them and create a bond far stronger than their ties to school or class. Friends who did not go to war—like Henry Adams who observed the war from London as secretary to his father who had been appointed ambassador to England—would never again enjoy the intimacy and trust that existed between those who survived military service.

Each of Holmes's friends who enlisted had his own reasons for going to war. Some joined in the conflict out of a sense of duty, others because they believed in the northern cause. For Holmes, it was a combination of influences. Although he would come to respect those who stood against him on the field of battle "with feelings not different in kind" from those he felt for men who fought by his side, his attitude toward southerners at the outset of the war was harshly negative. Late in his life, Holmes recalled his opinion of the "comparatively primitive intel-lectual condition" of "southern gentlemen . . . an arrogant crew who knew nothing of the ideas that make the life of a few thousands that may be called civilized."[3] The conflict between North and South seemed in-evitable to Holmes; slavery had lasted long enough, and it was impera-tive that the North should win. Holmes's decision to enlist was also influenced by the actions of his close friend, Norwood Penrose Hallo-well. A Philadelphia Quaker with strong convictions, Hallowell gave the "first adult impulse" to Holmes's youth; away from home and on his own at college, Hallowell served as an important example for Holmes as he struggled to achieve his own identity and independence.[4]

On 22 August, Holmes was ordered to join the regiment, which had pitched its tents at Camp Massasoit, eight miles south of Boston near the town of Readville. He arrived at camp on the twenty-third, just as news of the army's disastrous defeat at Bull Run reached the regiment. Despite difficulties in filling the ranks, it was clear that the regiment would soon be ordered south. The formation of the first regiments of Massachusetts Volunteers had seriously depleted the number of available men, and the news from the front had dampened the enthusiasm of many of those. Put on alert in mid-July, the regiment had been brought to nearly full strength through transfers from other units. When Holmes arrived, some eight hundred men were already assembled at Camp Massasoit.[5]

Assigned to Company A under the command of Capt. Henry M. Tremlett, Holmes joined a regiment markedly different from other Mas-sachusetts units. No attempt had been made to organize the Twentieth along the typical "county" basis of other units of volunteers. Unlike the Fifteenth Regiment, for example, which was known as the "Worcester" by virtue of the fact that it was formed of companies of men drawn from towns like Fitchburg, Clinton, and Grafton, the Twentieth enlisted men from throughout the commonwealth. Several individual companies in the Twentieth did have a particular composition, however. Companies B and C became known as the "German" companies because they were composed exclusively of German immigrants; Company I was composed primarily of men from Nantucket. Thus, the most notable characteristic of this "rag-tag" regiment was the fact that most of its officers were Harvard alumni representing the leading families of Massachusetts.[6]

The Twentieth had been organized by Col. William Raymond Lee, a West Point classmate of Jefferson Davis, who had left the army and established himself as a civil engineer in Roxbury, south of Boston. No relation to the governor's aide, Col. Henry Lee, he had been appointed by Governor Andrew to form and command the Twentieth Regiment, Massachusetts Volunteers, on 26 June 1861. Colonel Lee chose Francis W. Palfrey, the son of the famous historian John Gorham Palfrey, as his lieutenant colonel and second in command. Palfrey had served as a lieutenant in Company B of the Fourth Battalion at Fort Independence, and accordingly had firsthand knowledge of the qualifications and capabilities of those seeking officer commissions in the new regiment. Upon his recommendations, William Francis Bartlett and John C. Putnam received commissions as captains, Henry L. Abbott as a second lieutenant, and Norwood Penrose Hallowell as a first lieutenant. Not surprisingly, the regiment quickly came to be known as "the Harvard Regiment."[7]

The regiment also acquired another designation, however—"the Copperhead Regiment." Among its officers were numerous men who were bitterly opposed to the sentiments of both President Lincoln and Governor Andrew. Known as "Copperheads," men like Lieutenant Colonel Palfrey, Maj. Charles A. Whittier, Captain Bartlett, and Lieutenant Abbott opposed the politics of the newly formed Republican party, as well as the crusading morality of the Boston abolitionists. Supporters of Gen. George McClellan and the Democratic party, these men were skeptical of the capabilities of the political leadership in Washington and had no confidence in the Republican War Department; nevertheless, they were prepared to give their lives in the service of their nation in order to preserve the Union.[8]

Not all the regiment's officers were from Harvard or shared these views. Ferdinand Dreher and John Herchenroder had joined their compatriot George Adam Schmitt as captains in the regiment. Dreher in particular was uncomfortable with what he perceived as "an aristocratic clique" of young officers. A Prussian who had served as a major in the German revolution of 1848, Dreher had little respect for the military competence of the group, noting that he could "take all the military sciences out of these gentlemen, and put them in a private, and it would still not make the best sergeant" in the regiment. Although not included by Dreher as one of the group's leaders, Holmes was named by him as one of its members.[9] Other officers in the regiment were also concerned about Palfrey and his "protégés"; Governor Andrew had expressed his fear that under Palfrey's command, merit might "yield to favor," with advancement in the regiment reduced to "the private property of a few neighbors."[10] Palfrey himself was warned by a senior officer that the sooner he rid himself of "this blue-blooded notion," the better off he and his regiment would be.[11] Understandably, those officers who did not share the privileged world of the Harvard clique quickly became suspicious of a group they viewed as snobbish and exclusive.

Even though Holmes did not share the same political views as the Copperheads and maintained his special relationship with "Pen" Hallowell, he enjoyed the favor of the group and soon came to admire their cavalier attitude and animated comradeship. Holmes particularly respected the courage of Whittier and Abbott, who cared little for the cause, but devoted themselves exclusively to doing their duty. Consistent with his growing admiration for the officers who had served in the regular army prior to the war, his respect for those who quietly did their duty reflected Holmes's new appreciation of the standards of those who had chosen the profession of arms.[12]

Lieutenant Holmes's duties at Camp Massasoit were those of a junior officer putting a disorganized group of men into shape for immediate active duty. Already put on alert, the regiment was busy making its final preparations for departure when Holmes arrived in camp. Finding the men in his company only slightly trained, he drilled his charges in the same skills he himself had only recently mastered a few weeks earlier at Fort Independence. Near the end of the month, Governor Andrew led a large delegation from Boston to review the troops. The ladies of the city presented the regiment with a white silk standard, the governor made a speech, and the civilian assembly departed; it was to be their last review of the Twentieth, as it received orders to march on 4 September. With little notice of the regiment's departure, H. B. Sargent represented the governor as the troops were called into formation and marched to the train station at Readville. Having no opportunity to march to Boston to parade on the common, the Twentieth Regiment, Massachusetts Volunteers, went off to war, moving south to Groton, Connecticut, by rail.[13]

At Groton, the regiment was transported across Long Island Sound to New York City by the steamship *Commodore*. From New York, the unit traveled by train through Philadelphia and Wilmington to Baltimore. Despite persistent problems of discipline within the ranks, the troops became more serious as they marched through Baltimore from one train station to the other. Remembering the experience of the Sixth Regiment, the Twentieth marched with standards unfurled and rifles loaded, prepared to fight if the need arose. Arriving at their destination without incident, the men boarded cattle cars for the final leg of their journey to Washington, D.C. They arrived near the Capitol, and after forming into battle-line formation, marched out Pennsylvania Avenue to Camp Kalorama on Georgetown Heights.[14]

The trip south had taken several days, and as Holmes reported in his first letter home from Georgetown Heights, the passage was "very long and there was very little sleep or food." Perhaps to reassure his family, or perhaps out of ignorance, he added that he thought the regiment had "seen the worst of hardships, unless on special occasions."[15] The regiment, now under the command of Gen. Frederick W. Lander, spent two days at Camp Kalorama and then was ordered on 9 September to take up a position closer to the Capitol at Camp Burnside on Meridian Hill overlooking the city. For several days the regiment enjoyed a brief interlude of relative tranquillity, as it recovered from its trip south and concentrated on improving military discipline among the troops. Holmes, feeling "very well and in very good spirits," reported that he was "certainly trying" to learn all he could of "a regular soldier's life."[16]

On 12 September, the regiment received its orders to join Gen. Charles P. Stone's "Corps of Observation" on the front lines. The regiment struck its tents and prepared to march to its new camp near Poolesville, Maryland. Marching nine miles through Georgetown and along the Potomac River in the first day, the regiment reached its destination two miles from Edwards Ferry two days later. Responsible for keeping an eye on rebel troop movement across the river near Leesburg, Virginia, the regiment was assigned routine picket and guard duty along the canal that ran beside the river. With the exception of occasional rifle fire and verbal exchanges between Union and Confederate pickets along the river, the regiment occupied itself for the next several weeks in steady drilling which at times became grueling for the raw recruits. By the end of the first few weeks, Colonel Lee could boast that his regiment was ready to march upon the first order.[17]

While Holmes waited for the war to become real, he wrote his family concerning his experiences as a soldier. His father had already received at least one report of his "soldier boy" and his "pleasant smiles"; though a green recruit himself, Lieutenant Holmes was pleased with the air of neatness and discipline that pervaded the camp. Very soldierlike, he shared the confidence within the regiment of its generally superior quality. Nevertheless, only days away from seeing the brutality of war close up, the young soldier could end his letters with the salutations of a boy: "God bless you my darling [Mother]"; "Bestest love to Dadkin"; "Love to the babbies"; and "Goodnight my loveliest and sweetest [Mother]."[18]

On the evening of Sunday, 20 October, the quiet was broken by a new bugle call—the call to battle. Throughout the night, units of the Twentieth Regiment joined others from the Fifteenth Regiment, Massachusetts Volunteers, under the command of Col. Charles Devens, and crossed the Potomac River into Virginia. Harrison's Island, a few miles above Edwards Ferry, lay mid-stream, providing a convenient stepping-stone, but the current was swift and the river deep, and the troops had only four scavenged river scows to assist their crossing. By the following morning, some 2,000 of the 8,400 men in Stone's corps had crossed the river and taken up their position in a field known as Ball's Bluff at the top of a cliff rising a hundred feet from the riverbank. The men met no resistance as they formed a straight line across the field. Under the command of Col. Edward D. Baker, a former U.S. senator from Oregon, the Union forces included companies from the California and Tammany regiments. Within hours, Colonel Baker would lie dead, together with nearly 900 of his men and 300 of the enemy's.[19]

The Battle of Ball's Bluff was a needless minor engagement which was later dignified by being named a "battle" only because of the heavy loss of lives. Initiated by the Union as a reconnaissance maneuver, it was intended to provide information about the strength of the Confederate Seventh Brigade. Camped near Leesburg, Virginia, the brigade comprised four infantry regiments from Virginia and Mississippi, with three companies of cavalry and six artillery pieces, totaling in all about four thousand men. With little reliable intelligence concerning the true strength or location of his opponent's forces, General Stone ordered twenty-two companies—roughly a fourth of his command—across the river. Having been in the field for little more than a month and lacking combat experience, the field commanders were unacquainted with one another and unsure of the chain of command. With only the barest orders concerning their objective, the companies followed one another across the river; no one made any preparation for a possible retreat. In short, Ball's Bluff revealed the terrible consequences for the Union of fighting an "amateur battle."[20]

Shortly after 2:00 P.M. on the afternoon of 21 October, the engagement commenced in earnest; the various companies of the Twentieth

Regiment immediately sustained heavy casualties as a result of their forward position. Holmes's company was particularly hard hit, as it was among the front ranks. Whistling rifle balls "flew like hail," and company after company wilted under the terrible fire. As one survivor described the awful scene, "the ground was smoking, and covered with blood, while the noise was perfectly deadening. Men were dying underfoot, and here and there a horse struggling in death. Coats and guns were strewn over the ground in all directions."[21] Colonel Baker was hit by a volley of enemy bullets, but with so many officers either dead or wounded, and the general confusion of the battlefield, no one took command. The Union troops were forced back to the edge of the cliffs, faced with a choice of being shot advancing on the enemy or being slaughtered like sheep at the foot of the bluff. The river ran red with the blood of the dead and dying.[22]

After nearly an hour of deadly combat, Holmes was struck in the stomach by a spent ball; picking himself up from the ground to fire another round, he was hit again, this time by two live balls in his right chest. Among the fortunate men who were only wounded during the battle, Holmes was carried down the bluff and transported safely across the river to Harrison's Island, where a makeshift field hospital had been set up in two abandoned houses, Many did not fare as well. One boat loaded with wounded capsized mid-stream; all aboard drowned. Of the twenty-two officers in the regiment who took their positions on Ball's Bluff, only nine returned from the battle unharmed. Among these were Holmes's heroes—Bartlett, Abbott, and Whittier—and his closest personal friend, Hallowell. Colonel Lee and Major Revere were captured during the battle, after refusing to cross the river until they had seen to their wounded and dying men.[23]

On Harrison's Island, Drs. Haven and Hayward—surgeons for the Fifteenth and Twentieth Massachusetts regiments—did what they could in the chaos of the ghastly debacle. Using old doors ripped out of houses as litters, they moved as many of the wounded as possible by canal boat to Edwards Ferry, where they were transferred to wagons and carried overland to Camp Benton near Poolesville and more adequate hospital facilities. Moving the wounded was made more difficult as a result of the panic that had swept through the troops. Fearing capture by the enemy, many units had fled the vicinity; those who were still about simply refused to help move the wounded.[24]

On 23 October, Holmes sent his first letter home after the battle; it was straightforward and remarkably positive. He reported that though

43

he had thought he was going to die, it now appeared that he had a good chance of surviving his wounds. More important, he was "happy in the conviction" that he had done his duty "handsomely."[25] Lying in the hospital, the young soldier's most reassuring thought was that his parents could be proud of their son.

The Holmeses had been lucky; the rifle balls had passed clean through their son's chest, missing by only a fraction of an inch his heart and lungs. Other Boston boys had been less fortunate, and the death toll from Ball's Bluff continued to rise. Despite the carnage of the defeat, the Twentieth Massachusetts Regiment was praised for its courage. When other units broke and ran, the boys from the Bay State had stood their ground. In front of the fiercest fire, with everything against them, they had held their ranks, every man a hero. Confederate officers at Ball's Bluff reportedly said that fewer officers from the Massachusetts regiment would have been killed if they had surrendered.[26]

Soon after Holmes had written his parents, Nathaniel P. Banks visited the hospital at Camp Benton and sent an even more positive report to Dr. Holmes. He informed the worried father that he had found the patient cheerful and "full of manly spirit"; Lieutenant Colonel Palfrey confirmed the young man's favorable progress by writing that he had found Lieutenant Holmes "smoking and deriving much satisfaction from the contemplation of the photographs of certain young ladies."[27]

Throughout Wendell's ordeal, he was closely attended to by his friend, Pen Hallowell, who had escaped being killed or captured by swimming the river. When it was clear that Holmes was well enough to travel, Hallowell arranged to have his brother William, a civilian, escort Holmes to the Hallowells' home in Philadelphia, and the two traveled north on 31 October. A week later, Dr. Holmes arrived in Philadelphia and found his son "fat and in good spirits."[28] Returning to Boston, father and son made an overnight stop at the Fifth Avenue Hotel in New York City and arrived home on 9 November. Despite Wendell's outward appearance, it was clear to his father that he had changed. Had his confrontation with death taught him something about life that Dr. Holmes did not know? The thought certainly must have crossed the father's mind.

When they arrived at 21 Charles Street, Mrs. Holmes, a skilled nurse, took charge of her son's convalescence. Attended by Dr. Henry Jacob Bigelow, one of Boston's most prominent physicians, Holmes quickly began to recover his strength. He was visited by numerous callers, among the very first, his childhood companion, John Morse. Others included Ida Agassiz and Fanny Dixwell, two of the young man's favorite visitors. He was also honored by the visits of President Felton and Senator Charles Sumner, who were as interested in learning the facts about the Battle of Ball's Bluff from an eyewitness as they were about Holmes's health. In a letter to a friend, Dr. Holmes reported that "Wendell's experience was pretty well for a youngster of twenty," and that the boy was recovering nicely from his "narrow escape from instant death." Disgusted by what he characterized as the "stupid sacrifice" of the battle, Dr. Holmes noted proudly that "they did all that men could be expected to do." Revealing much about his own character, he concluded by saying he envied his "white Otello," the "young hero with wounds in his heart," surrounded by a "semi-circle of young Desdemonas about him listening to the often told tale which they will have again."[29]

Holmes spent the remainder of the winter at home, surrounded by his family and friends in comfortable quarters, recuperating from his near fatal wounds. By the first of the year, he was well enough to rejoin his unit, but received orders to stay in Massachusetts indefinitely, recruiting new men to fill the ranks of the decimated regiment. Colonel Lee and Major Revere were in southern prisons awaiting transfer for Confederate officers held by Union forces, and the regiment was not likely to see immediate action on the front. Holmes traveled throughout the state, urging young men to replace those who had already fallen defending the Union.[30]

On 8 March 1862, Holmes celebrated his twenty-first birthday with his family in Boston. Two weeks later, he received new orders to rejoin his regiment with the new rank of captain. Returning to the front, Captain Holmes was not the same boy who had gone off to war a year earlier. The terrible disaster of Ball's Bluff, and the experience of Harrison's Island where he had calmly awaited death, left Holmes a different person. As he wrote in his diary, he had been forced to distinguish between "a mind still bent on a . . . consistent carrying out of its ideals of conduct" and "the unhesitating instinct of a still predominant and heroic will."[31] Confronting death, Holmes wanted his parents and friends to know that he had done his duty, but he himself knew that he had done so instinctively rather than out of concern for his family's honor. He wrote that he was fully aware that given his opinions concerning God and religion, a "majority vote of the civilized world" declared he was "en route to Hell"; nevertheless, he was prepared to take "a leap in the dark," his only confession being "God forgive me if I am wrong." Ready to "die like a soldier," Holmes faced death unrepentant, asserting both to himself and to others that he had done his duty.[32] Unaided by a Christian faith in salvation which strengthened many of his comrades, Holmes returned to war, confident that he carried within himself sufficient courage to face death once again without fear. "Life must be viewed *sub specie Puritanica.* Man is born to strive, perhaps to lose, but the wages of the great-hearted are secure, and they know it. Let them be at peace, if they will only fight manfully."[33]

In late March 1862, Captain Holmes set out from Boston to rejoin his regiment. A very different man than the young Boston patrician who had set out on a great Christian crusade a year earlier, Holmes was clearly aware of what awaited him. General McClellan, fresh from victories in the West, had been put in command of the Army of the Potomac and had ordered the whole army to advance toward Richmond, Virginia, the Confederate capital. It was clear to everyone that a major new campaign would soon be underway, which it was hoped would put an end to the rebellion and secure victory for the Union forces. In his first letter home after rejoining the regiment, Holmes told his worried parents, "Whatever happens keep up your pluck."[34]

If Holmes's mood was markedly different from what it had been the previous year, the character of the regiment itself had changed during Holmes's absence. Under the command of Lieutenant Colonel Palfrey, serving in the absence of Colonel Lee who was still being held prisoner, the regiment had been plagued by political disagreements and personal jealousies. Holmes undoubtedly remembered the regiment's better days at Poolesville prior to Ball's Bluff and wished that Colonel Lee were still in command.[35] Another junior officer who had joined the unit during Holmes's absence, Lt. Henry Ropes, wrote his brother, John Ropes, of the regiment's growing problems. He was astounded by one of his senior officers' remarkable "obscenity and licentiousness." Commenting on another junior officer, Ropes described him as a "shockingly bad officer," and added that others in the regiment had told him that "Holmes is as bad"[36] That some in the regiment felt this way probably would not have surprised Holmes, who would later remark that he had "a very modest opinion" of his merits as a soldier.[37] Holmes was by nature a quiet and self-reflective individual with very little interest in the dynamics of group politics. Lacking the traditional attributes of a leader, Holmes had not particularly distinguished himself during his relatively brief tenure with the regiment. Nevertheless, as time went on, he gained a reputation for his steadfastness and courage under fire which earned him the respect of his fellow officers. Significantly, Ropes and Holmes became close friends, as Holmes grew into the sometimes difficult job of commanding his company.

Ropes was not alone in his initial judgment of Holmes's ability as an army officer. Henry Abbott, another young officer from Boston, reported soon after Holmes's return to the regiment that he was "most thoroughly and amazingly deficient in military knowledge."[38] Holmes's deficiencies may perhaps be explained by the fact that he had been seriously injured in his first engagement and had spent the past months recovering in Boston while his peers had spent the same time perfecting their knowledge of their craft. Whatever the cause of Holmes's failings as a leader, Abbott also grew to appreciate qualities not immediately observed in the new arrival. Within a few months, he would write that Captain Holmes was "a very good officer," who was "remarkably brave and well instructed."[39]

Two days after Holmes joined his comrades, the regiment traveled by water to Fort Monroe at the mouth of the James River. Part of General John Sedgwick's division of the Second Corps, the Twentieth Massachusetts joined the Army of the Potomac as it moved up the peninsula between the York and James rivers. The army's objective was clear—to take Richmond and end the war. It soon became equally clear that achieving this objective would not be easy. Heavy rains turned the rough roads into rivers of deep mud. Much of the terrain was swampy and covered with tangled underbrush. Making little headway despite great effort, the men soon became exhausted and discouraged. Holmes wrote home, "It's a campaign now and make no mistake. . . . No tents, no trunks, no nothing."[40] Alternately pushing and pulling artillery and wagons through the wilderness, and marching for hours through knee-deep mud, the troops frequently went days without removing their boots or changing their uniforms. In addition to other adversities and discomforts, many of the men—including Holmes—came down with dysentery.

Although Holmes had received his promotion to captain before leaving Boston, his actual commission did not reach the regiment until early May. Until then, he had continued to serve as a lieutenant in Pen Hallowell's company. But during the principal engagements of the Peninsula Campaign, Holmes commanded his own company—Company G. His promotion caused some grumbling in the regiment; Lt. George Perry, who along with Colonel Lee had been taken prisoner at Ball's Bluff, had more seniority than Holmes and by rights, should have received the captaincy before Holmes. Most of Holmes's fellow officers, however, probably shared the view of Lieutenant Abbott that Governor Andrew had properly passed over Lieutenant Perry, as the immediate needs of the regiment outweighed the peacetime niceties of military promotions.[41]

During the final weeks of April, the regiment camped below the Warwick River within sight and shot of the Confederate lines. General McClellan had decided to lay siege to Yorktown on his right flank before turning east for the final drive toward Richmond. By early May, the regiment had occupied earthworks outside Yorktown abandoned by retreating Confederate troops. The regiment was once again commanded by Colonel Lee who, together with Major Revere, had rejoined the regiment. Although his men were glad to see his return, it was clear that the months he had spent in prison had taken their toll. Once again, the costs of war were visibly impressed upon the junior officers.

The regiment did not see action during the unfortunate Battle of Williamsburg on 5 May but was ordered to proceed by boat to West Point, where the Mattapony and Pamunkey rivers join to form the York River. From there the regiment moved on to Camp Tyler along the Pamunkey River, where it prepared in earnest for the inevitable battle. Soon the regiment was on the move again, this time through mud and marshes, crossing the Chickahominy River, and reaching by 30 May a position only seven miles east of Richmond. Plagued by a series of small and isolated skirmishes, men had fallen by ones and twos during the past weeks, not by entire companies as at Ball's Bluff. By the time the regiment joined the rest of the Second Corps, a third of the men were sick, and the remainder tired and exhausted. Holmes, who had suffered an earlier bout of dysentery, had recovered sufficiently to take command of his company.[42]

On the evening of 30 May, torrential rains fell, swelling the Chickahominy which divided the Union Army. General Joseph E. Johnston, the Confederate commander, seized the opportunity to take the offensive. The Confederate Army attacked early the following morning, surprising McClellan who had not anticipated finding himself on the defensive and who had not yet consolidated his forces. By the afternoon of 31 May, the Twentieth Massachusetts Regiment had been ordered to advance, and soon joined in the Battle of Fair Oaks. Holmes's company entered a wood "firing hard" and trying not to cross the Union line of fire. A company of rebels was "knocked to pieces," as the fighting grew more intense. As the shadows lengthened, the growing dusk allowed the men "to see clearly the lines of flames from the different Regiments as they fired," a sight "splendid and awful to behold."[43]

During the first day of the battle, General Edwin V. Sumner's Second Corps had stopped Johnston's assault; General Johnston himself had been severely wounded, and General Lee had assumed command of the southern army. Holmes's company, along with hundreds of others, had held the line, turning what might have been a fatal Union defeat into a victory. The battle commenced again in earnest on the morning of 1 June, but mud and more rain hampered McClellan's efforts to take advantage of the Confederate retreat. The Twentieth Massachusetts Regiment held its advanced position for the next ten days, doing picket duty on short rations and standing and sleeping in the mud and rain. On 11 June, the regiment was relieved from the front and moved to dry land near the rear of the Union Army.

Captain Holmes was grimly satisfied by his experience in the battle. "We licked 'em," he wrote home soon after the fight had ended, noting in another letter to one of his lady admirers in Boston that "a bullet has a most villainous greasy slide through the air."[44] The young captain had done well; his men had cheered him after the battle, perhaps the first time in his life anyone had shown such appreciation and approval for his actions. The young officer also noted a change in his own attitude about his new profession: "It is singular with what indifference one gets to look on the dead bodies in gray clothes which lie all around. . . . As you go through the woods you stumble constantly, and, if after dark, . . . perhaps tread on the swollen bodies, already fly blown and decaying, of men shot in the head or bowels."[45] Holmes had survived the battle and in retrospect was resigned to doing the job of a soldier—killing the enemy.

On 26 June, General Lee moved to crush McClellan's right flank, of which Holmes's unit was a part. Lee had successfully used the interlude to bring up General "Stonewall" Jackson's troops from the Shenandoah Valley to reinforce his own. Rather than turn to meet the assault, General McClellan withdrew his army toward the James River. The Twentieth fell back, with McClellan's main force, and did not see action in the Battle of Mechanicsville (Beaver Dam Creek) on 26 June or the Union defeat the following day at Gaines's Mill. As McClellan consolidated the various components of his army and made good his move toward higher ground, Lee's troops were unsuccessful in their efforts to intercept him in the Battle of Savage's Station on 29 June and the Battle of Frayser's Farm (Glendale) the following day. By 1 July, the Union

Army was securely entrenched on the heights of Malvern Hill, a strong defensive position on the north banks of the James River some eighteen miles southeast of Richmond. From this position, the Union forces repeatedly repulsed a series of Confederate attacks in some of the hardest fighting of the war.

Holmes's regiment was in the thick of this series of confused engagements along the banks of the Chickahominy, generally referred to as the Seven Days' Battles. Engaged with particularly heavy losses at the Battle of Malvern Hill, the men of the Twentieth held their ground, adding to their growing reputation for bravery under fire. Tired to the point of exhaustion, the men were probably glad to hear that rather than continue the Union assault on Richmond, McClellan had decided to retire to Harrison's Landing on the James River. Lee's army had suffered heavy casualties and had failed to dismember the Union Army; but by taking the offensive, Lee had saved Richmond and proven that defeating the Confederacy would not be accomplished easily.

Years later, the intensity of those days caused Holmes to recall his experiences as a captain in "a dispirited army fighting by day and marching for the James by night."[46] In a letter to his family written only days after these battles, he provided the following account: "Hard work for several days—marched all night—lain on our arms every morning, and fought every afternoon—eaten nothing—suffered the most intense anxiety and everything else possible. I'm safe, though, so far."[47] In the aftermath of nearly a week of continuous fighting, Holmes was clearly exhausted. The satisfaction of victory gave way to a new fatalism. In a letter written to his parents on 5 July, Holmes described in detail the action of the previous week—the disgraceful behavior of a Michigan unit that broke and ran at Nelson's Farm, how the guns got so hot and dirty that they couldn't be reloaded or fired, and how Pen Hallowell had been cut on his side but not badly hurt at Malvern Hill. In the same letter, the eyewitness correspondent noted the destruction of valuable stores as the army retreated, and regretted that a Union field hospital full of wounded had to be left to the enemy at Savage's Station. Perhaps most significant, Holmes reminded his parents that he had already sent them two notes and a page of his notebook indicating what should be done in case he was killed. He concluded what must have been a difficult letter for his parents to read with the following lines: "It was thought of you dear ones sustained me in terrible trials. . . . The hardest seems over now—at any rate, I'm ready—God bless you all, Goodbye, OWH, Jr."[48] Engaging in nearly continuous battle across cornfields and through woods, hearing bullets splat against tree trunks inches from his head, feeling a dead man's rotting body under his foot—these things had changed Oliver Wendell Holmes, Jr. He would never again think of war as a gallant adventure. The grim Peninsula Campaign was over and 16,000 men were either dead or wounded. War had become for Holmes a terrible, dull business, and he knew he might well become its next victim.

The Army of the Potomac licked its wounds and stayed in camp at Harrison's Landing until mid-August. President Lincoln had visited camp on 8 July to confer with his generals. McClellan's moderation following the Battle of Malvern Hill had earned him the criticism of the Radical Republicans in Congress and the administration, and it was known that the president—if not the army—had lost confidence in the general. On 14 August, General John Pope assumed command of the newly constituted Army of Virginia, and General Henry W. Halleck was named general-in-chief of the Union forces. Both of these men were personal favorites of the Congressional Committee on the Conduct of the War. Within two days, the army was on the march. On 25 August, the Twentieth embarked from Newport News for the journey up the Chesapeake Bay and Potomac River to Aquia Creek. From there, the unit moved through several camps near the Union capital. While passing through Alexandria soon after the regiment had landed at Aquia Creek, Holmes learned that his Grandmother Holmes had died on 19 August in Cambridge. Sarah Wendell Holmes had died quietly in her sleep, with her sons, Oliver Wendell and John, by her side. As a boy, Holmes had listened to his grandmother's stories about the British occupation of Boston during the Revolution—she was six when taken to Newburyport for safety by her father, Judge Oliver Wendell. there is no account of how her grandson received the news of her death, but it is likely that it served to remind him of his forefathers' sacrifices and to confirm his own sense of duty.[49]

On 31 August, the regiment learned of the devastating defeat General Pope and forward units of the Army of Virginia had suffered the previous day at Bull Run. General Lee had again seized the initiative and boldly attacked the Union positions west of the capital before Pope could consolidate the regiments being moved north from Harrison's Landing. Lee followed up his victory by crossing the Potomac River into Maryland, establishing his headquarters near Frederick. On 1 September, President Lincoln restored General McClellan to the highest field command, hoping to restore the sagging confidence of the army in their commanding general. McClellan promptly moved to position all the troops at his disposal between Lee's army and the Union capital. Holmes's regiment was again assigned to General Sumner's Second Corps, as it had been during the Peninsula Campaign. Marching out from Washington, D.C., the regiment took its place on the right wing of the Union line. Reaching Antietam Creek near Sharpsburg on 14 August, the corps found elements of Lee's army massed on the other side. McClellan slowed his approach as the army neared the creek, and both sides prepared for battle. Early on the morning of 17 September, Holmes sat down and wrote his parents a letter by candlelight. The youthful talk of chivalry, honor, and noble causes had by now given way to the grim realities of the seasoned campaigner. "I don't talk seriously," wrote Holmes, "for you know all my last words if I came to grief. You know my devoted love for you—those I care for know it. Why should I say more? It's rank folly pulling a long mug every time one may fight or may be killed." Noting that he would not seek to justify his life or his beliefs, he concluded, "I have lived on the track on which I expect to continue travelling if I get through—hoping always that though it may wind it will bring me up the hill once more."[50] Before this letter had arrived in Boston, Dr. Holmes received an urgent telegram from Hagerstown, Maryland: "Captain Holmes wounded shot through the neck not thought mortal at Keedysville."[51]

At Antietam, McClellan had thirty-five brigades of infantry and a strong division of cavalry. Lee initially had only fifteen brigades, as he had divided his forces, sending General Jackson to capture the large Union garrison at Harpers Ferry. But on 15 September, the garrison at Harpers Ferry capitulated to Jackson, who immediately marched to re-join Lee's main force near Sharpsburg. Hoping to defeat Lee before his reinforcements could arrive, McClellan ordered his army to attack on the morning of 17 September 1862. Before sunset, some twenty-three thousand men would be dead or wounded, making it perhaps the blood-iest single day of the Civil War or of any war that the American nation has ever experienced.

The Twentieth Massachusetts Volunteers formed the center of General Sedgwick's division, and immediately began to sustain heavy artillery fire and sharp musket fire. All was in relatively good order until the Confederates turned the left flank, breaking through the Union line. Before the front line of the Twentieth knew what had happened, the enemy was behind them. They turned and tried to fire, but were soon ordered to "retire to the right." General Sumner had allowed the Second Corps to be marched "at the double quick" into an ambush. Flanked and attacked from the rear, the division was virtually mowed down, sustaining staggering casualties before they could regroup. In less than an hour, the division lost more than two thousand men; General Sedgwick and Captain Holmes were among the wounded.[52]

Well enough to write home on the eighteenth, Holmes noted that he had been hit in the neck and that the ball had entered "at the rear passing straight through."[53] Pen Hallowell was also seriously injured, and Holmes thought it likely that his friend would lose his left arm. In one of the incidents of the war that Holmes would later relate, Hallowell urged the field surgeon to amputate his shattered limb immediately; the doctor resisted the suggestion, stating that the arm could be saved if a suitable splint could be located. Holmes, wounded and groggy himself, looked up and saw a wall clock; without really thinking, he told the doctor to look in the clock behind the pendulum, where the surgeon in fact found a small piece of wood that made an excellent splint.[54]

Capt. William G. LeDuc, an officer on General Napoleon J. T. Dana's staff, had found Holmes on the field and ordered him carried to a field hospital near the front. Though nearly taken prisoner when the Confederate line advanced, Holmes was moved to safer quarters in Keedysville during the early evening. Captain LeDuc secured accommodations for Holmes in a private home and then notified his parents by telegram of their son's condition and whereabouts.[55] But for LeDuc's care and attention, Holmes would very likely have died; even after his wound had been cleaned and wrapped by an army doctor, his chances of surviving were slim.

By 20 September, however, Holmes felt strong enough to begin his long trip home. Walking through the streets of Hagerstown, he was offered lodging by Mrs. Howard Kennedy, an ardent Unionist who had opened her home as a refuge for wounded soldiers. A hospitable widow, Mrs. Kennedy attended to the young captain's wound, assisted by her cousin, Ellen Jones, who was visiting from Philadelphia. Holmes apparently enjoyed this feminine attention; two days later he dictated to Miss Jones a letter to his parents, informing them that he was "not yet dead," but on the contrary, "doing all that an unprincipled son could do to shock the prejudices of parents and of doctors—smoking pipes partaking of the flesh pots of Egypt swelling round as if nothing had happened" to him. He reported that he had "pulled up in good quarters" with "most charitable people," and "not feeling quite inclined to undertake the journey homeward immediately alone," had decided to remain for a few more days, "from which determination" his "having a good time" did "not much detract." Concluding by noting that he was "really disgracefully well," he firmly stated that he did not wish "to meet any affectionate parent half way" nor receive "any shiny demonstrations" when he reached his "desired haven."[56] In his own way, Holmes was asserting his emancipation by insisting that he would set his own schedule and travel to Boston under his own steam. No longer a boy, Holmes clearly expected that his family would abide by his wishes and await his return to Boston.

By the time Holmes sent his request, however, his father was already en route to collect his wounded son. Having received LeDuc's telegram close to midnight on 17 September, Dr. Holmes departed Boston the following morning. Driven by the instincts of a father and doctor, he traveled to the Hallowells' in Philadelphia, where he expected to find his son. There he found Pen Hallowell and his brother, Edward, as well as Lieutenant Colonel Palfrey who had been seriously wounded at Antietam; the house on Walnut Street was full of wounded Union soldiers, but his son was not among them. Beset by new fears, Dr. Holmes set out for the scene of the battle, hoping that his son was still alive. From Frederick, through Middletown and Keedysville, and finally Hagerstown, he searched through the dead and dying. After six exhausting days, Dr. Holmes finally found his son in Harrisburg, aboard a train headed for Philadelphia and points north.

Together, father and son traveled to the Hallowells', where they spent the night. The following morning, they boarded a special coach arranged by Dr. Holmes and rode to New York City; after once again spending the night at the Fifth Avenue Hotel, they departed for Boston.[57] No record remains of Captain Holmes's reception at Charles Street, but it seems likely that his family and friends were as glad to have him home as he was to be back in Boston. He had seen enough of death and dying; and by any accounting, he had once again done his duty.

4

THE SEASONED CAMPAIGNER

The Battle of Antietam had a sobering effect on northern supporters of the Radical Republicans in Washington. Neither side in the conflict had anticipated such staggering losses, nor that the war would continue despite them. Recognizing that the will of his supporters was wavering, President Lincoln took advantage of what was being called the Union victory at Antietam to announce the Emancipation Proclamation. This presidential order would have the effect of freeing slaves in states still in rebellion against the Union on 1 January 1863. Before the end of September 1862, the president had also suspended the writ of habeus corpus, an action that outraged many northern unionists. On 7 November, Lincoln further distressed many in the North by removing General McClellan and replacing him with General Ambrose B. Burnside. Once again, it appeared that political rather than military concerns were primarily responsible for decisions that would affect the lives of thousands of young men in the field.

During his six-week period of convalescence at home, Holmes apparently was an ardent supporter of the actions of the president and other "Union Republicans." He voted for the first time, casting his ballot for men like Governor Andrew and Senator Sumner.[1] His attitude toward General McClellan's removal, however, was more ambiguous. He shared the opinion of many of his fellow officers that the army was willing "to trust its life and reputation" to only "one man," and it was to General McClellan that he was referring.[2] Throughout the weeks and months of the previous year, Holmes had increasingly come to adopt the attitudes and opinions of the regulars in the army; although he continued to endorse the morality of the cause, he shared the view of the professional soldier that politics have no place on the battlefield.

Holmes departed Boston on 12 November 1862 and headed south to rejoin his regiment. He was fortunate in having his friend "Little" Abbott as his traveling companion. The trip was neither easy nor uneventful. Following a short stopover in the nation's capital, Holmes wrote that Washington was a "modern Gomorrah" which he found "stinks of meanness" and "absolutely loathsome." Elaborating more fully, the young captain explained that though a "democrat in theory," he loathed "the thick-fingered clowns we call the people—especially as the beasts are represented at political centers—vulgar, selfish and base." He concluded his comments by noting that there were only two civilized places in America—"Boston and Philadelphia."[3]

From Washington, Holmes and Abbott crossed the Potomac River to Alexandria, traveling west to Warrenton Junction. There they learned that the regiment had passed through town a few days previous on its way to Fredericksburg. Departing Warrenton Junction on the evening of 17 November, the pair walked some twenty-five miles during the next two days before joining the regiment in Falmouth on the nineteenth. The young officers enjoyed a happy reunion with the men of the regiment, who were glad to see the return of two of the most popular officers in the unit.[4]

Stationed at Falmouth, Virginia, along the north shore of the Rappahannock River, the regiment was preparing to cross to attack Fredericksburg when Holmes arrived. Still a part of Sumner's Second Corps, the regiment was among the three "grand divisions" General Burnside had assembled to march on Richmond. His plan was to cross the Rappahannock at Fredericksburg and then proceed south to Richmond. Delays in bringing up the necessary pontoons allowed General Lee the necessary time to move General James Longstreet's First Corps and General Jackson's Second Corps to high ground just south of Fredericksburg. Although Burnside's forces significantly outnumbered Lee's, it appeared that the Confederate general had once again outmaneuvered his opponent.

Understandably, the Union Army was experiencing serious morale problems. Although Lee's advance on Washington had been stopped at

Antietam, enabling the Radical Republicans in Congress to claim it as a victory, the army knew better. Thousands had been sacrificed, and McClellan's decision not to pursue Lee had ended any possibility of a decisive victory. Holmes's regiment was no exception. Decimated by previous battles, it prepared itself once again for the inevitable slaughter. Colonel Lee, broken by imprisonment and the toll of months in the field, was again commanding the regiment, having recently returned from sick leave in Boston. Lieutenant Colonel Palfrey, the second in command, was permanently disabled as a result of his wounds from Antietam. Many of the regiment's junior officers and enlisted men were suffering from dysentery and unable to look with much eagerness upon the prospects of another grueling campaign.

Shortly after his return to the regiment, Holmes wrote home that the army was "tired with its hard and terrible experience and still more with its mismanagement." Stating that he believed the Confederacy had virtually won its independence, he revealed the prevailing view of many of his comrades by concluding, "We shall never lick 'em. . . . We shan't do it—at least the Army can't."[5] Dr. Holmes apparently took his son's comments as a repudiation of the underlying principles he had held when he went off to war in 1861. Although no letter to his son remains to confirm this supposition, he received another letter from Captain Holmes explaining his position. An indignant son informed his father that there had never been "any wavering" in his belief in "the right of our cause," but that he did not believe "in our success by arms." Noting that he thought he had "better chances of judging" the matter than his father, he added that he believed he represented the "conviction of the army—and not the least of the most intelligent part of it." Holmes put the point bluntly by concluding, "I think you are hopeful because (excuse me) you are ignorant."[6]

The tone of Holmes's letter of 20 December undoubtedly reflected the despair of the army following the Battle of Fredericksburg, an emotion it would have been difficult for his father to share. On 13 December, Holmes was himself "stretched out miserably sick with dysentery," and his regiment was going into battle while he was forced to remain behind. Expecting "one of the great battles of the War," Holmes confessed regret that he was simply "too weak for the work."[7]

General Burnside, lacking any better plan of attack, had ordered his most reliable units to cross the river and establish a bridgehead, hoping that his superior numbers would win the day. Captain George N. Macy, acting in Colonel Lee's place, led the regiment into battle. Captain Abbott, in Holmes's absence, served as acting major of the regiment. The Twentieth, serving with other units in Colonel Norman J. Hall's brigade of Sumner's Second Corps, was ordered to advance against strong Confederate opposition. Moving by the flank in fours under intrepid leadership, the regiment moved up the south banks of the Rappahannock, and entered Water Street to face withering fire from the celebrated riflemen of the Twenty-first Mississippi Regiment, three companies strong. Forcing their way through despite incredible losses, the regiment demonstrated unflinching discipline. Platoon after platoon was swept away, but the head of the column did not falter. Ninety-seven officers and men were killed or wounded in the space of fifty yards. Despite the consequences, Burnside ordered Sumner's Second Corps to take Marye's Heights, a rise south of Fredericksburg heavily fortified with entrenched Confederate artillery. Wave after wave of courageous Union infantry assaulted the hill, each in its course being cut down by intense Confederate fire, until protests by Burnside's subordinates finally brought the carnage to an end. The Union forces withdrew across the river, having suffered some twelve thousand losses, more than twice the number inflicted upon the enemy. Without question, the Battle of Fredericksburg was a devastating and demoralizing defeat for the North.[8]

From his bed in the regimental hospital on Falmouth Heights, Captain Holmes watched, plagued by guilt that he was not leading his unit. Although he couldn't see his men, he could see the battle—"a terrible sight when your Regt is in it but you are safe." He reproached himself that he "could not help."[9] As the battle progressed, the sheer number of dead and wounded soon became apparent. Holmes observed, "it's odd how indifferent one gets to the sight of death."[10]

Although a terrible blow to Union hopes, the Battle of Fredericksburg added to the growing reputation of the Twentieth Massachusetts Volunteers. The courage of Captain Abbott soon became one of the proud legends of the regiment, and he became a popular hero. His fame was all the more significant as it was widely known that he was a staunch opponent of President Lincoln's policies and politics. Judge Josiah Abbott, the captain's father, was a leading member of the Democratic party in Massachusetts who openly fought Lincoln's election. Given his personal views, Abbott's bravery was all the more impressive. As Holmes would remember years later, "in action he was sublime . . . moving on in obedience to superior command to certain and useless death. . . . He was little more than a boy, but the grizzled corps commanders knew and admired him."[11] Holmes was undoubtedly thinking of Abbott when he wrote the following: "The faith is true and adorable which leads a soldier to throw away his life in obedience to a blindly accepted duty, in a cause which he little understands, in a plan of campaign of which he has no notion, under tactics of which he does not see the use."[12] It was in the spirit of this sentiment that Holmes informed his father following Fredericksburg that though he was "heartily tired and half worn out body and mind by this life," he believed he was "still ready as ever" to do his duty.[13]

With no confidence in their commander in chief, the Union Army settled into its winter quarters in Falmouth. Morale continued to decline as poor food, lack of pay, and innumerable other hardships beset various regiments. Personal disagreements among senior officers, many resulting from recriminations concerning who was to blame for the defeat at Fredericksburg, grew until there was talk of treason. With discipline increasingly hard to maintain in the ranks, General Burnside was removed from command on 28 January. General Joseph Hooker, his replacement, quickly moved to improve conditions and morale, with marked success.

In recognition of its distinguished service at Fredericksburg, the Twentieth was given provost guard duty at Falmouth. Holmes was appointed provost marshal of the town, a position he apparently enjoyed, although it was not without its problems. Armies are notoriously more difficult to control during lulls in the fighting than when actively engaged. Maintaining order, which was his principal charge, required diplomacy as well as firmness. Freed for the first time from the responsibilities of a company commander, Holmes renewed old friendships with officers from other units assigned to army headquarters. In particular, he enjoyed the company of Charles A. Whittier, aide-de-camp to General Sedgwick, who now commanded the Sixth Corps. Along with his new duties and associations, Holmes began to assume the manners and habit of a regular army officer.[14]

During this period, Governor Andrew was authorized by President Lincoln to recruit a regiment of volunteers made up of "persons of African descent" to be commanded by white officers. Robert Gould Shaw of Boston accepted the colonelcy and offered the lieutenant colonelcy to Pen Hallowell, who accepted the commission. The sole abolitionist among the officers of the Twentieth Massachusetts Volunteers, Hallowell would later receive a commission as colonel of another Negro regiment— the Fifty-fifth Massachusetts Volunteers. In late January of 1863, however, Hallowell was faced with the challenge of finding other capable white officers who would be willing to assume positions in Shaw's Fifty-fourth Regiment. That Hallowell asked Holmes to accept a major's commission in the new unit suggests that Holmes's antislavery principles were still strong. But although Holmes may have seriously considered the offer, he declined the position, which ultimately was filled by Hallowell's younger brother, Edward. Holmes may have been for equality in theory, but he apparently preferred to stand aside and let others test the principle in practice.[15]

The coming of spring marked the beginning of a new Union campaign to take Richmond. On 3 May, the regiment crossed the Rappahannock River into Fredericksburg, which had been taken with comparative ease by General Sedgwick's Sixth Corps. Through streets scarred from the prior heroic struggle, the regiment moved out of town toward Chancellorsville along River Road. Encountering a canal over which all existing bridges had been destroyed, the Union column came to a halt and paused in a field within range of a unit of Confederate artillery still in place on Marye's Heights. Holmes reported in a letter to his mother written on 3 May what happened next:

> Pleasant to see a d'd gun brought up to an earthwork deliberately to bear on you—to notice that your Co. is exactly in range—1st discharge puff—second puff (as the shell burst) and my knapsack supporter is knocked to pieces. . . . 2nd discharge man in front of me hit—3rd whang the iron enters through garter and shoe into my heel.[16]

The following day, Holmes wrote to his father, informing him that the ball had been extracted and "the foot didn't have to come off as was feared." He also told his father that he would be leaving the front for the Hallowell's in Philadelphia as soon as he could obtain medical leave.[17]

Holmes had again been fortunate; although seriously wounded, he was still alive. By sunset on the evening of 5 May, some seventeen thousand of his comrades were either dead or wounded. Although General Hooker's Army of the Potomac had outnumbered General Lee's Army of Northern Virginia two to one, the North had lost yet another decisive battle. The battle, however, had also been a costly one for Lee; in addition to casualties of dead and wounded approaching thirteen thousand, General "Stonewall" Jackson had been killed during the fighting.

Given the grim realities of the battlefield, it is understandable that Holmes may initially have hoped that his foot would in fact have to be amputated. Holmes's friend Whittier raised this point in a letter, noting that Dr. Hayward, surgeon for the Twentieth, had said that Holmes "seemed to be rather sorry that he wasn't going to lose his foot."[18] Late in his life, Holmes himself vividly recalled his prayers after the Battle of Chancellorsville that he might lose his foot "in order that duty might not a third time compel him to return to the front."[19] Clearly, the question of how long Holmes's luck would hold was one the young captain could no longer avoid considering.

As he had indicated to his family, Holmes traveled to Philadelphia, stopping to rest at the Hallowells', and then went on to Boston. Attended in Philadelphia by Dr. William Hunt, his wound was cleaned and bandaged. When he arrived in Boston, Dr. Bigelow looked after Holmes during his period of convalescence. For nearly eight months, Holmes would remain in Boston, until he was indeed sufficiently healed to return once again to the front.

Holmes used this extended period of convalescence to catch up on his reading in philosophy and social history. Among the works he took out of the Boston Athenaeum were John Stuart Mill's *Logic*, and Plato's *Dialogues*. Perhaps more significant, Holmes read Herbert Spencer's *First Principles*, which introduced him to the philosophy of social Darwinism, a view of social evolution that would become a fixed element of his own thought. Read by a participant in the most violent struggle the nation had ever endured, the work provided him with a philosophical context for understanding the war. Years later, Holmes expressed the judgment that only Darwin himself had done more "to affect our whole way of thinking about the universe."[20]

Holmes received frequent letters from his friends in the regiment during his absence. From Henry Ropes, he learned of the inadequacies of Col. Paul Revere, who had been placed in command of the regiment; from the same correspondent, Holmes was informed of the great promise as a military officer of his cousin, Lt. Sumner Paine. The son of Holmes's mother's sister, Paine, like Ropes, had been recruited by Holmes to fill the ranks of the Twentieth.[21]

From these letters, Holmes followed the progress of the war. During the month of June, General Lee had followed up his victory at Chancellorsville by moving his army north through the Shenandoah Valley and across the Potomac. By the end of the month, the Confederate Army had moved across the Mason-Dixon line into Pennsylvania near Chambersburg. The Union Army, under the command of Gen. George Meade—who had succeeded General Hooker on 28 June—moved his troops west through Maryland to meet Lee's challenge. By a fateful co-incidence, the armies clashed near the town of Gettysburg in a momen-tous battle that in retrospect would be seen as the turning point in the war. The battle raged for three days—1 July–3 July—and although there was no clear victory, Lee was forced to abandon his objectives and with-draw from northern territory. Together the armies had lost nearly fifty thousand men in one of the most important battles of the war.

The Battle of Gettysburg had taken a particularly high toll on the Twentieth Massachusetts Volunteers. Colonel Revere was killed and Lieutenant Colonel Macy lost an arm from wounds that were nearly fa-tal. But the greatest losses for Holmes were the deaths of both Lieutenant Ropes and his young cousin, Lieutenant Paine. One observer stated the obvious, reporting that the death of such gentle youths was "a sad and shocking sight."[22] Together with Pen Hallowell, Holmes served as a pall-bearer at Henry Ropes's funeral at King's Chapel. Although he had es-caped the physical terrors of Gettysburg's bloody battlefields, he could not escape its horror.

Colonel Revere's death posed serious problems for the regiment. By seniority and merit, Macy would be promoted to the colonelcy, and Holmes would take his place as lieutenant colonel. But as a result of their wounds, both were unavailable for active duty for an uncertain period of time. Abbott, barely twenty-one and holding only the rank of captain, was commanding the regiment as acting colonel. Holmes, os-tensibly concerned that it would seem improper for him to hold high rank in the regiment even though he was physically unable to rejoin his unit, suggested that Abbott receive his commission as lieutenant colonel. Abbott respectfully declined Holmes's offer, assuring him that his fellow officers all agreed that they couldn't afford to lose him.[23]

In August 1863 Holmes learned to ride horseback. It had not been necessary for him, as a company commander, to ride before, but as a field grade officer, it would be essential. It seems likely that as a result of his injuries, Holmes was seriously considering the desirability of obtaining a staff appointment. His friend Charles Whittier had suggested to Holmes the possibility of securing a position on the staff of General Sedgwick, who knew and liked Holmes.[24] During the same period, Holmes was considering yet another possibility. Colonel Shaw had been killed lead-ing the Fifty-fourth Massachusetts Volunteers at Fort Wagner, South Carolina, and Maj. Edward Hallowell had been gravely wounded. The Fifty-fifth Regiment, under the command of Col. Pen Hallowell had also sustained heavy losses. Holmes was once again asked by his close friend to consider taking a field rank commission in one of the "colored" regiments. For whatever reasons, he once again declined.[25] Rumors of Holmes's decision eventually reached his regiment; on 8 October, Abbott wrote to assure Holmes that his decision was "thoroughly right and proper," adding that it would have been absurd for Holmes to have wasted himself "before the shrine of the great nigger."[26] Holmes's reply to his friend—if there was one—has not survived; it is doubtful, however, whether Holmes would have openly agreed with such a frank statement of what might indeed have been his own private conclusion.

By early January 1864, Holmes's wound was sufficiently healed for him to again return to his regiment. Although he had received his commission from Governor Andrew as a lieutenant colonel, he could not be mustered into the regiment at that rank, as it was still technically held by Lieutenant Colonel Macy, whose promotion to colonel had not yet come through. Abbott's commission as major had taken effect, however, and there were no vacant captaincies in the regiment. The practical consequence of this confused situation was that Holmes was without a job when he arrived back in his regiment in late January. Thus, it is not surprising that he decided to act on Whittier's suggestion that he seek a staff position; by special orders of General Sedgwick dated 29 January, Captain Holmes was directed to report for temporary staff duty to the headquarters of Gen. Horatio Wright, divisional commander of the Sixth Corps. This new assignment ended for all practical purposes Holmes's association with the Twentieth Massachusetts Volunteers.[27]

Holmes's duties as General Wright's aide-de-camp, though different from those of a company commander, were no less dangerous. Staff officers might have been better dressed and better fed than officers of the line, but they were frequently exposed to hazards even greater than those of their regimental comrades. Assigned to such duties as reconnaissance and dispatch, staff officials often found themselves behind enemy lines. By Holmes's own account, General Wright "managed to keep himself and his staff pretty well in range of enemy fire."[28] On occasion so tired that he could hardly sit up in the saddle, Holmes put to good use the lessons in horsemanship he had received during his stay in Boston. As he would later remark, "the prize of the general is not a bigger tent, but command."[29]

In March 1864, Gen. Ulysses S. Grant assumed the command of the Union Armies, and the regiments prepared for yet another bloody campaign. From his headquarters at Culpepper, Virginia, Grant planned his offensive against Richmond, and on 4 May, the Army of the Potomac crossed the Rapidan. The Wilderness Campaign had begun, and within the space of a month, sixty thousand Union troops and twenty thousand Confederate would be dead or wounded. In the bloody battles of the Wilderness, Spotsylvania Court House, North Anna, and Cold Harbor, Grant waged a "sanguinary war" against his enemy, hoping that the losses would be more than the South was prepared to accept. But although Grant's strategy was largely successful and Lee lost over a third of his army, the war went on.

For Holmes, who now observed the war from the perspective of his commanding general, the bloody days and nights of slaughter were particularly grueling. Following General Sedgwick's death on 9 May, General Wright assumed command of the corps. Although Holmes himself escaped injury, he witnessed firsthand the Battle of Cold Harbor, where nine thousand men fell in the space of three hours, and saw the dead piled five and six deep in shallow trenches, "the wounded writhing under the superincumbent dead."[30]

In the midst of so much suffering, one death more than any other seemed to effect Holmes. It is unknown when or how Holmes learned of the death of his friend "Little" Abbott, who had lost his life on 6 May leading the Twentieth into battle. As Holmes would later observe, "for us, who not only admired, but loved [him], his death seemed to end a portion of our life also."[31] Confronted with the loss of his personal friend and hero, Holmes must have wondered whether anyone would survive the ordeal.

Following the cruel failure of the Union Army to destroy the enemy at Cold Harbor, Grant moved his forces across the peninsula to the James River, determined to take the town of Petersburg lying some fifteen miles south of Richmond. Lee successfully moved up reinforcements to defend the town, while dispatching Gen. Jubal Early north to threaten the Union capital which was protected by only "scare crow" defenses. Grant then sent the Sixth Corps to protect Washington, and General Wright and his staff arrived at Fort Stevens on 11 May. Anticipating battle, President Lincoln went to the fort to observe firsthand the fortunes of his army. The fort was already under fire from rebel sharpshooters when the president ascended the parapet to get a better view of Early's forces. Standing over six feet tall in his stovepipe hat, the commander in chief made a perfect target. Although General Wright suggested that the president get out of the line of fire, Lincoln remained where he was. Holmes, apparently unaware of the president's visit, soon joined the general's entourage, and seeing a civilian on the parapets, yelled, "Get down, you damn fool, before you get shot!" Retiring from the parapet, Lincoln is reported to have said, "Captain, I'm glad you know how to talk to a civilian."[32] Thus ended Holmes's only conversation with Abraham Lincoln.

Unwilling to attack Wright's fortified position, General Early retired from the field, and the Sixth Corps moved west from Fort Stevens to Poolesville, where they prepared to fight their way down the Shenandoah valley. Ironically, Holmes's military career had come full circle; as his three-year enlistment came to an end, he found himself back where he had begun his military service. Although the war was not yet over nor the outcome certain, Holmes had decided not to reenlist. During the worst days of the Wilderness Campaign, he had written his parents that if he survived the bloodshed, he was going to quit the service: "Nearly every Regimental officer I know or care for is dead or wounded. . . . I have made up my mind to stay on the staff if possible till the end of the campaign and then if I am alive, I shall resign." Haunted by the ghosts of his friends, Holmes tried to explain his decision: "I have felt for some time that I didn't any longer believe in this being a duty and so I mean to leave at the end of the campaign, as I have said, if I'm not killed before."[33] Apparently, Holmes's decision to leave the war before it had reached its inevitable conclusion was deemed unacceptable by Dr. Holmes. Receiving a letter from his father which he found "discreditable" to his "feeling of soldierly honor," Holmes informed his father that he no longer acknowledged the same obligation to duty he once had. The war had placed a greater strain on Holmes's mind and body than he could be expected to endure; he simply could not take any more killing.[34]

Clearly, Holmes was suffering from physical and mental exhaustion when he had written his parents in early May of his determination to resign. By early June, however, his battle fatigue was every bit as real, as he continued to do his duty more from the daily pressures of necessity than from any strength of his constitution. In another letter home, Holmes informed his parents that he had not simply been demoralized when he had announced his intention to leave the service if he survived the summer campaign. He had started the war as a boy, but he was now a man, entitled to reach his own conclusions and make his own decisions. He reported that for several months he had been coming to the conclusion that his duty had changed. "I honestly think the duty of fighting has ceased for me," Holmes wrote, "ceased because I have laboriously and with much suffering of mind and body earned the right . . . to decide for myself how I can best do my duty to myself, to my country, and if you choose, to God."[35] In short, he had gone off to war to do his duty, and in his mind, it was done.

On 17 July, Holmes received his final discharge from the army and began his trip home to Boston. Arriving on the nineteenth, he attended a dinner of the Harvard class of '61 at Young's Hotel on the twentieth, at which he was asked to speak as class poet. Although glad to be home and among his friends once more, the evening must have been a bitter-sweet one for the thrice-wounded veteran. Many in the class were either still at the front or deceased. When he rose to speak, his peers must have wondered what he would say. He did not disappoint them:

> How fought our brothers, and how died, the story
> You bid me tell, who shared with them the praise,
> Who sought with them the martyr's crown of glory,
> The bloody birthright of heroic days.
>
> But, all untuned amid the din of battle,
> Not to our lyres the inspiring strains belong;
> The cannon's roar, the musket's deadly rattle
> Have drowned the music, and have stilled the song.
>
> Let others celebrate our high endeavor
> When peace once more her starry flag shall fling
> Wide o'er the land our arms made free forever;
> We do in silence what the world shall sing.[36]

5

PREPARATION FOR DESTINY

When Holmes returned home from the war in the summer of 1864, he hoped he would be able to leave the fighting behind. But in an unexpected way, the more important struggle was just beginning. Holmes may have distanced himself from the battlefield, but he could not get away from his own memories of the war. For Holmes, there would always be "two Civil Wars," the "war in fact" and the more haunting and troubling "war in retrospect."[1] The evidence is overwhelming that the impact of the war and its horrors had a deep and lasting effect on this young veteran. Holmes in later life reflected on the experience:

> Through our great good fortune, in our youth our hearts were touched with fire. It was given to us to learn at the outset that life is a profound and passionate thing. . . . I think that, as life is action and passion, it is required of a man that he should share the passion and action of his time at peril of being judged not to have lived.[2]

Holmes had shared the "passion and action of his time" and had satisfied himself that he had done his duty. But the question of whether others might judge him more harshly would plague him throughout his life. Some fifty years later, he thought it still necessary to explain his decision to leave the war. Confronted with the horrible slaughter of a generation of his peers, he had relied on his "special faculties" as "a ground for not taking the chances of war." He admitted that he had applied a personal and subjective standard in measuring whether his three years of active service had satisfied his obligations as a soldier. He had repeatedly risked his life and had never flinched from doing his duty. Nevertheless, he was never thoroughly convinced, even in his own mind, that he had done the manly and honorable thing by leaving the war before the final battle was won.[3]

The war had changed Holmes's world in ways he had not anticipated. Nothing ever seemed quite right again. The North had won the war, but Holmes continued to question whether the South hadn't really had the better constitutional claim. Victory had been won, but was it worth "the butcher's bill"?[4] Things that had once seemed clear were now less apparent. For Holmes, only one ideal survived the war: "I do not know what is true. I do not know the meaning of the universe. But in the midst of doubt, in the collapse of creeds, there is one thing that I do not doubt, that the faith is true and adorable which leads a soldier to throw away his life in obedience to a blindly accepted duty."[5] Paradoxically, it was this very faith that Holmes had breached by deciding for himself the limits of his duty. Throughout the remainder of his life, the faces of his fallen comrades would haunt him: "young and gracious figures, somewhat remote and proud, but with melancholy and sweet kindness. There [was] upon their faces the shadow of approaching fate, and the glory of generous acceptance of it. . . . They cared nothing for their lives." Of one "beautiful boy," Holmes recalled: "The advance was beginning. We caught each other's eye and saluted. When next I looked, he was gone."[6] It would not be wrong to conclude that Holmes reproached himself for surviving the war and sought a means of vindicating his choice of life over death.[7]

Safely home in Boston, Holmes became plagued by self-doubt. The war "in fact" became a symbol of the endless struggle between death and life, while the war in Holmes's mind increasingly assumed the dimensions of a classical myth. Time and again, he would refer to his life in relation to this myth; his writings are full of war and battle imagery.[8] Holmes adopted a habit of thought and action that presumed that the only life befitting a gentleman was one built on the soldier's choice of honor over life.[9] "High breeding, romantic chivalry," wrote Holmes, "we who have seen these . . . can never believe that the power of money or the enervation of pleasures has put an end to them. We know that life may still be lifted into poetry."[10]

When Holmes had gone off to war, he knew he would have to do what was expected of a son of the Puritan aristocracy. When he returned, however, he had an even more difficult burden to bear—the guilt of having saved himself from the slaughter. As he prepared to get on with his life, he struggled with the choice of a career. What could he do to prove that he had been right to save himself? What success would vindicate his decision to survive the war? As he later wrote to a friend, "I always think that when a man has once had his chance . . . it does not matter much whether he has more or less time allowed him in that stage. The real anguish is never to have your opportunity. I used to think that a good deal during the War."[11] Holmes had experienced war firsthand, and having survived his enlistment, had decided not to allow any more of his life to be consumed "in that stage." During the late summer of 1864, he would anguish over the "opportunity" to which he should devote the remainder of his life.

To understand Holmes, it is necessary to understand that he self-consciously set out to justify his life by achieving some great success. Although only twenty-three, he was undoubtedly aware that his father had become famous at twenty-one as the author of the poem "Old Ironsides." Moreover, Dr. Holmes had increased his fame during his early years in the medical profession, both as a scientist and as an author. Known and respected for his wit and wisdom on both sides of the Atlantic, the "Autocrat of the Breakfast-Table" certainly provided a plausible role model for a young man seeking success. Whether Holmes's interest in medicine was the result of his father's example or, more likely, because of his own experience with doctors during the war, it is clear that he had not seriously considered making medicine a career before the war. He had styled himself a "law student" when he entered the service and had expressed his intention to study law if he survived the war, "at least as a starting point."[12] Moreover, those who knew Holmes tended most frequently to note the literary gifts of the poet of the class of '61. No less a judge of talent than John Lothrop Motley, Dr. Holmes's close friend, had remarked favorably upon the young Holmes's "brilliant, intellectual, and poetical spirits."[13] Another contemporary observer described Captain Holmes as a "poet, artist, Greek scholar [and] virtuoso."[14]

In addition to the pressure Holmes felt to make a decision about how to spend the rest of his life, he most certainly felt the strain that resulted from returning to his father's household. He had led companies of men into combat and had been recognized for meritorious service at the Battle of Chancellorsville, but now Captain Holmes was once again reduced to the status of a "Jr." in the daily affairs of 21 Charles Street. Once entrusted as provost marshall with the conduct of an entire town, Holmes now had difficulty asserting control over his own life. Predictably, he sought the advice of his older mentor, Emerson; the sage of Concord only added to his pupil's problems. Like a classical oracle, the philosophic old man spoke of moral purpose and of fulfilling destiny. The road mattered little so long as it led to the right destination. Although Holmes shared Emerson's disgust for men who chased after "vulgar prosperity," he knew he would never be content to devote himself solely to the life of the mind.[15] Holmes must have recognized that the crusade that gave meaning and purpose to Emerson's life was one that sought its justification in transcendent principles not readily susceptible to easy proofs. Such a life would not likely provide the kind of vindication Holmes so earnestly sought.

In the end, a combination of factors influenced Holmes to seek his fortune in the law. He was virtually surrounded by distinguished men who had begun their careers by studying the law. John Lothrop Motley, James Russell Lowell, Henry Wadsworth Longfellow—even Ralph Waldo Emerson—had benefited from their early training in the law. Closer to home, Holmes's favorite relative, Uncle John Holmes, had studied law and practiced briefly. Holmes had a very special affection for his uncle and must have been reassured by his example. If such a charming man could survive the rigors of the law, then surely, legal study did not necessarily foreclose the possibility of living a meaningful life.[16]

The family's legal tradition, however, was actually much richer than John Holmes's brief and undistinguished practice at the bar would suggest. Holmes could not have been unaware that although his great-grandfather, Judge Oliver Wendell, lacked a formal legal education, he had established a considerable reputation as probate judge for Suffolk County. Perhaps more important, Holmes's maternal grandfather, Charles Jackson, had enjoyed an active and notably successful career at the bar prior to his death in 1855. Serving as an associate justice of the Supreme Judicial Court of Massachusetts, Justice Jackson had been described by a colleague as the "American Blackstone." No higher tribute could have been paid to an American lawyer of the day.[17] Holmes's interest in pursuing a career in the law undoubtedly pleased his mother, who may have seen something of her father's nature in her son.

The most significant influence, however, was Dr. Holmes's urging that his son pursue a legal education. Years later, Holmes recalled that his "Governor" would not hear of his plans to study medicine or philosophy. Dr. Holmes "put on the screws" to have his son go to law school. Exerting "the coercion of the authority of his judgment," the father "kicked" his wavering son into Harvard Law School.[18] It is interesting to consider Dr. Holmes's motivation for intervening to resolve his son's doubts concerning a career. He himself had abandoned the study of law in his youth, finding it intellectually unpalatable. But he was also well acquainted with the financial uncertainties that had accompanied his medical and literary endeavors. Was he trying to assure his son's independence by urging him to pursue a career as a lawyer? Or was he perhaps concerned by his son's emotional reaction to the war and anxious to engage his energies in some practical course of study? Whether by conscious design or not, Holmes's choice of the law as his career had the effect of focusing his mind on a concrete objective and ultimately freed him from the long shadow of his father's considerable reputation.

Without a settled conviction that he would in fact make the law his profession, Holmes nevertheless enrolled in Harvard Law School in the fall of 1864. The atmosphere of the school was markedly different from that of Harvard College. Although an undergraduate degree was not a prerequisite for admission, law students were treated as having attained an age of responsible maturity. The faculty assumed that law students would have a more successful academic life if treated like gentlemen rather than children. As a consequence, there was little parietal discipline exercised by the faculty; class attendance was not mandatory, nor were any examinations required for graduation.[19]

Established in 1817, the law school had flourished during the years that Joseph Story—associate justice of the Supreme Court of the United States—had served on the faculty. From 1829 to 1845, Justice Story was the preeminent figure on the Harvard Law School faculty. "A man of great learning, and of a reputation for learning greater even than the learning itself,"[20] Story set the standard for those who would follow. During the years that Holmes was at the law school, "character was . . . all over the place, as it could scarce fail to be when the general subject . . . had become identical with the person of all its votaries."[21]

The faculty members who instructed Holmes, although probably not of the caliber of Story, were nevertheless quite distinguished. Theophilus Parsons, Jr., the son of Chief Justice Theophilus Parsons who had sat with Justice Jackson on the Supreme Judicial Court of Massachusetts, was a productive scholar whose name was well known as the author of numerous legal treatises. Judge Joel Parker, the senior member of the faculty and a former chief justice of New Hampshire, presided over the school, essentially exercising the duties of a dean. The third member of the faculty, Emory Washburn, was a former judge, senator, and governor of Massachusetts who had considerable practical experience as both a politician and a lawyer.

Each accomplished in his own way, these three men sought to prepare their students to become able practitioners of the law. At sixty-nine, Judge Parker was a veteran professor when Holmes sat in his classes in constitutional law along with Robert Todd Lincoln, the president's eldest son who was also a first-year law student. Parker, a strict constructionist, did not temper his criticism of the president's theory of executive authority simply because of the likely sympathies of his students. A singularly dry lecturer, Parker tended to intimidate weaker students and inspire stronger ones. Demonstrating "in the chair the same qualities that had made him famous on the bench," Judge Parker taught his students through example the importance of accuracy and detail. "Master of his subject," Parker challenged his students to share his love of the law, and "under his teaching a legal mind was formed."[22]

Professor Washburn's reputation was somewhat less secure among his students. One particularly disgruntled student wrote: "Washburn is detestable. His style is clumsy, obscure, inelegant, ungrammatical and ambiguous. . . . His thinking is but little more lucid than his style."[23] Others, however, welcomed Washburn's friendly and genial temperament and the warm affection he felt for his students. Untiring and enthusiastic, his "kindly ardor" did more "than the learning of Coke and the logic of Fearne" to make the subject of real property comprehensible. "Candidly confiding, especially as to his own pleasant fallibility," Professor Washburn's open manner endeared him to his young colleagues.[24]

Without question, Professor Parsons was the law school's leading light. The best lecturer and most popular member of the faculty, Parsons was an accepted authority on the law of contracts. But he achieved his principal distinction in the field of maritime law, having attained the reputation as a master of this difficult and elaborate subject. Possessed of considerable charm, Professor Parsons interspersed his lectures with personal anecdotes and recollections and little bits of professional gossip that made his students feel more like junior associates than pupils. "An illustrative figure . . . [his] tone, his unction . . . [were] rounded and compact, quite self-supporting, which gave it serenity and quality, something comparatively rich and urbane."[25] For many of his students, Professor Parsons represented all they hoped to become through their study of the law.

It is difficult to know with any certainty exactly which lectures Holmes actually attended while a student at the law school. But if he followed the course of study recommended by the faculty, which seems likely, he undoubtedly attended Professor Parker's lectures on agency, pleading, equity, and constitutional law; Professor Washburn's lectures on real property, wills, and criminal law; and Professor Parsons's lectures on contracts, evidence, and the law of nations.[26] Upon enrollment, Holmes began the intensive and laborious task of reading the numerous treatises on which the traditional course of legal instruction—"reading the law"—was based. Stephen on pleading, Greenleaf on evidence, Parsons on contracts, Jones on bailments, Byles on bills—such was the standard fare of a beginning student of the law. In addition to the treatises, the reading was rounded out by the leading commentaries on the common law—Blackstone, Story, and Kent—and volumes of case law— Smith's leading cases, and Allen's Massachusetts reports.[27]

The members of the law school faculty took seriously their dual responsibility to impart specific legal knowledge to their students while training their intelligence to the specific challenges of a career in the law. Although dedicated to producing men of learning, they were equally committed to producing young men who would think like lawyers. As a consequence, moot court activities were considered an important part of the law school curriculum. Some of these competitions between the students were organized and supervised by the faculty, but most were informal debates staged by student clubs. In November 1865, Holmes presented the plaintiff's claim in a case being tried before Professor Parker, in which Holmes was at least partially successful. He also participated in moot courts as a member of the Marshall Club, assuming the role of judge as well as advocate. It seems likely that while thus tempering a law student's dull preoccupation with reading dry legal texts, Holmes first became acquainted with the experience of sitting in judgment over the arguments of his peers.[28]

Although challenging, the course of study recommended by the Harvard Law School faculty was more concerned with legal tradition than with emerging new horizons in the law. The faculty members were old men, products of a legal culture little changed since the Middle Ages. In many ways members of a professional guild that prided itself more on perfecting its craft than on advancing legal scholarship, these men were content to share with their students the conventional wisdom of their trade. Holmes, however, was eager to press beyond the recommended reading. He explored such radical works as Walker's treatise, *American*

Law, and Bentham's *Defense of Usury,* texts that expressed views contrary to those of Harvard's conservative law school faculty. Also omitted from the suggested reading were Maine's *Ancient Law* and Spense's *Equitable Jurisdiction.* Such works suggested "many new and startling views of social progress," which had the effect of confirming "new generalizations which were beginning to arise . . . as faint suspicions."[29] From these progressive authors, Holmes first became aware that modern legislation might in time have a disturbing effect on the symmetry of Blackstone's magisterial common law.

By the end of his first year in law school, Holmes could write with some sense of accomplishment of his achievements: "I think my first year at law satisfies me. Certainly it far exceeds my expectations both as gymnastics and for its intrinsic interest." Nevertheless, he admitted that he was still tempted to skip his assigned reading on evidence or contracts in favor of reading "some new poem, or (worse) writing one." Acknowledging that "no caution can be given to a young man which is too great," he confessed, "I know the danger well and try to avoid it. . . . Truth sifts so slowly from the dust of the law."[30]

Throughout his first year, Holmes lived at home in his old room. His younger brother, Edward "Neddie" Holmes, was a sociable sophomore at Harvard who was achieving an enviable academic record. His twenty-one-year-old sister, Amelia, was still at home and served as a convenient conduit to a gregarious and entertaining social life. On 21 July 1865, Harvard honored those who had fought and died during the war. Holmes's contemporary, Maj. Gen. William Francis Bartlett, was the clear hero of the occasion, having lost both a leg and an arm in defense of the Union. James Russell Lowell wrote his famous "Ode" for the commemoration; Dr. Holmes composed a poem that once again drew on his son's experiences for its inspiration. Holmes was in uniform, prompting one observer to comment that Captain Holmes "was seen on the streets of Boston again . . . to the great delectation of the girls of the city. He was a romantic hero, [and] built for it."[31]

It is likely that others made similar comments on this occasion. Many of Harvard's sons had not returned from battle, and few if any were as eligible as Oliver Wendell Holmes, Jr. Throughout the war years, Holmes had shown an interest in several young ladies. He had forwarded a sonnet to Agnes Pomeroy, the elder daughter of Robert Pomeroy of Pittsfield. Whether merely an evidence of their friendship or a talisman of a summer romance, the poem represented the full extent of Holmes's attention. Holmes corresponded with several other young ladies while away from home, including Ellen Hooper and Eugenia Mifflin, and perhaps most frequently, Fanny Dixwell. It was a picture of Ida Agassiz, however, that "was like having an angel in his tent."[32]

Nevertheless, after his return home in 1864, Holmes frequently visited the Dixwells' home on Garden Street in Cambridge. Close to the law school and the Old Gambrel house where Uncle John lived alone, Holmes once again made the Dixwells his second family. On many Wednesday evenings, Holmes attended meetings of the Scientific Club held at the Dixwells'. Professors Gibbs, Agassiz, and Gray were all old friends and regulars at the gatherings. Undoubtedly, many of Holmes's young friends also attended. Henry Bowditch and his friend William James were both beginning medical studies; Charles Peirce, son of Professor Benjamin Peirce, had begun his work in philosophy; and John Ropes and John Gray were young lawyers just beginning their careers.[33] Obviously, Holmes needed little encouragement to visit the Dixwells—something interesting was always going on. But there is some evidence that Holmes was particularly attracted to Fanny Bowditch Dixwell, the eldest of the Dixwells' six children. Three months older than Holmes, she was the product of a cultivated home. If less than affluent, the Dixwells lived comfortably. Related to many of the first families of New England, they occupied a enviable position between the fashionable world of Boston and the learned community of Harvard.[34] As for Fanny, Holmes had known her all his life, and she was clearly among his most intimate friends. Described by William James as "decidedly A 1, and (so far) the best girl I have known," Fanny avoided the typical activities of Boston "society." Shy and rather plain in appearance, she was intellectually the equal of any of her male contemporaries. Claiming that she was "about as fine as they make'em," James accused "that villain Wendell Holmes" of keeping her "all to himself out at Cambridge for the last eight years"; James added that he hoped to "enjoy her acquaintance" now that he had finally discovered her.[35]

As Holmes's relationship with Fanny grew, he also extended his circle of male friends. Having first met John Gray while he was home on furlough from the Twelfth Massachusetts Regiment, Holmes immediately liked this friend of John Ropes. Both Gray and Ropes had gone to Harvard Law School before the war and were now starting out together as partners. Holmes enjoyed their company, and by the middle of his first year in law school, he was showing "a fondness for talking over his points while sipping a gin toddy and smoking a cigar" with these able young practitioners.[36] Increasingly, Holmes and Gray spent time with Henry and William James, and their charming cousin, Minny Temple. In time, an association of "ardent spirits" developed that would be very important for Holmes in particular. During August 1865, the group went on a holiday together to North Conway, New Hampshire. Henry James later recalled the pleasures of that summer: "the play of young intelligence and young friendship, the reading of Matthew Arnold and Browning, the discussion of a hundred human and personal things . . . the splendid American summer drawn out to its last generosity."[37] Thus did Holmes spend at least part of the summer between his first and second year of law school.

When Holmes returned in earnest to his studies in the fall, he had finally resolved to abandon literary pursuits in favor of a legal career. Despite his poetic ambitions and philosophic inclinations, Holmes was now prepared to settle down to the hard work he knew awaited him. "When I began," Holmes would later write, "the law presented itself as a rag-bag of details. . . . It was not without anguish that one asked oneself whether the subject was worthy of the interest of an intelligent man."[38] But soon after resuming his studies in October 1865, Holmes affirmed that the "law, of which I once doubted," had become his "enthusiastic pursuit—I am up to my ears in it all the time."[39] Clearly, Holmes's attitude had changed over the summer. Writing to Henry Howard Brownell, a well-known Civil War poet who had turned from law to poetry in his middle years, Holmes noted his interest in understanding "how men come to prefer a professional to a general reputation—and for the sake of the former, which hardly outlives the greatest except a few judges, will sacrifice every hope of the other."[40] Writing a few months later to Emerson, who "more than anyone else first started the philosophical ferment," Holmes made something of a confession: "It seems to me that I have learned, after a laborious and somewhat painful period of probation, that the law opens a way to philosophy as well as anything else, if pursued far enough, and I hope to prove it before I die."[41] Having searched his soul for a way to justify his continued existence, Holmes sensed that he had finally found the right road.

Although the typical course of study at the law school anticipated that students would attend lectures for two years, it was not uncommon for students to leave school early to complete their training in a lawyer's office. In December 1865, Holmes withdrew from Harvard Law School to continue his study in the office of Robert Morse, a well-regarded Boston attorney. Throughout the remainder of the term, Holmes occupied himself with the duties of a law clerk. On 30 June 1866, the law school awarded Holmes a degree along with the others in his class. Holmes did not attend commencement, but the theme of the ceremonies was the power of honor to bind men's lives together, an appropriate sentiment for young men who had witnessed firsthand the ravages of war.[42] Although the faculty would feel satisfied if their students used what they had learned to become respectable and prosperous members of the bar, Holmes had already set for himself a different agenda. His legal training had acted as fuel for the more speculative elements of his temperament; having confirmed in his mind the conviction that even a lawyer might become a chivalrous knight, Holmes took on no less a challenge as his personal crusade.

Having worked for several months as a law clerk in Morse's office, Holmes decided to take a break from his studies. Whether a trip to England and the Continent was his idea or his father's, it is likely that the subject had been under consideration for some time. It will be recalled that Dr. Holmes had prevailed upon his parents to allow him to go to Europe in 1833, arguing that "a boy is worth his manure as much as a potato patch."[43] As Holmes had no independent means of his own, it is clear that the cost of the trip was borne by his parents.

Holmes set sail for England in April 1866, carrying letters of introduction from such leading Americans as Senator Charles Sumner, James Russell Lowell, and John Lothrop Motley. Perhaps most important, he carried the name Oliver Wendell Holmes, a name well known and highly respected by cultivated Englishmen. Dr. Holmes in asking Motley for letters of introduction for his son, had described Holmes as "a presentable youth with fair antecedents" who was "more familiar with Mill's writings than most fellows of his years."[44] Motley willingly accommodated his friend's request, finding some satisfaction in writing among others a letter of introduction to John Stuart Mill. Strikingly handsome and clearly possessing a keen mind, Holmes was described by Motley as "a true representative of 'jeunesse doree,' not the electroplated article, but the true thing tried in the fiery furnace of a four year's war."[45] Acquainted with the insufferable arrogance of much of the British upper class, Motley was eager to see how these aristocrats would react to one of New England's finest sons.

When Holmes departed for England, he was certainly more than "a presentable youth." As a thrice-wounded veteran of the Civil War, he had survived one of the fiercest struggles the world had ever witnessed.

In addition to his record of bravery, his firsthand experiences would un-doubtedly be of considerable interest to those English gentlemen who followed military affairs. More important, Holmes had grown up in one of the most civilized homes in America, surrounded by a distinguished group of American poets, authors, scientists, and scholars. He had a keen and eager mind and was anxious to expand his intellectual horizons. The trip abroad represented in many ways the "pilgrimage of a maturing mind which had already found its tendencies."[46] For Holmes, the trip was more than the typical summer holiday of a sophisticated Bostonian with a cul-tivated appreciation of history and culture; it provided an opportunity to encounter for himself the men whose words and ideas were already shap-ing the future of the world.[47]

Holmes's reading during the winter preceding his departure for Eng-land suggests a predominant interest in works of a scientific and positivist nature. The essence of what Holmes had come to see as scientific inquiry was a concern with empirical causes rather than moral justification. As an undergraduate at Harvard College, he had written that "the law of cause and effect is absolute; if we know the data, the results are inevita-ble."[48] Years later, he reaffirmed the same view: "The postulate on which we think about the universe is that there is a fixed quantitative relation between every phenomenon and its antecedents and consequents. If there is such a thing as a phenomenon without these fixed quantitative relations, it is a miracle."[49] Holmes may have come to this conclusion as a result of his own insights, but his views were consistent with those of many of the leading authors of his day. Herbert Spencer, a writer Holmes read with great enthusiasm, asserted that intelligent men had a duty "to submit [themselves] with all humility to the limits of [their] intelligence, and not perversely to rebel against them."[50] Holmes was also impressed with the works of George Henry Lewes, who argued that the only legit-imate interest in the study of philosophy was a historical one. The notion that the truth might be revealed through philosophical speculation could no longer be defended; modern science had taught informed men that the truth could be discovered only through the careful observation and measurement of natural phenomena.[51]

This scientific approach to human experience was extended to a system of ethics and a theory of society by Jeremy Bentham and his dis-tinguished student, John Stuart Mill. Holmes eagerly read Mill's *Auguste Comte and Positivism* in preparation for his trip to England and was im-pressed by Mill's scientific rigor.[52] Holmes shared Mill's distrust of a priori principles. For Mill as well as for Holmes, the limits of a man's knowledge were of necessity set by the boundaries of his own experience, moral sentiment being merely the way one chose to feel about that experience. From such a perspective, it was clear that the source of all true knowledge must be found in an external and objective standard rather than in an internal or subjective one. Holmes would later summarize this point by observing that "a page of history is worth a volume of logic,"[53] a view he may well have accepted prior to his reading of Mill. In an installment of the "Breakfast-Table" series published in the *Atlantic Monthly* in 1859, Dr. Holmes had written: "A man's logical and analytical adjustments are of little consequence, compared to his primary relations with nature and truth; and people have sense enough to find it out in the long run; they know what 'logic' is worth."[54]

Holmes set sail for England on the *Persia* in late April and arrived in Liverpool on 7 May. He spent his first night in the Adelphi Hotel, which he described in his travel diary as "very poor."[55] He went on to London and upon his arrival made three calls familiar to all travelers of the time: first, he called on the Barings bank, second, the American legation, and third, a tailor. "All seemed an old story after the stereoscopes," he noted; "everybody tries to be a swell," but "few of the gentlemen are real ones." Holmes concluded these "first impressions" by adding some general observations: "Common people like ours. Swells finer. Two types. Saxon and dark. All dressed alike—lavender gloves and sailors ties. Evening, whores stop you everywhere."[56]

Soon after his arrival in London, Holmes made his way to the quarters of the family of his fellow Bostonian, Charles Francis Adams, American ambassador to the Court of St. James. Here Holmes needed no introduction. Holmes had been at Harvard College with Henry Brooks Adams, the ambassador's son, who had accompanied him to England as his personal secretary. Henry had always been too aware of being an Adams to have become a close friend of Holmes. The fact that he had witnessed the progress of the Civil War from the safety of the American embassy in London also put some distance between the two young men. Despite their differences, however, Adams welcomed Holmes warmly and served as an able guide to less obvious elements of British society.

If Henry Adams was eager to introduce Holmes to a certain group of young men in London, Mary Adams, the charming younger daughter of the ambassador, was helpful in obtaining for Holmes an enviable array of social invitations. Although there was no shortage of friends from Boston's Back Bay society visiting London during Holmes's visit, he chose to spend most of his time making new English friends. Through the Adamses, he found himself a guest in several of England's grandest homes. Soon after his arrival, he was a guest of Russell Sturgis at Walton-on-Thames. Mount Felix was a "regular English country place" with a broad green lawn running down from the mansion house to the river. At dinner, Holmes sat opposite Sir Edward Bruce Hamley, a general of the Crimean campaign and professor of military history at Sandhurst. Regarded in England as the highest authority on military tactics, General Hamley made it clear from his comments that he had very little regard for the discipline of the Union Army. "Colonel Holmes," he inquired sharply, "can you train your men to fight in line?" Holmes, fully aware that everyone was waiting for his reply, answered, "Why, General Hamley, you can train monkeys to fight in line." Spirited, modest, and quick-witted, Holmes was a success, and his exchange with the general was soon the talk of London's fashionable clubs. The evening was brought to a pleasant close with Colonel Holmes and General Hamley exchanging war stories over "cigars and hot toddy."[57]

Early in his visit, Holmes was also introduced by the Adamses to Lord and Lady Belper, who were not only staunch friends of the North during the war but also good friends of many of England's leading literary and political figures. At a dinner at Lady Belper's, Holmes first met Lady Trevelyan, Thomas Macaulay's sister, and numerous "other lords and ladies."[58] While Holmes clearly enjoyed his new celebrity, he was not completely overwhelmed by British social life. He recorded that he attended one party on Upper Belgrave Street "signalized by bad look, bad manners, and bad feed." He also noted that English ladies wore "lower necked dresses than at home," and that English manners were "not very good and rather repulsive."[59]

Even more important to Holmes than the rounds of social engagements was his acquaintance with men he had traveled to England to meet. During the last week in May, Holmes accompanied the Adamses to a reception at the prime minister's. He had "quite a long talk" with Gladstone and observed that he had "a voice like Emerson's" and seemed "like an American—He came out to meet you and had gusto."[60] Holmes also dined with Lord and Lady Cranworth. Lord Cranworth, the lord chancellor of England, invited Holmes to attend his chancery court at Lincoln's Inn. Appearing in court the following morning, Holmes was invited by the lord chancellor to sit with him on the high bench. Whether Lord Cranworth knew that Holmes's grandfather, Justice Jackson, had joined Lord Stowell on that very bench years before is not known, but Holmes could not have been unaware of the precedent.[61]

With Ralph Palmer, a friend of Henry Adams, Holmes visited Oxford University and stayed at Balliol College as his guest. Holmes dined with Benjamin Jowett, master of the college, whom the visitor described as "a delightful man," but "not an originator of large ideas."[62] Returning to London, Holmes also dined with Thomas Hughes, a distinguished essayist and friend of James Russell Lowell. An eager supporter of what he called "muscular Christianity," Hughes most likely shared the judgment of another member of his set concerning Holmes: "We were very much pleased with Colonel Holmes. . . . He seems a very intelligent, modest, young man; as little military as need be, and, like Coriolanus, not baring his wounds (if he has any) for public gaze."[63]

Holmes was unable to meet with Herbert Spencer, who was out of the city when he called on him, but he was more successful meeting with John Stuart Mill. On 1 June, he was received at the House of Commons by Mill, who invited the young American to join him for dinner at his club. They were joined by Fitzjames Stephen, the older brother of Leslie Stephen whom Holmes had met in Boston in 1863. Holmes and the elder Stephen hit it off immediately; following dinner, they walked the streets of London until nearly midnight, having "a good talk" on a wide variety of subjects.[64]

Like Holmes, Stephen put two virtues at the pinnacle of human achievement—manliness and wisdom. Neither man had much time for "do gooders," believing that "how you do your job and not how you think or feel about it afterwards" was what really mattered. The two men also agreed that neither Bentham nor Mill could provide a satisfactory answer to the man who would say boldly, "I am bad and selfish and I mean to be bad and selfish," for a true positivist could only reply, "Our tastes differ."[65] Holmes in later life would assert this point: "Do you like sugar in your coffee or don't you? You admit the possibility of difference and yet are categorical in your own way, and even instinctively condemn those who do not agree."[66] In even stronger language, Holmes would write: "Pleasures are ultimates and in cases of difference between oneself and another there is nothing to do except in unimportant matters to think ill of him and in important ones to kill him."[67] Both Holmes and Stephen were prepared to accept the consequences of their ethical relativism and anticipated what in time Bertrand Russell would offer as the definition of logical positivism: "Since no way can be even imagined for deciding a difference as to values, the conclusion is forced upon us that the difference is one of tastes, not one as to any objective truth."[68]

During the early days of June, Holmes met with Gladstone more privately at a breakfast attended by the Adamses, the duke and duchess of Argyll, Lord Houghton, and Lord Lyttleton. A few days later, Holmes had a final meeting with John Stuart Mill at the Members' Dining Room at the House of Commons.[69] Such private meetings with leading political figures of the British Empire must have been heady stuff for a young American law student. Being treated with respect by the foremost men of the realm was an exhilarating experience for Dr. Holmes's "presentable youth." Equally rewarding were the new friendships Holmes established with young men of his own age. Immediately accepted as a chum and included in various activities, Holmes developed relationships that would last a lifetime. Among these was the friendship that developed between him and the Stephen brothers. Holmes was invited to join them at a meeting of the exclusive Alpine Club, of which Leslie was president. Holmes accepted and while dining with the Stephens, made plans to join Leslie on a climbing expedition to the Swiss Alps. Such experiences of personal acceptance rounded out the more intellectually stimulating aspects of his visit to London.[70]

Holmes departed England for the Continent in mid-June, arriving in Paris shortly thereafter. On this leg of his journey, Holmes was a typical tourist; he could not have been unaware of the sharp contrast between his recent success in England and his complete anonymity in France. In Paris, Holmes made the typical circuit of famous sites, returning several times to the Louvre. Dining occasionally with other Bostonians he met in the city, Holmes, with appropriate filial piety, visited the places his father had frequented some thirty years earlier. There is no indication from the modest notes he made that he particularly enjoyed Paris, despite its famous galleries and infamous theaters.[71]

On 2 July, Holmes met Leslie Stephen at the Paris train station, and traveled with him to Basel, Switzerland. Holmes had read John Ruskin's account of the beauty and majesty of the Alps, and despite that author's description of the mountains as "sculptured Revelation," Holmes was apparently unprepared for the "great emotion" he felt upon confronting the towering peaks for himself. Reflecting something of Ruskin's deep reverence and Stephen's exuberance, Holmes exclaimed, "this is not the place for squirts."[72] "The best of fellows and companions," the two young men "made merry" as they set out from Basel to climb the Balme Horne. Stephen had gained quite a reputation as one of the finest and fastest mountaineers in Europe, and for him to have invited Holmes to join him on a climb was a signal honor. As the pair ascended the peak, Holmes made a valiant effort to keep up with the demanding pace set by his more experienced guide. Stephen appreciated his effort, describing Holmes as "limping like [a] pilgrim . . . but still getting through [his] day's march and coming up in time for the next."[73] For Holmes, the experience was something of an epiphany: "When we were nearly up, the finest sight I ever saw burst upon us beyond the precipice—vast rolling masses of cloud and, above and beyond that, a panorama of the greatest Alpine peaks."[74]

No record remains of what the two discussed as they worked their way up the Alpine slopes, but a special bond clearly existed between Holmes and Stephen. Each had recently experienced a significant metamorphosis which set them apart from many of their contemporaries. Leslie Stephen had studied theology at Cambridge and taken orders in the Church of England in anticipation of spending a life in Christian ministry. But as the time for him to enter the pulpit neared, the beliefs that had once sustained him began to dissolve into doubt. His "faith in anything like religion growing dimmer," Stephen took his leave of Cambridge and the ministry in 1865; asserting that he believed "in nothing," he committed himself "to live and die like a gentleman if possible."[75]

Holmes also experienced a similar kind of transformation during his final months of military service. In a letter thanking a friend for forwarding a historical essay on St. Louis, Holmes wrote that the story had arrived "most opportunely now when we need all examples of chivalry to help us bind our rebellious desires to steadfastness in the Christian Crusade of the 19th century." Holmes continued that "it would be hard indeed to keep the hand to the sword" if "one didn't believe that this war was such a crusade." He concluded this very telling letter with the following words: "I am thankful to read of the great dead who have 'stood in the evil day.' No—it will not do to leave Palestine yet."[76] Within a very few months, however, Holmes informed his disbelieving parents that he could no longer "acknowledge the same claims . . . that formerly existed."[77] Years later, Holmes would express a view of truth very similar to the one held by Stephen: "I mean by truth simply what I can't help accepting. . . . as I have said before, all I mean by truth is what I can't help thinking."[78]

When Holmes and Stephen came down from the mountain on 19 July, they parted company, Stephen joining a party of English friends and Holmes setting out for Geneva. At Chamonix, Holmes found some of his own friends from Boston and joined them for some leisurely climbs of Mont Blanc. Sipping champagne with Eugenia Mifflin and giving "her an arm down," Holmes found the company "very pleasant."[79] The group traveled from the south of France back to Paris, where Holmes took his leave to return to London.

Arriving back in England on 28 July, Holmes decided to devote the remaining month of his summer holiday exploring the English country-side. Traveling first to Ottery St. Mary in Devonshire, he stayed for several days at Escot House as the guest of Sir John Kennaway. Holmes had met Sir John and his eldest son, John Henry, earlier in the summer and had accepted their invitation to join them at their country home following his return from the Continent. In time, John Henry Kennaway would become one of Holmes's most intimate English friends. It is clear that while Holmes very much enjoyed his visit at Escot House, he found the comfortable life of the British aristocracy slightly troubling. "Everything smacked deliciously of feudalism," observed Holmes, hurriedly adding, "to the artist, that is, though hardly to the republican."[80] Holmes, who may once have shared the condescending attitudes of the British upper class, had learned "some great lessons" in the army. One of the most important of these he shared late in his life with a close friend: "The army taught me . . . to know that however fine a fellow I thought myself in the usual routine, there were other situations alongside and many more in which I was inferior to men that I might have looked down upon had not experience taught me to look up."[81] Although arrogant in many ways, Holmes at least believed that "the deepest cause" Americans had to love their country was "that instinct, that spark, that makes the American unable to meet his fellow man otherwise than simply as a man, eye to eye, hand to hand, foot to foot, wrestling on the sand."[82]

From Devonshire, Holmes traveled through Stratford-on-Avon on 2 August, where he paused and "gazed long at Shakespeare's bust" in the village church before taking the train the next day for Glasgow, Scotland.[83] On Sunday, 5 August, Holmes found himself in the town of Arrochar. "Compelled by moral pressure" to attend the local church service, Holmes wrote in his diary that he "made up for it" by making "some good love to a maiden by name Campbell" and later, getting fairly drunk on some good Scotch whiskey.[84] There is some evidence that the "maiden by name Campbell' was Elizabeth Campbell of Stonefield, whom Holmes had met in London in June and described as "the prettiest girl" he had ever seen. Whether Holmes acknowledged a serious romantic interest in her is difficult to assess, but he did return to Stonefield to spend the final days of his visit to Scotland.[85]

On 6 August, Holmes reached Inverary Castle, the seat of the duke of Argyll, who had invited Holmes to be his guest. Holmes arrived in time to join in festivities celebrating the coming-of-age of the duke's eldest son, Lord Lorne. The round of sporting events, hunt dinners, and colorful dances continued for several days, offering Holmes ample opportunity to enjoy the pleasures of the Scottish highlands. Among these was Jessie Robertson, the daughter of the duke's London agent, to whom Holmes recorded he "fain would have made love," had she not thrown him over for another.[86]

Holmes departed Inverary in late August, and after spending a few days in Stonefield and Edinburgh, he boarded the *China* in Liverpool for the trip home.[87] Although the record of Holmes's travels in Scotland is fragmentary, it provides glimpses of a vigorous and attractive young man fully capable of finding satisfaction in the pleasures of country life. Throughout his trip, and especially during the final month in Scotland, Holmes had found himself among discriminating people who had accepted him immediately. In short, he had felt more at home in England than he ever had in Boston. His English friends seemed more eager to share his intellectual, artistic, and professional commitments than did most of his peers at home. The fact that Holmes's tastes were strikingly similar to those of many young Englishmen he met during the summer of 1866 may perhaps account for the degree of intimacy he shared with them. It is also possible, however, that Holmes felt freer to be himself in England than he did under the often demanding and repressive expectations of his family and friends in Boston. Whether experiencing a joie de vivre with Leslie Stephen on the Alpine slopes or frolicking with Elizabeth Campbell on a pleasant Scottish summer evening, Holmes seemed to have put behind him the haunting faces of the ghosts of his past.

6

APPRENTICESHIP

Soon after Holmes returned from England in the fall of 1866, he began in earnest to prepare for the bar examination. As a result of his friendship with John Ropes and John Gray, he had become acquainted with Robert Morse, in whose office he had clerked during the early months of 1866. He also met George Otis Shattuck, with whom John Gray had clerked following his graduation from Harvard Law School. Through this association, Holmes received an invitation to clerk for the firm of Chandler, Shattuck, and Thayer, one of Boston's most distinguished firms. On Tuesday, 11 October 1866, Holmes noted in his diary that he had returned to Morse's office "till Chandler & Shattuck should have a place." A week later, Holmes began his clerkship with the new firm.[1]

Chandler, Shattuck, and Thayer was a firm engaged primarily in litigation before the courts. The firm represented various Boston business establishments; among its clients were banks, merchants, railroads, and shippers. In addition, the firm enjoyed an active practice in the Federal Court of Admiralty. Peleg Whitman Chandler, the firm's senior partner, had a reputation as a lawyer of great competence. Although his courtroom practice was shortened in the 1850s as a result of his increasing deafness, Chandler continued an active practice despite this handicap. Widely respected as a counselor-at-law, he advised substantial clients who appreciated and valued his experience with "the practical adminis-tration of the affairs of men."[2]

The junior partner in the firm was James Bradley Thayer. Ten years Holmes's senior, Thayer had taken his law degree from Harvard Law School in 1856. A close friend of Ralph Waldo Emerson and well re-garded by Boston's Brahmin elite, Thayer achieved prompt success as a practitioner of the law. In time, Thayer would receive an appointment as Royall Professor of Law at Harvard and establish himself as one of the greatest law professors of the period. Unlike many of his contemporaries, he did not stand in awe of judicial power. In one of his most important essays, Thayer wrote that "under no system can the power of courts go far to save a people from ruin." Favoring the formulation of social policy through legislation as distinguished from judicial creativity, Thayer was one of the first legal scholars to call attention to the political implica-tions of the growth of the common law through judicial decisions.[3]

Although more intellectually compatible with Thayer, Holmes quickly fell principally under the influence of George Otis Shattuck, the third partner in the firm. Holmes would later attribute to Shattuck much of the credit for shaping his legal career:

> Young men in college or at the beginning of their professional life are very apt to encounter some able man a few years older than them-selves who is so near to their questions and difficulties and yet so much in advance that he counts a good deal in the shaping of their views or even their lives. Mr. Shattuck played that part for me.[4]

Twelve years older than Holmes, Shattuck had been admitted to the bar in 1855. As Chandler's junior partner, he quickly succeeded to much of his associate's trial practice, earning an immediate reputation as an ad-vocate of great capacity. Holmes evaluated his skills with considerable admiration: "Profound and far-reaching in plan, he was vehement in attack and stubborn in defense"; perhaps more important, "he was fertile in resources and very quick in seeing all the bearing of a fact or a piece of testimony, a matter in which most men of weighty ability are slow."[5] A veteran trial lawyer, Shattuck shared Chandler's views on the proper focus of study for young lawyers. Under Shattuck's guidance, Holmes learned that the most important talent of a lawyer is the ability to deal with the actualities of daily life, "to think under fire—to think for action upon which great interests depend."[6] Although Shattuck did not entirely dismiss legal scholarship, his emphasis was clearly on the study of actual judicial opinions crafted to respond to the specific details of concrete cases rather than the theories of legal scholars, no matter how elegant or profound.[7]

Under such able instruction, Holmes's analytical and logical capacities were quickly honed through his diligent study of the law. Some question remained, however, whether his personal temperament was compatible with the practice of law in the traditional sense. Reporting at nine o'clock on 18 October for his first day of work at Chandler, Shattuck, and Thayer, he settled into briefing his first case, *Warner v. Bates,* then pending before the Massachusetts Supreme Judicial Court. Holmes researched relevant cases and prepared a legal memorandum for Shattuck concerning the strengths and weaknesses of their clients' claim to inherit property under their mother's will. Although the extent of Holmes's contribution to the case is unclear from the record, Shattuck's clients received a favorable judgment from the court.[8] Shattuck increasingly gave Holmes important briefs to prepare, offering his young clerk a wide variety of legal issues to consider. Walking and dining with Shattuck frequently, Holmes discussed subtle points of law with one of Boston's leading legal minds. Dealing principally with breach of contract, personal injury, and corporate law matters, Holmes quickly became immersed in the daily routine of an active and prosperous law firm. Frequently accompanying his mentor to court, Holmes took notes on legal process as well as the substance of the case at hand. He spent his evenings augmenting his observations through intensive reading of leading treatises on law and equity.[9]

Despite the satisfactions of this demanding professional regimen, Holmes questioned whether he was really cut out to be "a first rate lawyer": "This week I haven't felt very well and debauched on Mill accordingly, by way of removing an old incubus before endeavoring to immerse myself in the law completely—which Shattuck says a man must at some period of his career if he would be a first rate lawyer—though of being that I despair."[10] Holmes apparently found much of the daily routine of a law clerk discouragingly mundane. His evening reading included John Stuart Mill's *Political Economy* and *Logic,* as well as Friedrich von Humboldt's treatise on government. He also read such philosophically important works as John Locke's *Essay on Human Understanding* and Immanuel Kant's *Critique of Pure Reason.* Such works were not among the titles typically included in a young lawyer's preparation for the bar.[11]

Although Holmes continued to indulge his intense interest in abstract intellectual speculation, he resolved to immerse himself in the law completely. Some indication of this is provided by his note that he began his research in the admiralty case of *Richardson v. Winsor* by reading Parson's *Maritime Law* following dinner on Thanksgiving Day, 1866.[12] During his final weeks of preparation for the bar, Holmes studied with care Howe's *Practice in Civil Actions and Proceedings at Law in Massachusetts*, and Adams's *Equity Practice*. By the end of January 1867, Holmes believed he was ready to face the bar examiners, having recited the Statute of Frauds to his mother from memory.[13]

Holmes had hoped that he might be examined early in the month of February; however, it was not until the twenty-third that Judge Otis P. Lord appointed Asaph Churchill and Charles W. Huntington to examine him for admission to the Massachusetts bar. Both lawyers were Harvard men, well known to Holmes's family. Holmes was examined by Churchill a few days later, but could not arrange to be examined by Huntington until Saturday, 2 March. Nervous and unsettled by the delay, Holmes felt he had made "a devilish poor show" and worried about the results of his examination. Despite his concern, Holmes was admitted to the practice of law the following Monday by order of Superior Judge Morton upon the motion of his mentor, George Otis Shattuck. The young lawyer paid five dollars for his certificate, and settled into practice on Tuesday, 5 March 1867. Relieved and rather satisfied with his accomplishment, Holmes recorded that "the rush of clients" was "postponed on account of weather."[14]

During the following months, Holmes's legal practice attracted few clients. Perhaps the fledgling attorney recalled Professor Washburn's wise counsel that "a young lawyer who pays for his sign the first year and his rent the next can tell himself he is doing very well."[15] Clearly no businessman, Holmes had difficulty accommodating himself to the idea that most men engaged in the practice of law in order to make a living. He was far more interested in the publishing activities of his friends John Ropes and John Gray than he was in finding paying clients. In 1866, these talented and ambitious young lawyers had established the *American Law Review*, a legal periodical that quickly became one of the most important of its day. Primarily a journal devoted to the concerns of practicing lawyers, it was nevertheless hospitable to essays on theoretical developments in English as well as American law. The young editors seemed particularly interested in soliciting articles on the history of law, a subject that Holmes himself was beginning to explore more seriously.

In late November 1866, Holmes was asked to review Roscoe's *Digest*

of the Law of Evidence in Criminal Cases, receiving a copy of the book as
"plunder" for the effort. While Holmes's essay, published in January
1867, was written with the typical American trial lawyer in mind, it also
reflected his broader interest in comparative law. Relying on his own
study of English and French legal practices, Holmes's treatment of the
subject was far from parochial. Perhaps as a result of the favorable response to his first review, he was persuaded that the best chance of making a name for himself was through the publication of critically successful
legal essays; nine additional book notices by Holmes were published by
the *American Law Review* during the next two years.[16] Among these early
published articles, two deserve special attention. In Holmes's notice of
the sixth American edition of Dr. Alfred S. Taylor's *Manual of Medical
Jurisprudence,* he advised his readers that the work was not likely to be
very useful for the lawyer who wanted "to know under what circumstances the courts have admitted [a] defense in a criminal action."[17] Such
a focus suggests that as early as 1867, Holmes had already accepted a
positivist view of the law. His subsequent concern with "prophecies of
what the court will do in fact" and his dictum that "law is a statement
of the circumstances in which the public force will be brought to bear
upon men through the courts" are both entirely consistent with his earlier judgment of Taylor's work.[18]

One other early review strikingly anticipated yet another of
Holmes's most significant opinions about the nature of the law. While
writing his review of Judge Redfield's edition of Story's *Commentaries on
Equity Jurisprudence,* Holmes went back and reread Maine's *Ancient Law.*
It is not surprising that as a consequence, Holmes's note would incor-
porate Maine's conclusion that in modern times, equity and legislation
had more frequently been agencies of progress and instruments of social
reform than the common law. Consistent with this view, Holmes pro-
tested against Redfield's "habit of moralizing" points of law and challenged directly his reliance on religious authorities.[19] Throughout the
review, Holmes reflected an attitude about the law that he would later
summarize in one of his judicial opinions: "The law is not a brooding
omnipresence in the sky but the articulate voice of some sovereign . . .
that can be identified."[20]

In addition to his legal scholarship, Holmes managed to devote
some of his time to the actual practice of law. Having handled several
small and rather ordinary legal matters for a variety of clients, Holmes
argued his first case in the state's Supreme Judicial Court on 14 Novem-

ber 1867. As Judge Ebenezer R. Hoar, an associate justice of the high court, informed Dr. Holmes, the young counsel for the plaintiff made "a very creditable appearance." Judge Hoar noted certain aspects of the familiar "Jackson style and manner," and also commented that the young man used an expression of his father's from time to time. Despite an "ingenious and impressive argument," which had perhaps "a little savoring of experimental philosophy," the court found for the defendant.[21]

Following his return from England, Holmes had devoted himself primarily to professional matters; however, he did not cut himself off from the circle of friends he had established during law school. Three friendships in particular flourished during the period of his apprenticeship and preparation for the bar. Although Holmes had written Fanny Dixwell from England, the period of separation appeared to sharpen his interest in her. After his return, he called on her with persistent regularity. Nevertheless, he continued to maintain friendly relations with several other young ladies who appeared to enjoy his company. For some months, a Sunday afternoon walk with Clover Hooper—later Mrs. Henry Adams—was customary, and Holmes frequently called on Minny Temple when she visited the Jameses in Cambridge. In addition, Holmes more occasionally called on Nellie Shaw, Lily Winsor, Cora Crowninshield, and Anna Hallowell.[22]

Holmes's noted success with the ladies undoubtedly resulted from the fact that he took them seriously. A handsome and charming young man, he treated his female friends as his intellectual companions. His lively and often flirtatious talk could not disguise the fact that he was genuinely interested in what they had to say. Surrounded from birth by women of substance and high intellect, it is not surprising that Holmes would favor women with his own best thoughts. His relationships with these well-bred young women of Boston were of strikingly different character from those he had experienced with the young women he met abroad. Although the evidence is sparse, it seems likely that Holmes neither sought nor experienced in Boston the kind of sexual liaisons he enjoyed in Scotland. As a contemporary noted rather disparagingly, Holmes liked to "play with his mind"; if he was stimulated by the company of female companions, the object of his attraction was more likely intellectual than physical.[23]

In addition to Fanny Dixwell, Holmes's circle of intimate friends at this time included two others—John Chipman Gray and William James. A close friend of John Ropes, Gray was a Civil War veteran who had clerked with Chandler, Shattuck, and Thayer. Following the war, Ropes and Gray had formed a very successful partnership, as well as establishing the *American Law Review*. Soon to be appointed to a professorship at Harvard Law School, Gray was one of the most highly regarded young lawyers in Boston. While Holmes was a clerk for Shattuck, he and Gray frequently dined together, talking over various points of law. Sharing similar interests and experience, the two young lawyers became good friends. Over the years, their friendship would continue to grow, attaining a remarkable degree of intimacy and affection.[24]

Without question, the most dynamic of Holmes's relationships was his friendship with William James. Although Holmes had not known James before the war, the two young men quickly became close friends while Holmes was in law school. A medical student at Harvard, James had interrupted his studies in the spring of 1865 to go on a scientific expedition to Brazil with Professor Agassiz. When he returned a year later, he noted that Holmes was "the only fellow" in Boston he really cared about. Although Holmes was "perhaps too exclusively intellectual," James reported that Holmes saw things "so easily and clearly," and talked "so admirably," that it was "a treat to be with him."[25] Holmes and James increasingly spent time together, often joined by Fanny Dixwell, from whose company James "derived no mean amount of joy."[26] While Holmes was in Europe during the summer of 1866, his friend apparently flirted rather openly with Fanny; whether or not James's interest in her was serious, Mrs. Holmes apparently felt obliged to keep her son informed of his friend's activities.[27]

In the months between Holmes's return to Boston in the fall of 1866 and James's departure to Germany in April 1867, an affectionate companionship developed between the two. Speculative and sensitive by nature, each sought from the other some insight or perspective that might help explain the *vis viva*—the vital forces of life. Plagued by ill health, James decided rather suddenly to continue his study of physiology in Berlin, where he might be less troubled by his various physical afflictions. Throughout this period of self-imposed exile, James suffered serious bouts of depression; he also clearly missed the support of Holmes's friendship. The letters he sent to "Dear Wendy Boy," to whom he referred as "the most obtrusive ghost of all—namely the tall and lank one of Charles Street," suggest the depth of feeling James felt for Holmes:

> You had better believe that I have thought of you with affection since
> I have been away, and prized your qualities of head, heart and person,

and my priceless luck in possessing your confidence and friendship in a way I never did at home; and cursed myself that I didn't make more of you while I was by you.[28]

Holmes was undoubtedly struck by the intensity of his friend's feelings for him, but his letters to James focused primarily on his growing immersion in the life of the law. Although this is not to say that Holmes was unconcerned about his friend's welfare, it suggests that Holmes was less comfortable writing about his feelings than about his work. In one particularly telling reply, Holmes wrote: "Would that I could give back the spirits which you have given to me so often. At all events doubt not my love. . . . You know my sentiments—I will not repeat them."[29]

Perhaps James sensed that his friend's growing concentration on his legal career would leave little time for their friendship. At any rate, after his return to Boston in 1868, the familiar intimacy continued between the two, but each knew that something had changed. James initially informed his fellow medical student Henry Bowditch that "Wendell amuses me by being composed of at least two and a half different people rolled into one, and the way he keeps them together in one tight skin, without quarreling any more than they do, is remarkable. I like him and esteem him exceedingly."[30] But as time went on, Holmes became harder, more aggressive, and more self-centered; James ceased being amused and became increasingly concerned. Whether it was the law or something inherent in Holmes's personality, the change disturbed and troubled James. Perhaps unable to accept the distance that had grown between them, James commented bitterly in October 1869 that the more he lived in the world, "the more cold-blooded, conscious egotism and conceit" of his associates afflicted him. Speaking specifically of Holmes, he continued, "all the noble qualities of Wendell Holmes, for instance, are poisoned by them, and friendly as I want to be towards him, as yet the good he has done me is more in presenting me something to kick away from or react against than to follow and embrace."[31] Not surprisingly, James's sense of alienation from his former friend would increase; several years later, James described Holmes as "a powerful battery, formed like a planing machine to gouge a deep self-beneficial groove through life.'[32]

During this period, Holmes devoted himself almost entirely to his study of law. No record remains to indicate any interest in politics, civic, or charitable activities. He allowed himself few diversions, concentrating his considerable energies on preparing for the bar. The Holmes family summered in Nahant after selling their summer estate in Pittsfield. Renting various cottages, the family enjoyed the company of a summer colony of their friends which included the Longfellows, Lawrences, and Lodges. Undoubtedly, Holmes spent an occasional weekend with his family and friends at the shore. In May 1867, he took two weeks off from his studies to go on a fishing trip with friends to the backwoods of Maine, and in August, he joined the Jameses, Minny Temple, and John Gray for a holiday in New Hampshire. The following summer, he and Henry Cabot Lodge went on a one-week western hunting expedition. During the summer of 1869, Holmes and Gray traveled to Pomfret, Connecticut, to visit the Jameses, and although they "seemed in very jolly spirits at being turned out to pasture from their Boston pen," Holmes hurried back to his work without any additional vacation.[33]

By the close of 1869, it was clear to those who knew Holmes best that a period of his life was coming to a close. The events of his personal and professional life reflected a new sense of independence and maturity. Possessed by an increasingly compelling sense of urgency, Holmes troubled himself to see that not a moment should be wasted; driven by the conviction that he must "accomplish just so much each twenty-four hours," Holmes revealed feelings of responsibility consistent with his Calvinist ancestry.[34] He would later confess that though he didn't much enjoy reading, he felt "the necessity of sticking in fuel"; throughout his life, Holmes referred to knowledge as the fuel that kept life aglow.[35]

As the first month of 1870 came to a close, Arthur Sedgwick observed that Holmes knew "more law than anyone in Boston of our time, and works harder at it than anyone."[36] Sedgwick's judgment seemed to confirm John Ropes's earlier comment that he had never known anyone in the law "who studied anything as hard as Wendell"; even William James had suggested, perhaps half in jest, that such diligence "must lead to Chief Justice, U.S. Supreme Court."[37] Such remarks surely pleased Holmes, as he strived to achieve distinction among a group of unusually talented peers. But such expectations, even if not entirely serious, served to heighten Holmes's growing sense of urgency that he make his mark in the law.

In November 1870, the Holmeses moved from the house on Charles Street to a new residence Dr. Holmes had built at 296 Beacon Street. The tidal swamps along the Charles River had recently been filled—a project Dr. Holmes enthusiastically endorsed—creating a new residential district adjacent to the Longfellow Bridge. Conveniently located near Cambridge, the area soon became Boston's "fashionable West End." As a consequence of new construction, the Holmes's Charles Street home lost its view and access to the river; leading the exodus from Charles Street, Dr. Holmes built a three-story brownstone of refined elegance overlooking the Charles.[38]

Once again, a physical move marked the end of a significant period in Holmes's life. About the same time the family moved to Beacon Street, Holmes left the offices of Chandler, Shattuck, and Thayer at 4 Court Street and moved to a new office at 7 Pemberton Square which he shared with his younger brother, Edward, and another young attorney, Isaac Taylor Hogue. A member of the Harvard Law School class of 1869, the younger Holmes served as Senator Charles Sumner's private secretary in Washington, D.C., following graduation. Although Dr. Holmes had provided two small garret rooms on the third floor of the new house for his sons, Edward's engagement to Henrietta Wigglesworth in 1870 signaled his approaching emancipation from the household. Perhaps as a result of his engagement to the daughter of one of Boston's most traditional and straitlaced families, Edward became increasingly concerned with establishing a successful career. Although the two brothers shared offices together, they never formed a partnership; as the young Holmes concerned himself with the traditional legal fare of trusts, contracts, and investments, his older brother buried himself ever deeper in the study of the law.[39]

Within a year, the grand new house on Beacon Street had become strikingly silent. Holmes's sister, Amelia, married John Turner Welles Sargent, a very proper Boston widower. Her departure marked the end of the frequent visits of her gay young friends, who henceforth would call on Mrs. Sargent at her own home. Edward married Henrietta Wigglesworth in October and thus took his leave of his father's home. Although nearly thirty and the family's firstborn, Holmes was faced with being the last child to leave home. Living under his father's roof had always been difficult, but now it became particularly awkward. Financially dependent upon his father's generosity, however, Holmes was in no position to challenge his authority.[40]

Perhaps as a result of the inevitable tension between father and son, Holmes grew increasingly detached from the normal activities of daily life surrounding him. Refusing to accept the obvious reality of his extended adolescence, he turned to the satisfaction offered by the life of the mind. During this period, Holmes enjoyed the company of a distinguished group of young intellectuals. Together with John C. Gray, John C. Ropes, and Henry and William James, Holmes joined a dinner club whose early members included Henry Adams, John Fiske, Charles

Peirce, Nicholas St. John Green, and Chauncey Wright. Modeled after the Saturday Club, the group facetiously dubbed itself the "Metaphysical Club." Gathering together for lively conversation, these young lawyers and philosophers shared a common attitude toward the law and problems of philosophical inquiry. Skeptical of general propositions and a priori assumptions, they adopted a pragmatic and scientific habit of mind. In the congenial company of close friends, they "twisted the tail of the cosmos," developing their individual theories of the universe.[41] In such company, Holmes quickly realized that he could never be happy pursuing the traditional opportunities offered by a legal career.

In 1870 another part of Holmes's life came sadly to an end. Minny Temple, the Jameses' charming cousin, had never enjoyed good health; somewhat frail and susceptible to illness, she died during the winter of 1870 at the age of twenty-five. Whether John Gray or Wendell Holmes ever really loved her, both were deeply affected by her death. More than simply "the heroine" of their "common scene," she had been the one spark of life in Boston that seemed to set Holmes on fire. During the years immediately following her death, he withdrew from the larger society of Boston, increasingly confining himself to his work.[42]

By the close of the year, Holmes had clearly embarked on a lonely journey of his own choosing. If his younger brother had identified himself with the merchant class of Boston through his marriage and pursuit of prosperous business clients, Holmes's own behavior reflected a significant affiliation of mind and sympathy with the less worldly scholarship of the Brahmin class. Occasionally representing a client in court, Holmes devoted most of his energy to his work as a coeditor of the *American Law Review,* a responsibility he had assumed with another former Chandler, Shattuck, and Thayer clerk, Arthur G. Sedgwick. During the winter of 1870, Holmes had been invited by Charles Eliot, Harvard's new president, to present a series of undergraduate lectures on constitutional law at the college. Most likely, the income such a lectureship would provide was more an inducement for Holmes than the subject matter, as he had not previously evidenced much interest in the subject of public law.[43] In fact, his complete indifference to politics struck many of his contemporaries as somewhat odd. Visited in 1870 by two distinguished Englishmen—James Bryce, Regius Professor of Civil Law at Oxford University, and Albert Venn Dicey, a cousin of Leslie Stephen's and prominent London barrister—Holmes undoubtedly realized the extent to which he was isolating himself from the affairs of the world. Caring little for the subject these men found so stimulating, Holmes accepted that his choice of profession was a matter of deep "personal aptitudes and preferences"; having chosen the law as his route to the world of ideas, he was committed to sticking with it exclusively.[44]

About this same time, an opportunity presented itself that would have a significant impact upon Holmes's career. Shortly before Holmes left the firm of Chandler, Shattuck, and Thayer, James Bradley Thayer had been retained to edit the twelfth edition of Chancellor Kent's famous *Commentaries.* Busy with other matters, Thayer had asked Holmes if he would like to become associated with the project as a junior partner in the enterprise. As originally discussed with the chancellor's grandson, James Kent, both Thayer's and Holmes's names would appear with Kent's on the title page of the revised edition, but it was clearly understood that Thayer was to serve as senior editor of the work.[45]

From Holmes's perspective, the timing of this offer could not have been better. Eager to make his mark as a rising young legal scholar, he seized the opportunity to make the new edition his own, transforming the intended joint venture into his own individual achievement. Ambitious in a way markedly different from either his father or his brother, Holmes rejected modesty in favor of public recognition; prepared to sacrifice the next two years of this life to the task at hand, he was unwilling to share any of the credit. When the work was finally published, only Holmes's name would appear on the title page. Despite an acknowledgment by Holmes to Thayer in the closing paragraph of the preface, his former colleague was understandably bitter. Nearly a decade later, Thayer still had not forgotten his sense of betrayal; recognizing Holmes's solid achievements and superior qualities, he noted traits he believed evidenced a serious weakness of character: "selfish, vain, thoughtless of others."[46]

Confident that the excellence of the product would justify his unilateral decision to assume responsibility for the project, Holmes set out to write a work that would attract the attention of serious legal scholars. Distinguished by concise and well-written annotations, Holmes's commentary threatened to eclipse the original text. Unwilling to overlook any topic of relevance to the subject matter at hand, he painstakingly checked references and citations, intent that no point or case be overlooked. The further he went, the more absorbed in the work he became. Holmes expanded and extended many of the ideas suggested through the preparation of his notes into articles which he published anonymously in the *American Law Review*. In order to give more authority to his work, the note would include a reference to the corresponding published article.[47]

As month followed month, Holmes became increasingly obsessed with the project, and the intensity and concentration of the editing began to take their toll. Carrying the manuscript with him everywhere in a canvas bag, he never let it out of his sight. Instructing his family and friends that in case of a fire, it was to be saved at all costs, Holmes attached a value to his work that was not always appreciated by others. Invited to dinner at the Jameses', Holmes took his manuscript with him; Mrs. James could not help commenting to her son that Wendell's "whole life, soul and body" was "utterly absorbed" in his work on Kent: "His pallid face, and this fearful grip upon his work, makes him a melancholy sight."[48]

Mrs. James was not alone in her concern. No one in Holmes's inner circle of friends could quite take Holmes's total devotion to his work seriously. While other young men were getting on in the world, establishing families and making their fortunes, Holmes was ruining his health and reputation over a book. Never able to detach his writing from his personal life, Dr. Holmes gave his attention to the question of his son's aberrant behavior. In March 1872, an installment of his "Breakfast-Table" series appeared in the *Atlantic Monthly* which introduced a new central character—the young astronomer: "a strange unearthly being, lonely, dwelling far apart from the thoughts and cares of the planet on which he lives, an enthusiast who gives his life to knowledge."[49]

Typically, Dr. Holmes—father and author—was not prepared to leave it at that. Probing deeper into the astronomer's psyche, he discovers that the young man's ambition serves a deeper need for solitude revealed by his "almost studied search for heartlessness." Despite the tender devotion and deepest affection of a character identified as "Scheherazade" and, more directly, "the young girl," the astronomer preserves a "cold indifference" to the world. For this, the author reproaches the lonely thinker, urging him to stop and warm his hands "just for a little while in human consciousness," and tempting him to feel "the breath of a young girl against his cheek."[50] But the astronomer refuses. The story ends with a conclusion that must have been shared by many who knew Holmes well:

> But our young man seems further away from life than any student whose head is bent downwards over his books. . . . If he would

only fall in love with her, seize upon her wandering affections and fancies as the Romans seized the Sabine virgins, lift her out of herself and her listless and weary drudgeries. . . . I am afraid all this may never be. I fear that he is too much given to lonely study, to self-companionship, to all sorts of questionings, to looking at life as a solemn show where he is only a spectator.[51]

Although perhaps not intended as a psychological profile of his son, Dr. Holmes's perceptive analysis of the young astronomer's condition suggests a judgment of Holmes that is unavoidable.

In many ways, Holmes's lonely journey stood in stark contrast to his father's insatiable quest for popularity and celebrity. In 1897, Holmes offered a tribute in remembrance of George Otis Shattuck which provided him with an opportunity to reflect on what properly constitutes greatness in a man. In what can only be viewed as a comment upon his father's career, Holmes observed that "a small man may be remembered for some little felicity which enabled him to write a successful lyric, or in some way to charm the senses or emotions of a world always readier with its rewards for pleasures than for great thoughts or deeds." Holmes stated that he knew of no other measure of a man's life except "the total of human energy" it embodied, and that "the final test" of such energy was "battle in some form." He concluded that "many of those who are remembered have spared themselves this supreme trial. . . . It is one thing to utter a happy phrase from a protected cloister; another to think under fire—to think for action upon which great interests depend."[52] Extremely sensitive to criticism—especially from his father—Holmes was capable of his own stinging critique.

Despite the obvious differences of temperament and personality, Holmes may have received a greater intellectual inheritance from his father than he was prepared to acknowledge. Dr. Holmes's conviction that "a man may fulfill the object of his existence by asking a question he cannot answer, and attempting a task he cannot achieve" was a sentiment shared by his son, who believed that "no man has earned the right to intellectual ambition until he has learned to lay his course by a star which he has never seen,—to dig by the divining rod for springs which he may never reach."[53] Both men praised action. For Holmes, Sr., "every event that a man would master must be mounted on the run. . . . No man ever caught the reins of a thought except as it galloped by him." Holmes, Jr., expressed the same idea slightly differently: "If you want to hit a bird on the wing, you must have all your will in a focus, you must not be thinking about yourself, and, equally, you must not be thinking about your neighbor; you must be living in your eye on that bird. Every achievement is a bird on the wing."[54] But most important, neither father nor son could escape the judgment of their Puritan ancestors that "the rule of joy and the law of duty" were one. Both accepted the conclusion that the command "Whatsoever thy hand findeth to do, do it with thy might" more important than the Christian injunction to love one's neighbor as oneself.[55]

Although those around him may not have recognized it, Holmes was fighting a private war with very high stakes. "To fight out a war," he would later write, "you must believe something and want something with all your might. . . . More than that, you must be willing to commit yourself to a course, perhaps a long and hard one, without being able to foresee exactly where you will come out."[56] Holmes was willing to wager the pleasures of a lifetime for the chance to establish himself quickly as a serious scholar. Striving "to hammer out as compact and solid a piece of work" as he could, and trying to make it truly "first rate," everything else in his life would simply have to wait.[57] Convinced that "a man of high ambitions" must "leave even his fellow adventurers and go forth into a deeper solitude" in order to "face the loneliness of original work," Holmes accepted the conclusion that "no one can cut out new paths in company. He does that alone."[58] Although unable to explain himself to the satisfaction of his family and friends in 1872, Holmes would later write of the "secret isolated joy of the thinker," a joy he obviously had experienced. With great satisfaction, he offered this insight into the inspiration that sustained him during those lonely years: "a hundred years after he is dead and forgotten, men who never heard of him will be moving to the measure of his thought—the subtile rapture of a postponed power . . . which to his prophetic vision is more real than that which commands an army."[59]

Holmes was clearly eager that his work be a success. Demonstrating an intense longing for recognition, he worked anxiously to complete the *Commentaries*. During the summer of 1872, he sent Judge Doe of the New Hampshire Supreme Court a copy of his as yet unpublished article on the theory of torts. Another outgrowth of his work on Kent, Holmes had written the essay with a view toward publishing it at some future date. To Holmes's surprise and indignation, Judge Doe delivered an opinion in a case that had been before the court—*Stewart v. Emerson*—which drew heavily upon Holmes's argument without acknowledging Holmes's contribution. Rather than being pleased that his work had found an important and practical application in the court's decision, the young scholar was offended that he had not received sufficient credit.[60] Ten years later, Holmes would accuse another author of appropriating without proper acknowledgment material he believed to be his own original work.[61] Equally sensitive to the occasional scholarly criticism his articles received, Holmes's relationships with other authors and scholars were frequently strained by an extreme sensitivity suggesting a more fundamental intellectual insecurity.

On 13 March 1872 Holmes announced his engagement to Fanny Dixwell. Coming after his father had written the story of the young astronomer but prior to its publication, the announcement ended speculation among family and friends concerning the nature of Holmes's relationship with the woman he had for many years described as "his most intimate friend."[62] Although Fanny's affection for Holmes was well known, and at least one young lady who knew them both rather well thought Fanny "just the wife for him,"[63] some question remained as to Wendell's feelings for his future wife. That they understood and respected one another was obvious enough, but Holmes had always treated Fanny rather differently from his other lady admirers, more like a sister than a lover. Perhaps Fanny knew better than anyone else how significantly the war had changed him and was prepared to accept a marriage where devotion to duty would predominate over moments of private passion. Both were mature adults when they finally made the decision to marry—Holmes was thirty-one and Fanny a few months older. Whether goaded by his father into proposing to Fanny out of a sense of obligation and responsibility or encouraged to take a spouse by his dear Uncle John who well knew the loneliness of unmarried life, Holmes married Fanny Bowditch Dixwell on 17 June 1872 in a nominally Unitarian service conducted by Phillips Brooks at Christ Church in Cambridge. If the couple went on a honeymoon trip, it was a very brief one; within a few days of their wedding, Fanny moved into Wendell's room under his father's roof, converting Ned's room across the hall into her sitting room.[64]

Marriage did not outwardly seem to have much effect on Holmes. From first to last, Fanny was dedicated to his welfare, much as Mrs. Holmes had devoted herself to taking care of Dr. Holmes and their children. As a wife, Fanny must have reminded her husband a great deal of his own mother. Whatever needed doing, Fanny managed to see that it got done. For nearly the first ten years of their marriage, she actively supported her husband's aspiration for intellectual achievement, frequently becoming quite involved in his work, discussing ideas and reading rough drafts. Whether she shared her husband's aversion to the conventional responsibilities of marriage and family life is less clear. Holmes himself apparently found his marriage to Fanny quite agreeable. After many years together, he wrote a friend that "a man as well as a woman finds life enlarged and glorified by marriage. The adjustment of personality is easy to people who think nobly, and I feel confident that you will reach a new and higher plane of life."[65]

Like his father and grandfather before him, Holmes found himself finally married and relatively settled rather late in life. But unlike them, he seems to have been indifferent to beginning a family. Neither Holmes nor his wife was particularly fond of children; she is known to have "hated" several of her younger siblings, and despite his own special affection for Uncle John, Holmes virtually ignored his only nephew, Edward Jackson Holmes, Jr. More than once, Holmes expressed the view that he was "so far abnormal" as to be glad that he had never fathered a child. Despite Holmes's remarks, however, the fact that his wife regretted never having children suggests that for whatever reason, the couple may simply have been physically unable to have a family.[66]

In March 1873, Holmes renewed his professional relationship with his old mentor, George Otis Shattuck, who invited him to form a new partnership with himself and William Munroe. Munroe was a quiet and industrious young lawyer who had become Shattuck's junior partner in 1870. Two years younger than Holmes, he remained the junior partner in the new firm. From a different social world altogether, Munroe was very active in organizations like the Baptist church, as distinguished from the Metaphysical Club. Although the two young men had very little in common, Holmes enjoyed a friendly if not intimate relationship with Munroe, whom he respected as a competent and hard-working colleague. Shattuck by this time was a recognized leader of the Boston bar, having distinguished himself both as a trial lawyer and as a legal counselor to a host of distinguished clients. Although Holmes preferred men who cared more for "a fruitful thought" than "a practical success," the necessity of making a living was becoming more pressing. It is likely that his marriage to Fanny was at least partially responsible for both Shattuck's offer and Holmes's acceptance.[67]

In December 1873 the *Commentaries* were finally published. In a review of the work by Russell Gray, John C. Gray's younger brother, Holmes was characterized as "a disciple of the new school (if, indeed, he be not . . . the prophet of one yet newer)."[68] Generally heralded as a great success, Holmes's efforts to trace the subtle thread of theory through careful analysis and historical insight was most appreciated by an emerging generation of new legal scholars. Together with his new partnership with Shattuck, publication marked Holmes's return to the active practice of law as distinguished from the period of relative inactivity that characterized his association with his brother.

With new resources at his disposal, Holmes finally acquired his own "estate," purchasing a small summer home at Mattapoisett, a somewhat remote and unfashionable summer resort on Buzzard's Bay. During the first year of Holmes's marriage, Shattuck had loaned his future partner the use of his summer home at Mattapoisett. Spending an occasional weekend alone at Shattuck's cottage, the young couple enjoyed the only real privacy they experienced during a particularly difficult period in their marriage. Located not far from Shattuck's property, the house that Holmes purchased was situated on thirty-seven acres along the shore; the residence was a double house, one half of which was occupied by a farmer-caretaker who maintained the property for Holmes. Continuing their practice, Holmes and his wife spent as many weekends as they could occupying the other half.[69]

Having lived the first two years of their married lives in the most modest fashion, Holmes used the summer of 1874 to indulge his own neglected urge to return to England and the Continent. Although his wife was a timid traveler and as a consequence reluctant to make the trip with him, the two departed in early June. Arriving in London, Holmes quickly renewed and extended his circle of English friends. Preferring London society to any other, Holmes enjoyed seeing Tom Hughes and Leslie Stephen again; he met Frederick Pollock and went to court with Judge Pollock, Frederick's father. He visited Middle Temple and breakfasted with John Lothrop Motley and Sir Henry Maine. No longer requiring letters of introduction, Holmes met Carlyle and spent several evenings with James Bryce and Albert Venn Dicey. Holmes explained his fascination with London this way: "You have to pay your way in London. No one takes you on faith—and I love it. . . . London is hard to get into, not from any requirement of 16 quarterings, but because . . . there are too many interesting people in London. You must interest . . . people who, being in the center of the world, have seen all kinds of superlatives."[70] Perhaps Holmes's real reason for preferring London to Boston was that whereas he was forced to prove his intellectual superiority in Boston through grueling labor, he was free in London to be his father's son. Enormously gifted as a conversationalist, Holmes "could catch a subject, toss it into the air, make it dance, and play a hundred tricks, and bring it to solid earth again."[71] Once again a great success, Holmes reveled in his acceptance.

Mistrustful of the social and intellectual fashions of London, Mrs. Holmes was something less than a success. Shy and retiring by nature, she nevertheless accepted the hectic pace set by her enthusiastic husband. Holmes was undoubtedly aware of the strain on his wife; he would later explain to a friend that his "Mrs." was "a very solitary bird," who would likely have become "an absolute recluse" had not her "notion of duty" compelled her to do otherwise.[72] Preferring the simplicity of their cottage at Mattapoisett to the subtle complexities of London, she would undoubtedly have been happier at home. She may also have had considerable difficulty adjusting her behavior from the devoted servant of a virtual monk, cloistered in his third-floor cell, to the charming and gregarious wife of an international socialite.

Following a trip to the Continent that included visits to Paris, Geneva, Milan, Venice, and Turin, the couple returned to London in early August. After several short trips to visit old and new friends in Bedfordshire, Oxford, Cambridge, and Devonshire, the Holmeses sailed for home. Holmes's first trip to England had revealed a powerful and in some ways reckless zest for living; perhaps as a result, Holmes had denied himself that kind of life when he returned to Boston, devoting himself instead to achieving an ambitious eminence through his scholarship. By the end of 1873, Holmes had become more confident than ever before that great success still lay ahead of him. Prior to forming the new partnership with Shattuck, he had relinquished his lectureships at Harvard and transferred the editorship of the *American Law Review* to Moorfield Story and Samuel Hoar. By the time he sailed for Europe with his wife, Holmes had cleared the decks for future action. Concluding three years of essentially intellectual and academic activities, he relaxed and refreshed himself in preparation for the rather different challenges that would confront him as an active trial lawyer. Despite his acceptance of the necessity of making a living, it seems entirely likely that Holmes had resolved by the end of the summer of 1874 to find his "final distinction" as a thinker and not as a practitioner.[73]

Oliver Wendell Holmes, Jr., with his
sister, Amelia (center) and his
brother, Edward (left).
Courtesy of Harvard Law Art Collection

The "Autocrat"—Dr. Holmes in the
late 1850s.
Courtesy of Harvard Law Art Collection

Having earned the rank of "Brevet Colonel,"
Holmes leaves the Army in July 1864.
Courtesy Harvard Law Art Collection

Holmes presenting "The Common Law" at the prestigious
Lowell Lectures in November 1880.
Courtesy of Harvard Law Art Collection

Fanny Dixwell Holmes.
Courtesy of Harvard Law Art Collection

An engraving of Holmes, who became Chief
Justice of the Supreme Judicial Court of
Massachusetts in July 1899.
Courtesy of Harvard Law Art Collection

Justice Holmes, circa 1910.
Courtesy of The Supreme Court
Historical Society

Justice Holmes's library at his residence
at 1720 Eye Street, Washington, D.C.
Courtesy of Harvard Law Art Collection

Holmes in casual attire during one of his summer
trips abroad in the early 1900s.
Courtesy of Harvard Law Art Collection

Associate Justice Holmes and the White Court of 1916.
Courtesy of The Supreme Court Historical Society

Justice Holmes routinely walked the roughly two miles
between his home in northwest Washington and the Capitol.
Courtesy of Harvard Law Art Collection

Old friends, Justices Holmes and Brandeis were frequently
seen walking together near the Capitol after Brandeis
joined the Court in 1916.
Courtesy of The Supreme Court Historical Society

Holmes and Chief Justice Taft in the late 1920s.
Courtesy of The Supreme Court Historical Society

Members of the court stand in silence as the bugle sounds
and the flag is folded during Holmes's internment at Arlington National
Cemetery on 8 March 1935.
Courtesy of The Supreme Court Historical Society

7

THE SCHOLAR JUDGE

As the summer of 1874 came to a close, Holmes and his wife returned to Dr. Holmes's household at 296 Beacon Street. It was undoubtedly hard on the young couple following the freedom of their European trip to resume the dependent status that such arrangements suggest. Holmes was lean as ever, but had let his mustache grow "to cavalry proportions"; having never lost an army officer's bearing, he became more strikingly distinguished as he grew older and the look of a man replaced the appearance of a boy. His eyes sparkled with a charming wit and intelligence, but his manner suggested the urgency of his purpose and revealed a hard masculine ambition.[1]

Soon after their return home, Fanny Holmes set about to find more suitable quarters; by early spring, she had located an apartment above the drugstore at 10 Beacon Street. Located within a minute's walk of the law offices of Shattuck, Holmes, and Munroe, their new rooms were next door to the Boston Athenaeum at the crest of Beacon Street near the common. Although far from lavish, the apartment afforded the young couple a sense of independence and identity they had not previously enjoyed. Only a couple of blocks from Dr. Holmes's elegant brownstone, the rooms at 10 Beacon Street provided Holmes, Jr.—and perhaps more important, his wife—with a place of their own. Emancipated really for the first time from his father's household, Holmes could come and go as he pleased without first having to discuss the matter with his father. Moreover, he and his wife could entertain their friends on their own terms, free from the dominating personality of Dr. Holmes and his ubiquitous chatter. The young couple frequently ate dinner together at the Parker House, often joining friends afterwards. Holmes had his dinner club, and Fanny her sewing circle. Although they lived rather simply and quietly, the two demonstrated a remarkable sense of enthusiasm and adventure for a married couple in their thirties.[2]

By the beginning of 1875 Holmes was completely absorbed in the practice of law. His personal ethic may have rejected the traditional moral teachings of his Puritan forebears, but with them he shared a dogged respect for hard work. Always suspicious of any form of weakness, he quickly established a reputation as a tough and effective advocate. Joining a firm that spoke for the dominant interests in the community, there is no record that Holmes ever represented the oppressed or downtrodden of Boston. If the partners of Shattuck, Holmes, and Munroe had a social conscience, their practice did not reveal it.[3] Holmes was exceedingly fortunate to have as a mentor one of Boston's greatest attorneys. As Holmes later acknowledged, Shattuck "taught [him] unrepeatable lessons"; in a revealing statement, Holmes said he "owed to Mr. Shattuck more" than he owed to "anyone else in the world" outside his immediate family.[4]

Working side by side, the two men represented an impressive list of business clients—merchants, insurance companies, bankers—appearing frequently in the Federal Court of Admiralty. Evidence suggests that Holmes was impressed by the qualities of mind and temperament characteristic of his more prominent clients, whom he described as "fierce" and "splendid old Philistines" who had "fought" their way to wealth and power.[5] However little he might wish to dine with such men, he couldn't help but respect those "who do big things."[6] Not surprisingly, Holmes's energy and intellect in turn were respected by such men, and in 1875, he was invited to become a member of the Harvard Board of Overseers, a position he would hold until 1882. Holmes derived considerable satisfaction from his appointment; in addition to being a position of great trust and distinction, as Harvard professors could not become overseers, it was a position Dr. Holmes had never held.[7]

As Holmes became increasingly absorbed in his work, the next few years were unusually demanding ones even for him. As his reputation as a lawyer grew, his cases became more significant. In 1877, Shattuck and

Holmes took on the distinguished Henry Dana, Sr., and his son, Henry Dana, Jr., in a particularly hard-fought legal battle. The case—*New Orleans Mutual Insurance Co. v. Nickerson, et al.*—was an admiralty case involving the ship *Concordia*. Argued before Justice Nathan Clifford sitting on circuit in August 1877, the case revealed a side of Holmes that few in Boston recognized; tough and hard-hitting, he relentlessly pressed his client's cause to the point of provoking some bitterness on the part of opposing counsel. Such powerful and effective advocacy had not previously been associated with the bookish and reclusive legal scholar.[8] A year later, in the case of *U.S. v. Ames*, Holmes skillfully argued his first case before the U.S. Supreme Court in the October term, securing a decision in the favor of his client in what was considered by many to be a rather difficult equity matter.[9] In these and similar cases, Holmes quickly gained the respect of his colleagues and distinguished himself as a rising member of the bar.

While her husband worked hard to establish his legal career, Fanny Holmes labored over her embroidery; perfecting a technique that would be acclaimed as "the most remarkable needlework ever done," she created a collection of embroidered panels that eventually were exhibited by the Boston Art Museum and the New York Ladies' Decoration Arts Society.[10] The couple had few close friends; spending most of their evenings at home with their respective labors, they looked forward to the occasional weekends they could get away to Mattapoisett. Holmes particularly enjoyed sailing and walking with Shattuck on the cape, where the two men could be more relaxed than on State Street in Boston.

In 1877 Amelia Holmes Sargent's husband died, and Holmes became involved in the administration of his brother-in-law's estate. There is no indication that Holmes considered this matter any differently from other legal business; he had never been particularly close to his sister and had spent little if any time with her after her marriage to John Turner Welles Sargent in the spring of 1871. Nor is there any evidence that Holmes felt any special sympathy for his brother, Edward, who was compelled to give up his law practice as a result of extremely severe asthmatic attacks. Despite efforts to find relief in various American and European spas, Edward died in 1884 at the age of thirty-eight.[11]

Although it is certainly true that Holmes displayed a traditional New England reticence regarding personal emotions, his reaction to his brother's misfortune suggests a wider gulf than might be expected. Holmes would later "reproach [himself] a little for not loving [his] fellow men in general enough." He wrote to a friend that he often felt "like a worm" when he read of men "whose dominant motive is love of their kind," but consoled himself "by thinking that most of the great work done in the world comes from a different type." His comments about a friend's financial problems might equally well have been made about his brother's plight: "almost ashamed to be well and in good condition," Holmes observed that "the condition of others is primarily their business and certainly is beyond our power, whence the futility of the command to love one's brother as oneself."[12]

In July 1878 George F. Sheply of Portland, Maine, died, creating a vacancy on the federal First Circuit Court. District Court Judge John Lowell of Boston was the likely candidate for the post, and his appointment would create a vacancy on the federal district court. Championed by Shattuck, Holmes's candidacy was supported by several of the leading men of the Boston bar. Holmes's close personal friend John C. Gray—Judge Horace Gray's half brother—was the prime mover in the campaign to secure the appointment for him. Writing to a friend, Holmes expressed considerable interest in the appointment. "The place . . . would enable me to work in the way I want," Holmes explained, "and so I should like to have it although it would cost me a severe pang to leave my partners."[13] President Hayes advanced Judge Lowell to the First Circuit as expected and initially considered Holmes as the leading candidate to fill the district court vacancy. However, Massachusetts's junior senator, George Frisbie Hoar, objected to the appointment, and urged President Hayes to appoint Thomas J. Nelson instead. After some debate between the president and his advisers, Hayes acceded to Hoar's recommendation despite his earlier preference for Holmes.[14]

Holmes was undoubtedly disappointed by losing the nomination, but the fact that he had come so close must have been encouraging. Barely thirty-seven years old and having only recently returned to the serious practice of law, Holmes realized that even to have been considered for a federal judgeship was a mark of high distinction. He was perhaps less aware that his concentration on scholarly work, his isolation from the larger world of Boston society and politics, and his aggressive personal style of advocacy had alienated him from an important part of the community. Although he had friends and supporters, he had also made enemies; for whatever reason, a great many important men in Boston mistrusted this ambitious Oliver Wendell Holmes, Jr., a young man they really didn't know.

It soon became an "article of faith" for Holmes "that if a man is to do anything he must do it before 40."[15] In later life he elaborated upon his belief that "men reach their highest mark between thirty and forty." Having "settled down to their permanent occupation by thirty," men are likely to have found "such leading and dominant conceptions as they are going to find" in the course of the next ten years. "The rest of life," said Holmes, "is working out details."[16]

Although Holmes had worked hard to establish himself as a first-class lawyer, it is certain that he did not intend to remain a courtroom attorney for the rest of his life. His breeding and status as a leading member of Boston's Brahmin class made him particularly sensitive to the coarseness of the cultural tone of the American nation in the decade following the Civil War. The crass values of the businessmen and lawyers who devoted themselves to the pursuit of wealth were simply not Holmes's values. Such men might be grudgingly admired for the sheer force of their wills; their motives, however, were hardly acceptable to a gentleman who still considered personal honor the proper standard for judging behavior. Disgusted by the excesses of the Gilded Age, Holmes shared Henry Adams's contempt for "the crude, raw, careless throb" of American life.[17] In short, any active participation in the political or commercial arenas of that period would simply have been incompatible with Holmes's aesthetic sensibilities and genteel upbringing.

Thus, the distinction he drew between men of learning and men of wealth was a telling one. "Where shall chivalrous faith rise above the cynicism of business," Holmes queried, "if not in the scholar?"[18] Content to tolerate what he could not mend, Holmes preferred the life of the isolated thinker to that of an active participant. In many ways, Holmes chose to "step out of life," withdrawing from the challenges of the courtroom in favor of the life of a detached observer of events. Comfortable with the role of a spectator, Holmes increasingly withdrew behind a carefully constructed "public mask."[19]

During Holmes's tenure as coeditor of the *American Law Review*, he published six unsigned essays and some sixty notes or comments, and after relinquishing the editorship, he published five more signed essays in the journal. As a result of this significant body of work, he was invited by Boston's Lowell Institute to present the Lowell Lectures in 1880. Holmes seized upon this opportunity to make his mark and set out to present a definitive series of lectures on the common law. Years later he suggested that the impetus behind his acceptance of the challenge was "the passionate demand . . . that the law should be proved, if it could be, to be worthy of the interest of an intelligent man."[20] He would also write that he had always believed "that not place or power or popularity makes the success that one desires," but rather "the trembling hope that one has come near to an ideal."[21] Accepting that "to be this is to be not that," Holmes made it clear to those around him that his lectures on the common law were to be the achievement by which he intended to be judged.[22]

Holmes delivered the Lowell Lectures on successive Tuesday and Friday evenings at Huntington Hall on Tremont Street. The first lecture was presented on 23 November and the series of twelve lectures ran through December. The lectures incorporated material Holmes had already published in the *American Law Review*, but reworked and substantially expanded. In addition, several of the lectures included entirely new material. It is likely that many if not all the Harvard Law School faculty attended the opening lecture, and that many of Boston's leading lawyers and judges were also in the audience.[23]

Although Holmes's early writing had relied upon traditional forms of legal reasoning, and his focus had been primarily upon the structure of the law, his published articles after 1875 had begun to stress a new historical perspective. The dominant syllogistic form of legal reasoning Holmes initially accepted assumed that logical deductions could be made from established intellectual principles. This formalistic way of thinking about the law accepted Sir William Blackstone's assertion that the law was "permanent, fixed and unchangeable."[24] It also informed Rufus Choate's definition of law as "invisible, omnipresent, a real yet impalpable existence," which he poetically characterized as "the whispered yet authoritative voice of all the past and all the good."[25]

As Holmes became more interested in the historical origins of the common law, he began to reject this static view of the law in favor of a more dynamic one. As early as 1872, Henry Adams had asserted that the common law of England was based primarily on Germanic rather than Roman law. Implicit in this assertion was the conclusion that English common law had evolved over time from the practices of the past. Having become a student and scholar of Roman law, Holmes learned German and began to investigate the new materials Adams had emphasized in his work.[26] This new perspective on the development of English common law immediately appealed to him. Consistent with Darwin's theory of evolution and natural selection, it provided Holmes with a "scientific way of looking at the world."[27] A "historian before he was a judge,"

Holmes became increasingly more interested in understanding the historical explanation for existing legal arrangements than with formulating legal fictions that might provide the illusion of a philosophically consistent legal system.[28]

It was this new conception of the common law that Holmes attempted to establish through his series of lectures. From the outset, both the lecturer and his audience must have been aware that Holmes was attacking directly the prevailing legal orthodoxy and, specifically, the way the law was perceived and taught at Harvard Law School. In an article published in 1879, Holmes had focused on "the paradox of form and substance in the development of law," noting that while in form such development might appear logical, in substance it was evolutionary. "The secret root from which the law draws all the juices of life" was in fact "considerations of what is expedient for the community," Holmes asserted, and not any a priori legal "ideal."[29] He concluded his article by pointing to the "failure of all theories" that considered the law only from its "formal side," whether they attempted to deduce the law from an established set of principles or fell into "the humbler error" of assuming the law to be the *elegantia juris*"—or "logical coherence of part with part."[30]

Holmes had made this point even more directly in a 1880 review of a new contracts textbook authored by Christopher Langdell, the dean of the Harvard Law School. "Mr. Langdell's ideal in law [and] the end of all his striving," wrote Holmes, "is the *elegantia juris* or logical integrity of the system as a system. He is perhaps the greatest living legal theologian."[31] In such bold language, Holmes attacked the intellectual leader of his own alma mater, heralding a new attitude and approach to the study of law. Those who had read Holmes's recent work must have sensed that they would hear a distinctly new voice speaking an exciting new language of the law. At least one local newspaper noted that Holmes's lectures stirred particular interest among the younger men of the legal community.[32]

From the outset of the first lecture, Holmes made it clear he would extend the argument he had begun to develop in his attack on Langdell. "The life of the law has not been logic," he informed his audience, "it has been experience." For Holmes, the law "embodies the story of a nation's development through the centuries"; accordingly, it could not be dealt with as if it contained "only the axioms and corollaries of a book of mathematics," but rather as the essence of "organic living institutions transplanted from English soil." Thus, the true significance of the law was "vital not formal"; the meaning of legal principles could not be properly understood "simply by taking the words and a dictionary," but required an understanding of "their origin and their line of growth." The law as Holmes perceived it was alive and growing; it was something completely different from the static and fixed set of formal propositions with which Langdell was concerned.[33]

Through a careful historical study of such legal concepts as fraud, malice, and negligence, Holmes attempted to establish that every law had its origins in the actual struggle of a prior time, and not "in the mind of God or the will of the Prince."[34] Holmes may have found John Austin's view of sovereignty inadequate, but he must certainly have applauded Austin's judgment concerning "the childish fiction employed by our judges that . . . common law is not made by them, but is a miraculous something made by nobody."[35] "Law is administered by able and experienced men," asserted Holmes, who knew "too much to sacrifice good sense to a syllogism." Holmes was "pretty certain" that such men would make laws that seemed "convenient" without "troubling themselves very much with what principles [were] encountered by their legislation." As far as Holmes was concerned, "the substance of the law is legislative," and as a consequence, "the first requirement of a sound body of law is that it should correspond to the actual feelings and demands of the community, whether right or wrong."[36]

Underlying Holmes's series of lectures was his desire to bring legal study into the mainstream of the scientific movement by establishing a system of jurisprudence based on the observation of social phenomena as distinguished from a system of law based on intellectual abstractions and formal logic.[37] Holmes rejected Lord Coke's maxim that "reason is the life of the law," insisting instead that "the *ultima ratio*, not only *regnum*, but of private persons, is force, and at bottom of all private relations . . . is a justifiable self-preference."[38] Challenging the quasi-religious view supported by the German philosopher Immanuel Kant that men should never be treated as means but only as ends, Holmes stated boldly that "no society has ever admitted that it could not sacrifice individual welfare to its own existence."[39]

Intent on "smashing fixed systems of the universe and substituting a fluid one," Holmes sought to replace theory and logic with history and practice.[40] Although he had not read Darwin's revolutionary *Origin of the Species*, he accepted entirely the theory of evolution in the law as espoused by Sir Henry Maine in his *The Ancient Law*. Moreover, Holmes was an enthusiastic supporter of the work of Herbert Spencer. The "scientific way of looking at the world . . . was in the air," and Holmes's wartime experience had confirmed what he had already accepted in theory. All life was a struggle between the weak and the strong; it was inevitable that this fundamental reality be reflected in law as well as in every other aspect of life.[41]

In addition to his development of a scientific history of the common law, Holmes emphasized in his lectures a concern of particular interest to practicing lawyers. It was important to Holmes that above all else, the law be predictable. More likely the result of his critical examination of Austin's jurisprudence than of his intellectual affiliation with the philosophical pragmatism of the Metaphysical Club, his argument was that "the end of all classification should be to make the law *knowable*."[42] Throughout his lectures, he returned to this point, insisting that the movement of the law was away from internal/subjective standards of behavior based on notions of morality toward external/objective standards based on the community's notions of desirable public policy. Properly understood, the law was concerned with what is, not with what ought to be.[43]

Even if Holmes's purpose in stressing the acceptance of an external and objective standard was to increase the extent to which the operation of the law could be predicted with accuracy, his argument had the effect of separating law from morality. A lawyer's chief concern was not a matter of right or wrong, or even of determining what was the will of the sovereign; a lawyer's true task was to anticipate the actual decisions of the courts and the likely consequences to his client. Although Holmes was prepared to acknowledge that the history of the law "is the history of the moral development of the race," his principal focus was on the fact that "the merit of the common law is that it decides the case first and determines the principle afterwards."[44]

Concerned that others might take the ideas he had presented during the Lowell Lectures and publish them as their own, Holmes rushed to get his lectures published himself. Shortly before his fortieth birthday in March 1881, he delivered an autographed copy of *The Common Law* to his father, mimicking a practice Dr. Holmes had started in 1847 when he presented his seven-year-old son with an autographed copy of one of his books.[45] Critical reaction to the book was favorable, the work being called "most valuable" and "almost indispensable . . . to the scientific student of legal history." In June 1882, the London *Spectator* hailed *The Common Law* as "one of the ablest and most philosophical" works of legal speculation since the publication of Maine's *The Ancient Law* in 1861.

American reviews commented on the work's "series of scientific observations," and the extent to which Holmes had brought the operation of the law "into unaccustomed clearness." Within a decade, a legal commentator would announce that *The Common Law* was "everywhere regarded as a scientific work."[46] Evidence of the influence of the work is the fact that Holmes's arguments quickly found expression by leading American theorists. Although the words are those of J. Allen Smith, the ideas expressed in 1885 could just as well have been Holmes's:

> It would be impossible, even if it were desirable, to bind the country by unaltering laws a century old. It is of little moment whether the meaning of our great charter is slowly construed away by the ingenuity of lawyers, or whether it is roughly thrust aside by force; its fate is sealed; it must yield where it obstructs. . . . In our country and our age that which the majority of the people want will be the law.[47]

Largely as a consequence of the success of *The Common Law*, President Eliot of Harvard offered Holmes a new position at the Harvard Law School on 1 November 1881. Holmes was anxious to secure the position, but he conditioned acceptance of the offer on several specific conditions. In addition to requiring an annual salary of forty-five hundred dollars, Holmes made it clear he would consider himself free to consider a judgeship should one be offered to him. These conditions were apparently acceptable to the university, which began an immediate campaign to raise the necessary funds to endow the new position. The task of raising the approximately $100,000 needed proved more difficult than expected; embarrassed by the rather awkward campaign to get him a position at Harvard, Holmes withdrew his conditional acceptance of Eliot's offer.[48] However, through the good offices of Louis Brandeis, a graduate of the Harvard Law School and recent law clerk to Judge Gray, William F. Weld, Jr., offered to endow the new chair. After some discussion, the university nominated Holmes as the first incumbent at Weld's request, and President Eliot officially notified Holmes of his selection on 11 February 1882.[49] Dr. Holmes had retired from the faculty of the Harvard Medical School in 1880 after thirty-five years; now his son would succeed him as "Professor Holmes."[50]

Holmes assumed his position at Harvard in the spring of 1882, and his addition to the faculty was met with some considerable interest by both his students and at least one of his colleagues—his old associate, James Bradley Thayer. There is some evidence that the dean of the law school, Christopher Langdell, and his young protégé, the brilliant James Barr Ames, were less excited by his appointment to the school.[51] With his place on the Harvard Law School faculty secure and no longer engaged in the active practice of law, Holmes took the opportunity to return to England, leaving Boston on 20 May 1882. After visiting old friends in London, he traveled to France, Switzerland, and Germany. He returned to England in mid-August and Boston a month later, resuming his teaching at the law school during the fall term. On 3 January 1883, however, he submitted his resignation from the faculty, effective immediately.[52]

The law school and university were stunned by Holmes's abrupt departure. They were of course aware that Judge Otis Lord had resigned from the Massachusetts Supreme Judicial Court in early December 1882 and that Holmes would likely receive serious consideration by Governor Long to succeed him. They were apparently not aware, however, that the governor had offered the position to Holmes on 15 December with the caveat that Holmes either accept or decline the appointment immediately. Holmes accepted, but informed only his mentor, George Otis Shattuck, and his closest personal friend, John Chipman Gray, of his decision, allowing the students, faculty, and administration of the university to read of his appointment in the papers. Harvard was understandably upset by his behavior, as it adjusted to the extremely awkward and burdensome consequences of his sudden departure. There was sufficient ill will for Holmes to consult legal counsel concerning any possible obligation he might have to return some portion of the annual salary he had already received; satisfied with his lawyer's opinion that no legal obligation existed, Holmes made no offer of restitution.[53]

Two weeks after his appointment to the court, Holmes wrote a friend concerning his decision to leave Harvard. Commenting on the opportunity to gain "an all around experience of the law," Holmes stated that he did not think he could "without moral loss decline any share of the practical struggle of life which naturally offered itself" and for which he "believed himself fitted." Now "as happy as a man could desire," Holmes added that he felt that if he declined "the struggle" offered him, he "should never be so happy again"—he would feel that he "had chosen the less manly course."[54] Years later, he expressed a similar sentiment to a junior colleague: "Academic life is but half-life—it is withdrawn from the fight in order to utter smart things that cost you nothing except the thinking them from a cloister."[55] No matter how Holmes chose to justify his decision to himself and others, however, those who knew him best undoubtedly saw his departure from Harvard in favor of a judicial appointment as further evidence that he was continuing to "gouge from life a deep and self-beneficial groove."[56]

Holmes was appointed to the Massachusetts Supreme Judicial Court—the highest appellate court in the state—on 15 December 1882 and took his seat on 3 January 1883. At forty-one, he was the youngest of the seven judges on the high court. His colleagues, Judges Field, Morton, Devens, Colburn, and two Allens, were white-haired men of advanced years. They undoubtedly shared Holmes's view that his appointment was "a stroke of lightning" which would change his life and theirs.[57]

For Holmes the appointment marked a critical juncture in both his personal and his professional life. Shortly after he had completed *The Common Law,* he had become seriously ill and suffered "symptoms that for the moment" he "mistook for a funeral knell."[58] Although no record remains to document the nature of Holmes's medical problem, it is likely that the strain of completing his book, coupled with the difficulties associated with his appointment to the Harvard faculty, adversely affected his health. Sufficiently recovered by the spring of 1882 to make his trip to Europe, he was nevertheless chastened by his bout with mortality; his appointment likely served to bolster his conviction that he had once again been spared for some great work.

Professionally, putting on judicial robes removed Holmes from the classroom and thrust him into the courtroom. It also called attention to the fact that his route to the high bench had not been the traditional one. Although Judge Field had taught briefly at Dartmouth College, all the members of the court except Holmes had been appointed after years of experience as practicing lawyers. Judge Charles Allen had written the prestigious *Allen's Reports,* but his place on the court was secured by his practical professional record rather than his scholarly achievements.[59] In contrast, Holmes could claim experience in only thirty-four cases which had come before the high court during the fifteen years of his legal practice. Such reputation as he enjoyed among Boston's lawyers was based almost entirely upon his work as a legal scholar—as editor of *Kent's Commentaries* and author of *The Common Law.* Although he was the grandson of a distinguished jurist, many in the bar must have wondered whether the governor had chosen wisely in putting young Oliver Wendell Holmes, Jr., on the high bench.[60]

Among Holmes's own crowd there was less doubt concerning the appointment "The world is made up of very few *real* people, only a few score, I think," wrote Henry Adams to Holmes shortly after his appointment to the court, "and anything which encourages in the hope that we are one of these realities is the highest encouragement."[61] Reflecting the views of the rising generation of Boston Brahmins, Adams's comment suggests Holmes's own understanding of the significance of his appointment.

Despite his new prestige, Holmes could not escape the consequences of his family's prominence; he was continually confronted by the fact that he was the son of the "original" Oliver Wendell Holmes. Dr. Holmes's poem on the occasion of a public dinner held in recognition of his son's achievement was widely quoted, and news of the son's appointment was routinely accompanied by mention of the father's fame. Despite Holmes's elevation to the high court, his father's attitude toward him remained unchanged: "To think of it, my little boy a judge and able to send me to jail if I don't behave myself."[62]

With his appointment, Holmes left the quiet of academic life to enter the active world of a judge. The work of the court was extremely demanding; in addition to appeals which the judges heard together, Holmes sat alone in equity matters, hearing divorce and probate cases. Early in his tenure as a judge, Holmes expressed some pleasure at the prospect of "confirming some theories" he had developed as a legal scholar. Writing that he "enjoy[ed] the work so far extremely," he admitted to a friend that he liked the work "far more" than he had "dreamed beforehand."[63] But after initially finding the work challenging and intellectually stimulating, Holmes soon realized that the great bulk of the court's work was repetitious and relatively trivial.

The summer following his appointment to the court, he and his wife moved to a new home at 9 Chestnut Street, which was located between Beacon Street and the Charles River. With a salary of six thousand dollars a year, and an additional five hundred dollars for traveling expenses, the couple could finally afford to establish a proper household. Fanny Holmes engaged a young woman newly arrived from Ireland as a cook and hired a local girl as a housemaid. She also indulged her fondness of pets by acquiring two small brown finches, two nightingales, and a mockingbird.[64]

While his wife concerned herself with domestic details, Holmes became increasingly absorbed in his court work. In many ways he simply replaced the austerity of the solitary life of the scholar with the detached and isolated life of an appellate judge. Younger by a decade than the next youngest member of the court, and distanced by his position from the professional and academic worlds he had once frequented, Holmes had few regular companions. One notable exception was Owen Wister, who graduated from Harvard Law School in 1882. Nicknamed "Whisker" by the judge, Wister was a frequent guest at 9 Chestnut Street. The first of many bright young men who would attract Holmes's attention and interest, Wister was for many years one of the couple's closest friends.[65]

On the bench, Holmes devoted himself to his work. Although neither the cases nor the issues they raised were particularly significant, he labored to prove himself equal to the task. His early opinions were competent and thorough, but lacking in the tight, epigrammatic style that would come to distinguish his later cases. Undoubtedly, institutional constraints such as the tradition of collegiality and the norm of unanimity exerted considerable pressure upon Holmes's individuality. Somewhat surprisingly, Holmes espoused strict adherence to precedent in contract cases: "In view of the nicety of the distinctions which have been taken in the cases, and the desirability of certainty . . . we shall follow [prior decisions] without considering the matter anew."[66] During his early years on the court, neither his decisions nor his opinions revealed any particular departure from the jurisprudence of his peers.

In June 1886 Judge Holmes received an honorary doctor of laws degree from Yale University.[67] But once again, he found it impossible to compete with his father for prizes or honors. In April, Dr. Holmes had set out with his daughter, Amelia Holmes Sargent, for an unprecedented visit to England. At seventy-six, he was almost as well known in London as in Boston, and perhaps more loved abroad than at home. Greeted by the American ambassador, Dr. Holmes was entertained by Alfred Lord Tennyson and Robert Browning. Invited to attend the derby as the personal guest of the Prince of Wales, Dr. Holmes traveled to Epsom aboard the prince's private train. The crowning glory of Dr. Holmes's triumphal visit, however, was his receiving honorary degrees from Oxford, Cambridge, and Edinburgh.[68]

When Dr. Holmes returned home in August, he found his wife ill and disoriented. Although she recovered slightly, she never fully regained her health and slowly began to slip away. She died in February 1888. As Dr. Holmes wrote a friend, "we cannot disguise the fact—the keystone of our arch has slid and fallen, and all we can do is to lean against each other until the last stone is left standing alone."[69] Although Judge Holmes had revealed little emotion when his younger brother, Edward, died in the summer of 1884, he was deeply affected by his mother's death. He had been profoundly influenced by her guiding hand and had come to depend upon her gentle tenderness. She was also the one thing in life that linked father to son and the one who had kept the family together through the years.

After Mrs. Holmes's death, Amelia Sargent, herself a widow, moved home to look after her father. She too became ill, however, and died in April 1889. Following his sister's death, Holmes and his wife sold their home on Chestnut Street and returned to live with "the Governor" at 269 Beacon Street. It was a bitter decision for a man who had lived the better part of his life under his father's roof, but there was no one else left. Dr. Holmes, however, was quite pleased with the arrangement; as he wrote a friend, "my daughter-in-law, a very helpful, hopeful, power-ful, as well as brilliant woman, is with me, and my household goes on smoothly, and not without a cheerful aspect." Interestingly, he referred to his son in the same letter as "her husband, the judge."[70]

Prior to returning to his father's house, Holmes had planned to travel with his wife to England and the Continent. Knowing how much her husband had been looking forward to the trip, Fanny insisted that he go as planned, but without her; she would take Dr. Holmes to his summer house at Beverly Farms, Massachusetts. Reluctant to make the trip alone, the judge invited Owen Wister to accompany him. When Wister declined, Holmes decided to go anyway.[71] While he renewed old friendships abroad, his wife tended Dr. Holmes and the roses, petunias, and marigolds that grew alongside the old brown shingled house on the shore. As Dr. Holmes would comment, "Mrs. Judge knows how to make me comfortable, and does it perfectly well."[72]

In 1890 Chief Justice Morton retired from the court, and Judge Field took his place. But Field's health soon began to fail, and Holmes assumed a larger share of the court's work. A quick worker, Holmes produced opinions of enviable quality with incredible speed. Despite the departure of Judges Morton, Devens, and William Allen, and the appointment of their respective replacements, Holmes remained in 1891 the court's youngest member. In the nearly ten years he had sat on the court, he had dissented only twice.[73] During those years, Holmes had become ab-sorbed in "the actualities and immediacies" of the cases that came before him; although they had entailed "no very great or burning questions," he reported that there had been "a good many fairly interesting ones."[74]

Perhaps as a result of the nature of these cases, Holmes's attitude toward judging underwent a marked change. When he had first joined the court, he was confident that individual judges could have a significant impact on the development of the law. Over time, however, he concluded that "the glory of lawyers, like that of men of science, is more corporate than individual."[75] He also asserted that "the greater part of the work of the world is anonymous work. . . . Even in matters of general import we owe vastly more to the forgotten than to the remembered."[76]

Reconciled to the collective nature of the judicial enterprise, Holmes concentrated on conquering the seemingly endless work and perfecting his own style of writing opinions. Having once praised the "terse and polished subtlety of speech" and the "half-hidden wit" of a well-known Boston lawyer, Holmes himself set about pruning the rhetorical excesses of his judicial prose.[77] In addition to whatever literary merit resulted from his efforts, Holmes's new style of writing served a political purpose as well. By 1891, he was beginning to reflect a more individualized approach to some of the cases, but he contented himself with giving only "a hint" of his underlying rationale. Writing to a friend, Holmes reported that "it was thought advisable to cut down the discussion in which I aired some of my views."[78] Holmes's perfection of an epigrammatic style was thus an efficient and effective means of keeping abreast of the work while suggesting if only indirectly his own judicial views.

During the 1890s Holmes's opinions were in the main indistinguishable from those of his brethren on the court. In a few instances, however, he was prepared to distance himself from his colleagues. In *Commonwealth v. Perry* (1891), Holmes dissented in a case challenging an act of the Massachusetts legislature protecting workers' wages. "I cannot pronounce the legislation void as based on a false assumption," wrote Judge Holmes, "since I know nothing about the matter one way or the other."[79] In the battle between workers and employers, Holmes took a neutral position and was not as prepared as his fellows on the court to nullify labor's hard-won legislative victory.

In a pair of cases involving freedom of speech, *McAuliffe v. New Bedford* (1892) and *Commonwealth v. Davis* (1895), Holmes wrote for the majority, but exhibited a particular deference to legislative rule making. In *McAuliffe*, a case that upheld the right of the town of New Bedford to discharge a police officer for undesirable political activity, Holmes wrote, "The petitioner may have a constitutional right to talk politics, but he has no right to be a policeman."[80] In the *Davis* case, the court upheld a prohibition against unlicensed speech making on the Boston Common. As far as Holmes was concerned, "for the legislature absolutely or conditionally to forbid public speaking in a highway or public park is no more an infringement of the rights of a member of the public than for the owner of a private house to forbid it in his house."[81]

Without question, however, Holmes's most notorious decision during this period of his judicial career was his dissenting opinion in *Vegelahn v. Guntner* (1896). The case involved a 1894 strike by furniture workers demanding a nine-hour day and wage increases. Holmes, sitting alone, had initially issued a comprehensive injunction forbidding the workers to strike or to disrupt their employer's business in any way. But following a hearing in which evidence was presented establishing that the picket had in fact been peaceful, Holmes modified his order to allow the workers to resume their peaceful picketing. Holmes's amended order was appealed, and the initial injunction was reinstated by the full court. In his dissent to the court's decision, Holmes argued that it was "plain from the slightest consideration of practical affairs . . . that free competition means combination, and that the organization of the world, now going on so fast, means an ever-increasing might and scope of combination." As a consequence of what Holmes asserted as a natural fact, he viewed collective action by workers as "a necessary and desirable counterpart" to combination by capital, "if the battle is to be carried on in a fair and equal way."[82] Holmes's opinion in *Vegelahn* marked his first radical departure from the views of his colleagues and attracted a cold and hostile response from the more prosperous and respectable members of Boston's legal community.

During the summer of 1894, Dr. Holmes's health had begun to fail. By October it was clear he would not recover; sitting in his chair, he said to his son, "Well, Wendell, what is it—King's Chapel?" Somewhat surprised, the judge responded, "Oh—yes, Father." "All right then, I am satisfied," answered the old man. "That is all I am going to say about it."[83] Dr. Holmes died on 7 October 1894, and services were held at King's Chapel three days later. Freed at last from the reign of the "Autocrat," Holmes expressed solemnity rather than sorrow.[84]

For whatever reason, Judge and Mrs. Holmes decided to stay on at 269 Beacon Street after Dr. Holmes's death. Fanny was fond of collecting small china animals—frogs, ducks, and kittens—and had settled into her regular routine on Beacon Street. She had hardly recovered from nursing Dr. Holmes when she herself became seriously ill; she suffered a severe case of rheumatic fever in 1896. She regained her health slowly and, even after she was well again, chose to become a virtual recluse. Boston society soon became accustomed to seeing the judge attending functions alone and accepted what had become apparent—that Mrs. Holmes preferred to stay at home.[85]

While Mrs. Holmes added two marmosets and three flying squirrels to her pet collection, the judge resumed his legal research in earnest.[86] Holmes had never completely stopped writing and publishing important articles; among his most noted works are "Early English Equity," "Agency," and "Privilege, Malice, and Intent".[87] But during his early years on the bench, much of his most important nonjudicial writing took the form of public addresses rather than technical legal articles. These speeches provided an outlet for ideas and feelings that Holmes was unable to express in his judicial work.

In 1884 Holmes was invited by Sedgwick Post No. 4, Grand Army of the Republic, to give the Memorial Day address in Keene, New Hampshire. Although it is not clear from the record how or why Holmes was invited to be the principal speaker, his speech has been ranked by at least one critic with Lincoln's Gettysburg Address.[88] Four years earlier, Holmes had spoken at Harvard's commencement dinner in Memorial Hall. Surrounded by the names of those who had given their lives for their country, Holmes recalled publicly for the first time his personal experiences of war, remembering those who had not returned.[89] His speech in Keene, however, was of a different quality. There in front of a crowd of strangers, Holmes created detailed vignettes of his fallen comrades, verbal pictures of haunting vividness. He seemed almost to be talking to his old comrades in arms rather than the assembled citizens of a small New England town. The speech provided Holmes with the occasion to deal with emotions more personal than patriotic.[90]

A decade later, in 1895, Holmes returned to some of the themes he had sounded in that Memorial Day address. In "The Soldier's Faith," a speech delivered on Memorial Day before the graduating class of Harvard University, Holmes extolled a knightly sense of honor and challenged his young listeners to remember that "war, when you are at it, is horrible and dull—it is only when time has passed that you see that its message was divine."[91] He attacked those who concerned themselves only with acquiring riches: "In this smug, over-safe corner of the world . . . we may realize that our comfortable routine is no eternal necessity of things, but merely a little space of calm in the midst of a tempestuous untamed streaming of the world." Urging his audience to "be ready for danger," Holmes argued that "high and dangerous action teaches us to believe as right beyond dispute things for which our doubting minds are slow to find words of proof." Students at Heidelberg, with their "sword-slashed faces," inspired in Holmes's "sincere respect," and if "once in a while," in the rough riding of a polo match, "a neck is broken," it was not for Holmes "a waste," but the "price well paid for the breeding of a race fit for headship and command."[92]

In perhaps the most memorable passage of the entire speech, Holmes came as close as he ever would to stating his personal creed:

> I do not know what is true, I do not know the meaning of the universe. But in the midst of doubt, in the collapse of creeds, there is one thing I do not doubt, that no man who lives in the same world with most of us can doubt, and that is that the faith is true and adorable which leads a soldier to throw away his life in obedience to a blindly accepted duty, in a cause which he little understands, in a plan of campaign of which he has no notion, under tactics of which he does not see the use.[93]

For Holmes, being thought "a gentleman" was inextricably linked to "the soldier's choice of honor rather than life."[94]

In addition to these important public speeches, Judge Holmes frequently addressed special gatherings of lawyers and law students. In January 1897, he delivered the dedication address at Boston University School of Law. Entitled "The Path of the Law," the speech reflected an important shift in Holmes's legal thinking. *The Common Law* had emphasized that every man rightly prefers his own interests and that consequently it is the judge's job to impose an external standard of judgment that will result in the most desirable social consequences. As a judge himself, however, Holmes had been unable to discover any consistently reliable means of determining which outcome would produce the most desirable social ends. As a consequence, he generally abstained from any explicit consideration of public policy, choosing instead to defer to legislative decisions expressed as law.[95]

Holmes's argument in "The Path of the Law" reflected this evolution in his thinking. The law was "not a mystery, but a well-known profession"; he asserted that "the prophecies of what the courts will do in fact, and nothing more pretentious were in fact "the law."[96] Holmes refined this definition several years later: "Law is a statement of the circumstances in which the public force will be brought to bear upon men through the courts."[97] Since law is essentially a matter of predicting what courts will do, Holmes insisted that if someone really wanted to know "the law and nothing else," he should look at things "as a bad man who cares only for the material consequences which such knowledge enables him to predict."[98] Holmes's emphasis on the distinction between law and morality—between what is and what should be—distinguished his view of the law from that of virtually all his contemporaries. One of the first American positivists, Holmes's name in time became associated with a school of legal thought known as legal realism. For Holmes, and the young legal scholars who came to admire his jurisprudence, the law was viewed simply as "a judgment as to the relative worth and importance of competing legislative grounds," backed up by the physical power of the state.[99]

Two years later, in January 1899, Holmes delivered another important speech, this time before the New York Bar Association. "Law in Science and Science in Law" was a philosopher's plea that theory be founded upon fact and a historian's argument that experience provides a more reliable foundation for truth than does logic's most eloquent proof.[100] In 1895, Holmes had observed in a speech dealing with a similar topic that "so far as it depends upon learning," the law "is indeed . . . the government of the living by the dead."[101] But he had insisted that "the present has a right to govern itself as far as it can [as] it ought always to be remembered that historic continuity with the past is not a duty, it is only a necessity."[102] Returning to this theme, Holmes became even more explicit. Concluding that "the justification of a law" could not "be found in the fact that our fathers always have followed it," Holmes asserted boldly that there was no alternative for modern judges but "to exercise the sovereign prerogative of choice."[103]

During the winter of 1899, Judge Holmes and his wife suffered two difficult losses. John Holmes, with whom his nephew had shared a particularly close relationship, died and was buried next to his famous brother in Boston's Mt. Auburn Cemetery. Not long after, Epes Sargent Dixwell, Holmes's old schoolmaster, friend, and father-in-law, died at the age of ninety-two. Not yet sixty himself, Holmes was now the family's lone survivor.[104]

In July 1899 Chief Justice Field died, and Holmes was chosen to succeed him in the center chair. As Holmes had acquired seniority through the years, the number of his written opinions had increased noticeably. Following his appointment as chief justice, his work load increased even more. Although it was perhaps partly due to the court's growing caseload, it was more likely the result of Holmes's compulsion to stay busy. Writing his English friend Sir Frederick Pollock several months after becoming chief justice, Holmes noted that he "had more to do than ever," explaining that the increase was "partly from [his] own fault in assigning perhaps rather a lion's share" to himself.[105]

The Bar Association of Boston honored the new chief justice with a dinner on 7 March 1900, the day before Holmes's fifty-ninth birthday. Following the dinner, which was attended by all the city's leading men, Holmes made a short speech. "I ask myself," said the new chief justice, "What is there to show for this half-lifetime that has passed. . . . A thousand cases, many of them upon trifling or transitory matters . . . a thousand cases when one would have liked to study to the bottom and to say his say on every question which the law has ever presented." It is impossible to know how the speech was received by those who heard it, but to those who read it, it contains an unmistakable strain of pathos: "Alas, gentlemen, that is life. I often imagine Shakespeare . . . summing himself up and thinking: 'Yes, I have written five thousand lines of solid gold and a good deal of padding—I, who would have covered the milky way with words which outshone the stars!'"[106] Holmes concluded this part of his message by stating, "We cannot live our dreams—we are lucky enough if we can give a sample of our best, and if in our hearts we can feel that it has been nobly done."[107]

It was another theme of his address that particularly irritated Holmes's old friend, William James. Reminiscent of his Memorial Day addresses, Holmes had again celebrated "the rule of joy and the law of duty." "With all humility," Holmes thought the injunction "'Whatsoever thy hand findeth to do, do it with thy might' infinitely more important than the vain attempt to love one's neighbor as one's self." Holmes admitted that from his point of view, "life is action, the use of one's powers," and that "the end of life is life."[108] It was this repetition of Holmes's creed that James found particularly provoking. "I must say," he wrote to a friend, "I'm disappointed in O.W.H. for being unable to make any other than that one set speech which comes out on every occasion."[109] Explaining himself more fully, James continued:

It's alright for once, in the exuberance of youth, to celebrate mere vital excitement, *la joie de vivre,* as a protest against humdrum solemnity. But to make it systematic, and oppose it as an ideal and a duty, to the ordinarily recognized duties, is to pervert it altogether. . . . Mere excitement is an immature ideal, unworthy of the Supreme Court's official endorsement.[110]

125

The cases that came before the court during Holmes's tenure as chief justice were not significantly different than those that had dominated the court's docket in previous years. From time to time, there might be a significant personal injury case or an important commercial case, but in the main the cases were routine. By now, Holmes had developed a rather perfunctory manner of handling the work before him; he adopted the habit of stating the appellant's argument, rejecting the claim stated because of some flaw in the argument, and finally rejecting the premises of the argument altogether.[111] Holmes became increasingly convinced that a judge's first duty was to decide the case, and not to bring about any particular outcome. He explained his view in a case decided in 1900:

> The improvements made by the courts are made, almost invariably, by very slow degrees and by very short steps. Their general duty is not to change but to work out the principles already sanctioned by the practice of the past. No one supposes that a judge is at liberty to decide with sole reference ever to his strongest convictions of policy and right. His duty in general is to develop the principles which he finds, with such consistency as he may be able to attain.[112]

If Holmes had once considered judicial law-making through common law adjudication an important and intellectually challenging enterprise, by 1900 he had come to the conclusion that neither the decisions nor the opinions in individual cases were of much significance in themselves. Holmes's understanding of the evolution of the common law should have caused him to accept responsibility for the development of legal principles and beneficial social policy; as a seasoned jurist, however, Holmes increasingly relied on legal technicalities and a method of historical analysis that focused attention on the past to avoid making difficult choices.[113] In virtually every case, he answered the question of which interests should prevail in the case by referring to the dominant power in the community, which for Holmes was synonymous with the legislative majority.

In an important case in 1900, *Plant* v. *Woods*, Holmes reiterated his position that, as a general rule, once the court had decided a legal question, "a dissenting judge, however strong his conviction may be, should thereafter accept the law from the majority."[114] In this particular case, however, he dissented. The case involved the right of labor to organize;

Holmes explicitly denigrated the efficacy of labor's organizing tactics, and personally believed the workers to be misdirected. Nevertheless, he upheld the workers' right to attempt to increase their share of the benefit of their labor. Holmes argued that the workers' effort to affect the behavior of their employers through a strike was "a lawful instrument in the universal struggle of life."[115]

Those familiar with Holmes's early writings should not have been surprised by his dissent. He had asserted in *The Common Law* that "the *ultima ratio* . . . is force," and that "public policy sacrifices the individual to the general good."[116] More particularly, in 1873, he had published in the *American Law Review* an unsigned comment on the London "Gas-Stokers Case" of the previous year. In that case, leaders of the gas-stokers' union had been convicted of the common law crime of conspiracy to break a contract of employment and had been sentenced to one year in jail. Liberal English commentary on the case had characterized the decision as a classic example of abuse of the judicial system by judges sympathetic to the ruling class. Such sentiment seemed premised upon the notion that the law should be neutral, a view Holmes criticized harshly in his article. Explicitly rejecting the utilitarian philosophy that legislation should produce the greatest good for the greatest number, Holmes asked, "Why should the greatest number be preferred? Why not the greatest good of the most intelligent and most highly developed? The greatest good of a minority of our generation may be the greatest good of the greatest number in the long run."[117] Continuing his attack, Holmes made the following assertion: "If the welfare of the living majority is paramount, it can only be on the ground that the majority have the power in their hands. The fact is that legislation . . . is empirical."[118] Stating his point succinctly, Holmes concluded that, "having the power," those in the majority "put burdens which are disagreeable to them on the shoulders of someone else."[119] For Holmes, the nub of the problem was not whether the court had imposed a burden upon one class of society but whether the court had assessed accurately the dominant power in the community and resolved the conflict to reflect that balance of power.

Despite his early explanation of his position, and the fact that he was not personally sympathetic to the social reforms making their way through the state legislature, Holmes's decisions in the labor cases had an immediate effect on his professional reputation. Several reviewers labeled him a "radical," relying on his decisions in *Vegelahn* v. *Guntner* and *Plant* v. *Woods* as evidence. These reviewers found the language of these opinions "strange" for someone of Holmes's social class and background.[120]

In June 1902, Associate Justice Horace Gray of the U.S. Supreme Court let it be known that he was planning to retire. Appointed to the Court in 1881 by President Arthur, Gray had served as a judge on the Supreme Judicial Court of Massachusetts for seventeen years, and as chief justice of that court for eight of those years. The elder half brother of the distinguished Harvard Law School professor, John Chipman Gray, Justice Gray had served with distinction for twenty years in what had come to be known as "the Massachusetts seat" on the nation's highest Court. Gray's declining health had been well known to Boston insiders for some time. Gray had considered retiring the previous year, when President McKinley had quietly expressed his intention to appoint Alfred Hemenway of the Boston Bar to replace Gray on the Court. But an assassin's bullet killed McKinley in September 1901, and the eventual Supreme Court nomination fell to his vice president, Theodore Roosevelt.[121]

In February Gray suffered a debilitating stroke, prompting Eben S. Draper, a prominent Boston textile manufacturer, to write Henry Cabot Lodge, Massachusetts' junior U.S. senator, concerning a possible successor. Draper suggested that U.S. Circuit Court Judge Francis Cabot Lowell, a member of an old and distinguished family, should be the senator's first choice. In reply to Draper's letter, Lodge agreed that Lowell had much to recommend him, but informed Draper that he favored Chief Justice Oliver Wendell Holmes.[122] Draper's reaction was violent. Such an appointment would be "a grave mistake," Draper argued; leading members of the state's legal establishment found Holmes "erratic," and the chief justice could not be considered "safe" for such an important appointment. Referring Lodge to Holmes's opinions in *Vegelahn* v. *Guntner* and *Plant* v. *Woods*, Draper suggested that Samuel Hoar, the nephew of Massachusetts' senior U.S. senator, George Frisbie Hoar, would be a far more appropriate candidate to receive Lodge's endorsement for the appointment.[123]

Nevertheless, as chief justice of Massachusetts, Holmes was an obvious candidate for the appointment. He had served on the court for twenty years and had written some thirteen hundred opinions. The real question, however, was not whether Holmes was qualified, but whether President Theodore Roosevelt would nominate him. Lodge, a close friend of the president, pressed Holmes's candidacy in early July. Lodge may have felt personally obligated to Holmes; in 1884, when most of Boston's prominent men were openly scornful of Lodge's politically expedient support of James Blaine's unsuccessful bid for the presidency, Holmes was one of the few who had stood up for him and continued to treat him cordially. Thus convinced of Holmes's loyalty, Lodge told Roosevelt that it would be "hard to pass him by—hard on him [Holmes]." Moreover, Lodge added that he was "very fond" of Holmes, and thought him clearly "in line for the promotion." Mentioning that not everyone would support Holmes's nomination, Lodge stressed the importance of Massachusetts Attorney General Knowlton's support. Lodge failed to inform the president, however, that the probable reason for Knowlton's support was Governor Crane's promise to appoint Knowlton to succeed Holmes as chief justice.[124]

Despite Lodge's enthusiastic endorsement, Roosevelt was not immediately certain that Holmes was the man for the job. The president admitted that the "father's name entitles the son to honor," and recognized that even "if the father had been an utterly unknown man, the son would nevertheless now have won the highest honor." But the president was also concerned about Holmes's labor decisions, and more particularly, a speech Holmes had made about Chief Justice John Marshall which suggested a "total incapacity to grasp what Marshall did." It was imperative that Holmes be a solid "party man," a staunch nationalist who could be counted on to support Roosevelt's new initiatives. To nominate a man "who was not absolutely sane and sound on the great national policies" would constitute "an irreparable wrong to the nation."[125] In order for the senator to convince Roosevelt that Holmes was, as Lodge put it, "our kind right through," he arranged for Holmes to meet with President Roosevelt at Oyster Bay on 25 July 1902.[126] The meeting was a complete success, and as Holmes reported to a friend, "the way [Roosevelt] put his wishes to me . . . was a reward for much hard work."[127]

Others were not as pleased by the news of the president's choice. In unusually harsh language, Senator Hoar denounced the nomination to both Lodge and Roosevelt. "His accomplishments are all literary and social . . . not judicial," he wrote Lodge; "no decision of his makes a great landmark in jurisprudence." His letter to the president was even more blunt: "I have never heard anyone speak of Judge Holmes as an able judge. He is universally regarded as a man of pleasant personal address . . . but without strength, and without a grasp of general principles."[128] Hoar, however, was in a delicate position; he could not publicly challenge the legal qualifications of the chief justice of his own state, especially as his own nephew was known to be interested in gaining the appointment for himself. Hoar was finally forced to agree with Roosevelt that Holmes's nomination would "be greeted by the general public as entirely respectable," and that the state of Massachusetts would be well served by the appointment. Having done all that he could to scuttle Holmes's nomination, Hoar concluded with resignation that "those members of the profession whose opinion is of any value will have to make the best of it."[129]

On 11 August 1902, President Roosevelt officially announced Holmes's nomination to the Court. The announcement generated the ordinary reaction of the press. Newspaper articles, which invariably identified the nominee as Dr. Holmes's son, mentioned Holmes's labor dissents if they mentioned any of his decisions at all. "His striking originality of mind will help him when it does not hinder," wrote one editor; others called the appointment "a wise and admirable choice," and characterized Holmes as a judicial "ornament."[130] Holmes was bitterly disappointed by what he considered "the flabbiness of American ignorance." Writing Pollock, he vented his "unreasoning rage" over the "stack of notices," the "immense majority" of which were extremely favorable, but completely devoid of "personal discrimination or courage." "It makes one sick," Holmes wrote, "when he has broken his heart trying to make every word vital and real to see a lot of duffers, generally not even lawyers, talking with the sanctity of print in a way that at once discloses to the knowing eye that literally they don't know anything about it."[131] The thrust of Holmes's complaint was the fact that no one seemed aware of the real purpose of his years on the bench. "If I haven't done my share in the way of putting in new and remodeling old thought for the last twenty years, then I delude myself. Occasionally someone has a glimpse, but in the main, damn the lot of them."[132] It was also frustrating never to be free from the shadow of his father's fame. Holmes had met Andrew Lang, the famous Scottish scholar and author, while traveling in England during the summer of 1900. "So," quipped Lang, "you are the son of the celebrated Oliver Wendell Holmes." "No," replied Judge Holmes tersely, "he was my father."[133] Even as the headlines announced Holmes's appointment to the U.S. Supreme Court, it was Dr. Holmes's son that received the honor.

Although he was nominated by the president in mid-August, Holmes was not confirmed by the Senate until early December, and ever cautious, he did not tender his resignation as chief justice of the Supreme Judicial Court of Massachusetts until shortly before he was sworn in as an associate justice of the U.S. Supreme Court. As Holmes prepared himself for the challenge awaiting him, he reflected on what he had accomplished so far. "One feels as if the second stage of one's life—one's twenty years of work as a state judge—were up for judgment . . . and that there must be a few who will take the trouble, or find it worth the trouble, to consider it with discrimination or to discover one's aims." But in words that reveal Holmes's deepest needs, he concluded that "a man is pretty sure to get his due share of appreciation, for whether he speaks or is silent, the world generally finds him out."[134]

8

MR. JUSTICE HOLMES

Holmes's nomination was confirmed by voice vote in the U.S. Senate on 4 December 1902, only two days after President Roosevelt had formally presented the nomination for Senate consideration. Holmes arrived in Washington, D.C., on 5 December, accompanied by James Doherty, his Irish clerk and messenger from the Massachusetts court. They were met at the train station by John Craig, Justice Gray's black messenger. Mrs. Holmes followed a week later, after Holmes had set up temporary quarters in a rented house at 10 Lafayette Square, across from the North Gate of the White House.[1]

Holmes took the oath of office and joined the Court as associate justice on Monday, 8 December 1902. The court Holmes joined was neither a brilliant nor a particularly enlightened one. Holmes admired John Marshall Harlan, a pro-Union southern aristocrat, whom Holmes once described as the Court's "sage." But in a letter to a friend, he observed that Harlan was "a man of real power," who "did not shine either in analysis or generalization." Holmes concluded his comments by suggesting that Harlan's intellect was like "a powerful vise the jaws of which couldn't be got nearer than two inches to each other."[2] Holmes also felt some kinship with Edward Douglass White, a Confederate soldier who had been captured and imprisoned during the Civil War. Writing more favorably about White's abilities, Holmes concluded that although

White's writing left "much to be desired," his thinking was "profound"; Holmes was particularly impressed by White's capacity in "the legislative direction," which though not generally recognized as an important judicial requirement, Holmes considered especially significant for justices of the Supreme Court.[3]

On the whole, relations with his colleagues on the Court were cordial. In time, however, a rivalry of sorts developed between Holmes and Joseph McKenna, an Irish Catholic, whom Holmes described as "a truly kind soul" possessing a "sweet nature."[4] McKenna worked hard to match Holmes's unprecedented pace in turning out opinions and became one of the most severe critics of the "exuberances" of Holmes's judicial style. More fundamentally, however, McKenna could not accommodate himself to Holmes's repudiation of the natural rights of tradition. Holmes was aware of the problem, concluding that as a Catholic, McKenna could not look favorably upon his own "Darwinian" views.[5]

Although both White and McKenna were only a few years younger than Holmes, it was with Chief Justice Melville Weston Fuller that Holmes developed the closest friendship. Fuller, a member of Phi Beta Kappa at Bowdoin College, was a fellow alumnus of the Harvard Law School. Holmes enjoyed Fuller's company and frequently visited the chief justice on Sunday afternoons at Fuller's rambling Victorian mansion on the northwest corner of Eighteenth and F streets. More than any other member of the Court, Fuller eased Holmes's transition from chief justice of the Supreme Judicial Court of Massachusetts to junior associate justice of the U.S. Supreme Court.[6]

Unlike many of his colleagues on the Court who had achieved their place as a result of political acumen or professional reputation, Holmes brought with him the experience of twenty years as an appellate state court judge. While it may be the case that in retrospect, these years of judicial service added little to Holmes's professional stature or reputation, it would be incorrect to conclude that they were an unimportant part of his history. These years served as a period of transition between Holmes's active career as a legal scholar and his nearly thirty-year tenure on the Supreme Court. During these years on the state court, it had become increasingly apparent that there was an underlying tension or paradox in Holmes's jurisprudence. As a scholar of the common law, he had insisted that judges accept the inherently legislative nature of their work and assume greater responsibility for the policy choices reflected in their decisions. As a sitting judge, however, Holmes rejected the opportunity to consider the wisdom of policy choices reflected in laws passed by democratically elected legislatures, choosing instead to defer in most cases to the will of the political majority. If in *The Common Law* Holmes had struggled to work out a consistent system of legal rules that emphasized objective and external standards of liability, Holmes's judicial opinions stressed the relative unimportance of individual cases in the organic evolution of the law.[7]

Thus, by the time Holmes departed Boston for Washington, two important aspects of his behavior as a judge had become clear. "In cases of this sort," Holmes said in a 1899 case, "what ultimately is to be worked out is a point or line between conflicting claims, each of which has meritorious grounds and would be extended further were it not for the other. . . . The two desiderata cannot both be had to their full extent, and we have to fix boundaries as best we can."[8] Two years later, Holmes added an important addendum to this judicial guideline: "It may be that it would have been better to say definitely that constitutional rules, like those of the common law, end in a penumbra where the legislature has a certain freedom in fixing the line."[9] For Holmes, the essential problem confronting a judge was where to "draw the line," and in resolving this problem, he was inclined to let the dominant power in the community resolve the issue through regular legislation.

This view of jurisprudence continued to inform Holmes's decisions as a justice of the U.S. Supreme Court. In an early opinion, Holmes noted that "general propositions" could not carry the Court very far; a few years later, he was even more specific:

> We have few scientifically certain criteria of legislation, and as it is often difficult to mark the line where what is called the police power of the State is limited by the Constitution of the United States, judges should be slow to read into the latter a *nolumnus mutare* [limiting order] as against the law-making power.[10]

Holmes was fully aware of the fact that his approach provided for less certainty in the law and became increasingly exasperated by the challenges of his colleagues; "Where are you going to draw the line?—as if all life were not the marking of grades between black and white."[11] In another early opinion, Holmes had asserted that "great constitutional questions must be administered with caution," and had argued that "some play must be allowed for the joints of the machine," as "it must be remembered that legislatures are ultimate guardians of the liberties and welfare of the people in quite as great a degree as the courts."[12] Admitting that "now and then an extraordinary case may turn up," Holmes was prepared to accept the conclusion that "constitutional law, like other mortal contrivances, has to take some chances," and that "in the great majority of instances no doubt justice will be done."[13] Despite repeated affirmations of his position, Holmes apparently felt it necessary to clear the air once and for all on the issue of line drawing. "I do not think we need trouble ourselves with the thought that my view depends upon differences of degree," wrote Holmes in a particularly stinging opinion; "the whole law does so as soon as it is civilized." As evidence for this point, Holmes continued: "Negligence is all degree . . . and between the variations . . . that I suppose to exist and the simple universality of the rules in the Twelve Tables or the Leges Barbarorum, there lies the culture of two thousand years."[14]

Mr. Justice Holmes and Mrs. Holmes soon became part of the better part of Washington society. As an associate justice, Holmes's salary was ten thousand dollars—a considerable sum of money in 1902. In addition, he had received a not inconsiderable inheritance from his father's estate. Within a year of their arrival, the Holmeses established their permanent residence in a comfortable four-story brick house at 1720 Eye Street. Not far from Lafayette Square and the White House, their new home was in many ways not unlike the house at 269 Beacon Street. Furnished with the familiar Jackson and Oliver heirlooms carefully shipped from Boston, the house had a New England air about it. But in one very significant aspect, this house was quite different. As Holmes confided to a friend in November 1903, "the Boston house never ceased to be my father's. . . . [Now] we are in my house."[15]

Not surprisingly, Holmes became part of a group of men referred to in Washington as "Roosevelt Familiars," which included Henry Cabot Lodge, Henry Adams, and Owen Wister. These Harvard men were frequent guests at the White House, and together with other regulars like John Hay and Albert Beveridge, constituted Teddy Roosevelt's brilliant and vigorous inner circle. Although Mrs. Holmes seemed more at ease in Washington than she ever had in Boston, social life bored her, and she tolerated rather than enjoyed her husband's new celebrity. Outspoken and possessing a dry wit, her conversation was terse and frequently withering. "Washington is full of famous men and the women they married when they were young," was Mrs. Holmes's curt reply to President Roosevelt's polite question concerning her initial reaction to Washington society.[16] Caring little for the smart company and conversation her husband so enjoyed, Mrs. Holmes soon resumed her self-imposed exile;

with the exception of Sunday evening dinners with her husband at the Willard Hotel, which perpetuated their habit of dining weekly at the Parker House in Boston, and important public functions, Mrs. Holmes preferred to remain at home. In time, securing Justice Holmes as an extra man at their social functions became the challenge and triumph of Washington's reigning grande dames.

Holmes's friendship with Roosevelt came to an abrupt and permanent end in 1904 as the result of the justice's dissent in the *Northern Securities* trust case. With the exception of his concern over how Holmes might vote in the so-called Insular Cases, no issue was of greater concern to Roosevelt than making certain that the Court would uphold his efforts to "bust" the nation's great commercial monopolies. The importance of this particular case was apparent, as Mrs. Holmes joined the wives of President Roosevelt, Attorney General Knox, and Senator Lodge to listen to John G. Johnson, the renowned Philadelphia lawyer, argue that the Court should not permit the government to break up the infamous railroad cartel.[17]

While the majority upheld the Roosevelt administrations's position, Holmes dissented. Infuriated, an outraged president screamed that he could "carve out of a banana a judge with more backbone than that."[18] In a more reflective moment, Roosevelt wrote to Henry Cabot Lodge: "From his antecedents, Holmes should have been an ideal man on the bench. As a matter of fact he has been a bitter disappointment, not because of any one decision, but because of his general attitude."[19] As Holmes recalled the incident years later, his opinion in the *Northern Securities* case "broke up" his "incipient friendship" with the president, as Roosevelt "looked on my dissent" as a "political departure (or, I suspect, more truly couldn't forgive anyone who stood in his way.)" In the same letter, Holmes reported that "if [Roosevelt] had not been restrained by his friends, I am told that he would have made a fool of himself and would have excluded me from the White House."[20]

Even though Roosevelt was not a lawyer, he should have expected and understood Holmes's dissent, as it was entirely consistent with the views Holmes had expressed in the Massachusetts labor cases that had so concerned the president. What Roosevelt and so many others could neither grasp nor accept was the fact that Holmes completely divorced his personal political opinions from his work as a judge. Holmes believed it "a misfortune if a judge reads his own conscious or unconscious sympathy with one side or the other prematurely into the law," forgetting that what "seem to him to be first principles are believed by half his fellow men to be wrong." Judges needed to learn to "transcend [their] own convictions" and "to leave room for much that [is] dear to be done away with short of revolution by the orderly change of law."[21]

Following his nomination to the Court, Holmes wrote a friend that "some . . . of the money powers think me dangerous, wherein they are wrong."[22] Labor equally misunderstood the kind of support they could expect from Justice Holmes. Sometime after his dissent in the *Northern Securities* case, Holmes was invited to a dinner at the White House, at which several prominent labor leaders had been "spouting [off] about the judges." In reply to their complaints about a recent decision, Holmes said crisply, "What you want is favor—not justice. But when I am on my job I don't care a damn what you want—or what Mr. Roosevelt wants." In a subsequent letter to a friend, Holmes observed that his behavior may have seemed "a trifle crude," but he explained that he "didn't like to say it behind his [Roosevelt's] back and not to his face."[23]

Holmes had attempted to explain his position in his dissenting opinion in *Northern Securities Co.* v. *U.S.*: "Great cases, like hard cases, make bad law. For great cases are called great, not by reason of their real importance in shaping the law of the future, but because of some accident of immediate overwhelming interest which appeals to the feelings and distorts the judgment."[24] Holmes consciously attempted to resist the "hydraulic pressure" partisan politics and public opinion exerted, preferring instead to concentrate on more fundamental structural developments in the law. Despite repeated attempts to make this point clear in his opinions, few observers ever really understood that as far as Mr. Justice Holmes was concerned, how the case was decided was far more important than which side won.

Perhaps because Holmes was less concerned with specific outcomes than many of his colleagues on the Court, he perceived the challenge of being a justice somewhat differently. "I long have said there is no such thing as a hard case," Holmes wrote after years on the bench. "I am frightened weekly, but always when you walk up to the lion and lay hold the hide comes off and the same old donkey of a question of law is underneath."[25] Rather than struggling to keep up with his portion of the cases, Holmes worked quickly and frequently asked for additional work. His opinions were lively and poetic; compact and unusually brief, they often relied heavily on the use of ingenious epigrams. A master of "the pointed phrase," Holmes frequently used only a sentence where most judges would have written a paragraph. His style suggested that judicial opinions need not be heavy to be weighty; he complained that the court reports were "dull" because judges had "the notion that judicial dignity required solemn fluffy speech, as when I grew up, everybody wore black frock coats and black cravats."[26] Believing that "the eternal effort of art, even the writing of legal decisions, is to omit all but the essentials," Holmes wrote opinions that expressed the "essentials" with stinging brevity, and openly admitted that his goal was "to try to strike the jugular."[27] He also freely admitted that his real interest was not in the so-called great questions and great cases, but in "the little decisions that the common run of selectors would pass by because they did not deal with the Constitution or a telephone company," but which contained in them "the germ of some profound interstitial change in the very tissue of the law."[28] Prepared to "recognize without hesitation that judges do and must legislate," Holmes believed that they do so "only interstitially; they are confined from molar to molecular motions."[29] Fully aware that much of his best work went unappreciated, Holmes wrote somewhat smugly that he was "very hard at work . . . preparing small diamonds for people of limited intellectual means."[30]

Despite his conscious attempt to write intellectually satisfying opinions, Holmes never lost sight of the true purpose of judicial opinions and was prepared to sacrifice his own literary standards if necessary to obtain a majority vote of the Court. Writing to a former associate concerning his decision in the *Pipe Line* cases,[31] Holmes admitted that "vanity" compelled him to explain that the language of the opinion caused him "some discomfort." The case had "hung along in other hands for months," and Holmes was prepared to "strike out anything between title and conclusion" that would enable him "to get the case off per contract." The result was that he put his name on "something that [did] not satisfy or represent [his] views." Holmes confessed that the outcome truly distressed him, but he thought it his "duty to let it go as the majority was content." On the margin of his own copy of the decision, Holmes noted that he regarded the reasoning of the opinion "inadequate," but that he was "compelled" to "strike out" what he thought was the "real argument" in order to prevent the case from being held over to the following terms.[32]

Upon joining the Court in 1902, Holmes had continued the practice begun by Justice Gray of inviting a law student from Harvard to serve for a year as his private secretary. From 1902 until his death in 1915, John Chipman Gray selected clerks for his old friend Wendell Holmes as he had previously for his half brother, Justice Gray. In succeeding years, another distinguished professor at the law school and future Supreme Court justice, Felix Frankfurter, made the selection from among Harvard's best for Justice Holmes. For Holmes, these young men became in many ways the sons he never had. Preferring the company of bright young men to that of his own contemporaries, Holmes thrived on the smart talk of the younger generation, surrounding himself with his clerks' friends and associates. Mrs. Holmes took responsibility for introducing her husband's clerks—thirty in all—to those it was important to know in Washington and made certain they were comfortably settled into their bachelor quarters.[33]

In addition to this group of men, who in time would become partners of the most prestigious law firms, professors at the leading law schools, and prominent government officials, Holmes renewed his friendship with Owen "Whisker" Wister, and corresponded regularly with several other young men, including Harold Laski and Lewis Einstein. This correspondence frequently took on the character of urbane conversation, providing an important outlet for Holmes's cultivated sense of humor. He liked to write with a flourish about "wicked" French novels—"now for some French indecency to restore the tone of my mind."[34] Considering himself to be a man of the world, he paraded just a little his taste for champagne and his ready susceptibility to the attraction of a charming woman. He enjoyed attending an occasional burlesque show in Washington, and facetiously "thanked God" that he was "a man of low tastes."[35] In time, his wistful comment "Oh, to be eighty again"—uttered in his nineties when the skirt of an attractive young woman was caught by a gust of wind—would be appropriated with a knowing smile by the very "lads" who helped keep the justice young.

Whatever else Holmes found in these friendships, they clearly served as means of keeping the aging jurist in touch with provocative new ideas. Writing to Wister after reading a Hemingway novel his young friend had recommended, Holmes confronted directly the distance in manners and sensibilities that separated his generation from the next:

There is something quite remarkable about the author. . . . It is singular. An account of eating and drinking with a lot of fornication accompanied by conversation on the lowest level, with some slight intelligence, but no ideas and nothing else—and yet it seems a slice of life, and you are not bored with the details of ordinary life. . . . I sometimes say that if a man contributes neither thought nor beauty to life—as is the case with the majority—I would let Malthus loose on him. But then this lad could write this book and it must be a work of art. It can't be an accident or naivete. So let him survive—but as you promised he would, let him leave his garbage.[36]

Characterized perhaps ironically as "St. Thomas Aquinas plus Plymouth Rock" by one young associate, Holmes admitted that he was just a "poor Calvinist gone wrong" who had difficulty appreciating a culture that seemed to replace reason with an explicit appeal to the senses.[37]

If Holmes's personal sensibilities reflected a man who had come of age during the Civil War, so did his views on economics. A confirmed social Darwinist, Holmes had "never read a Socialist yet from Karl Marx down" that he didn't "think talked drool."[38] Nevertheless, consistent with his view of the role of a judge, Holmes refused to allow his personal economic convictions to affect his decisions. When late in his career, a friend parted with Holmes on the steps of the Supreme Court, saying, "Well, Sir, Good Bye—Do justice!" Holmes replied, "that's not my job! My job is to play the game according to the rules."[39]

It was this same attitude that informed his consideration of cases involving economic policy. As early as 1906, Holmes had written that the Sherman Anti-Trust Act was "a humbug based on economic ignorance."[40] Beginning in 1916, the government began to litigate a series of important cases involving the Sherman Act. A bit annoyed, Holmes inquired of John W. Davis, the solicitor general, "How many more of those economic policy cases have you got?" Davis replied, "Quite a basketful." "Well, bring 'em on and we'll decide 'em," said Holmes. "Of course I know and every other sensible man knows that the Sherman law is damned nonsense, but if my fellow citizens want to go to hell, I am here to help them—it's my job."[41]

Throughout Holmes's career on the Court, his decisions in cases involving economic issues made it clear that his reply to Solicitor General Davis had been entirely serious. In one of his first opinions for the Court, Holmes had signaled that he was prepared to give state legislation a broad margin of judicial toleration, even if such legislation involved new forms of state regulation of private economic transactions.[42] His dissenting opinion in Lochner v. N.Y. (1905) reaffirmed his position that, regardless of the Court's view of economic policy, states had a right to make their own social experiments, so long as those experiments were the product of legislation properly enacted:

> This case is decided upon an economic theory which a large part of the country does not entertain. If it were a question whether I agreed with that theory, I should desire to study it further and long before making up my mind. But I do not conceive that to be my duty because I strongly believe that my agreement or disagreement has nothing to do with the right of a majority to embody their opinion in law.[43]

Some twenty years later, Holmes had occasion to repeat essentially the same argument in yet another dissenting opinion:

> I think the proper course is to recognize that a state legislature can do whatever it sees fit to do unless it is restrained by some express prohibition in the Constitution of the United States or of the State, and the Court should be careful not to extend such prohibitions beyond their obvious meaning by reading into them conceptions of public policy that the particular Court may happen to entertain. . . . I am far from saying that I think this particular law a wise and rational provision. That is not my affair. But if the people of the State of New York speaking through their authorized voice say that they want it, I see nothing in the Constitution of the United States to prevent their having their will.[44]

For Holmes, the law was not "a brooding omnipresence in the sky," but "the articulate voice of some sovereign or quasi-sovereign that can be identified."[45] Nor was the law a set of "mathematical formulas having their essence in their form"; rather, "the provisions of the Constitution" were "organic living institutions transplanted from English soil," whose significance was "vital not formal." Their meaning could not be gathered simply "by taking the words and a dictionary," as it is essential to consider both their "origin" and their "line of growth."[46] As Holmes had said in "The Path of the Law," the law must be viewed instrumentally:

> It is revolting to have no better reason for a rule of law than that so it was laid down in the time of Henry IV. It is still more revolting if the grounds upon which it was laid down have vanished long since, and the rule simply persists from blind imitation of the past.[47]

141

Holmes repeatedly urged his brethren on the Court to examine seriously their reasons for invalidating state legislation. Was such legislation really forbidden by the Constitution, or did the Court simply not agree with the judgments concerning public policy implicit in such legislation? "We fully understand," wrote Holmes in an opinion for the Court in 1911, "the very powerful argument that can be made against the wisdom of the legislation, but on that point, we have nothing to say, as it is not our concern."[48] Holmes also urged his colleagues to think like statesmen in considering the long-term consequences of their decisions:

> We must realize that [the Founding Fathers] have called into life a being the development of which could not have been foreseen completely by the most gifted of the begetters. It was enough for them to realize or to hope that they had created an organism; it has taken a century and cost their successors much sweat and blood to prove that they have created a nation. The case before us must be considered in the light of our whole experience and not merely in that of what was said a hundred years ago.[49]

Frequently, however, Holmes could not convince a majority of the Court either to exercise judicial self-restraint or to exhibit judicial statesmanship, Dissenting in *Coppage* v. *Kansas* in 1915, Holmes argued that "whether in the long run it is wise for the workingmen to enact legislation of this sort" was not properly the Court's concern and that he was "strongly of the opinion that there [was] nothing in the Constitution to prevent it."[50] Three years later in another dissent, Holmes again argued that "the propriety of the exercise of a power admitted to exist" was not for the Court to decide, as it had no right "to intrude its judgment upon questions of policy and morals."[51] In similar language, Holmes dissented in *Truax* v. *Corrigan* in 1921:

> There is nothing that I more deprecate than the use of the Fourteenth Amendment beyond the absolute compulsion of its words to prevent the making of social experiments that an important part of the community desires, in the insulated chambers afforded by the several states, even though the experiments may seem futile or even noxious to me and to those whose judgment I most respect.[52]

Acknowledging in his minority opinion in *Adkins* v. *Children's Hospital* (1923) that "pretty much all law consists in forbidding men to do some things that they want to do," Holmes directed his attention to whose rules should govern.[53] On this point, Holmes's conclusion had changed little over a quarter century. In dissent in *Louisville Gas Co.* v. *Coleman* (1927), Holmes reaffirmed his view that "when it is seen that a line or point there must be, and that there is no way of fixing it precisely, the decision of the legislature must be accepted unless we can say that it is very wide of any reasonable mark."[54]

Holmes's career on the Supreme Court coincided roughly with the Progressive Era in American politics. Characterized by its sweeping attack on the dominant social mores of the late nineteenth century, the Progressive movement challenged directly the status quo and was impatient to achieve social progress. It is not surprising that as a result of Holmes's dissenting opinions in important economic cases, and his emphasis on social experimentation, that he would become one of the Progressives' heroes. One respected writer said of Holmes in 1921 that the justice had "firmly set himself against a slack universe of legal conceptions and a rigidly fixed social order" in order to "give man room to express his advancing needs in an orderly progressing society."[55] No less an authority than John Dewey accepted Holmes's credentials as a leading Progressive: "impatient with the attempt to settle matters of social policy by dialectic reasoning from fixed concepts," Holmes had demonstrated a Progressive's faith that "our social system is one of experimentation, subject to the ordeal of experienced consequences."[56]

It is ironic that at the time and frequently since, Holmes has been considered a leader of the Progressive movement, for he was anything but a reformer. Writing in 1915 to John Wigmore, dean of the Harvard Law School, Holmes confessed that "the squashy sentimentalism of a big minority" of people about the condition of human life made him "puke." He was particularly sickened by those "who believe in the upward and onward—who talk of uplift, who think that something particular has happened and that the universe in no longer predatory. . . . Oh, bring me a basin."[57] Holmes's unconcealed disdain for "do-gooders" reflected his underlying contempt for those who did not share his understanding of the fundamental unimportance of man. "I doubt if a shudder would go through the spheres if the whole ant-heap were kerosened," Holmes wrote in 1909.[58] Convinced that "men are like flies," he questioned whether man had any more cosmic significance than "a baboon or a grain of sand."[59]

Nor did Holmes share the hope of the Progressives that men might find peaceful ways of resolving their differences. Concerning the political debate over the desirability of American participation in the League of Nations, Holmes's position was unambiguous:

> Man at present is a predatory animal. I think that the sacredness of human life is a purely municipal idea of no validity outside the jurisdiction. I believe that force, mitigated so far as it might be by good manners, is the *ultimate ratio,* and between two groups that want to make inconsistent kinds of worlds, I see no remedy except force.[60]

Holmes, who liked "to see someone insist . . . that the march of life means a rub somewhere," had little sympathy for those who believed that life could be comfortable and safe "without much trouble or any danger."[61]

Holmes's response to World War I provides an insight into his understanding of man's plight in the world. As far as Holmes was concerned, the war demonstrated convincingly that "classes [of men] as well as nations that mean to be in the saddle have got to be ready to kill to keep their seat," and that "the notion that all that remained for the civilized world was to sit still, converse, and be comfortable, was humbug."[62] For Holmes, war was "not absurd," but "inevitable and rational." "When men differ in taste as to the kind of world they want, the only thing to do is to go to work killing," Holmes observed coldly. "All society rests on the death of men—if you don't kill them one way, you kill 'em another."[63]

There is little question that Holmes's stark acceptance of the role of force in society grew out of his own experience as a soldier. It was undoubtedly strengthened, however, by his philosophical skepticism. Although he hated "to discourage the belief of a young man in reason," Holmes instructed one student of the law that "its control over the actions of men when it comes out against what they want is not very great."[64] Concluding that moral and aesthetic preferences were "more or less arbitrary," Holmes observed that as he grew older, he had come to realize "how limited a part reason has in the conduct of men. . . . They believe what they want to."[65] Reason was merely a gloss that men applied to mask their arbitrary wills, and the mind, "a bribed witness."[66]

Consequently, "law" for Holmes was inextricably linked with the capacity to enforce certain rules—"All law means I will kill you if necessary to make you conform to my requirements"—and the fundamental "foundation" of all jurisdiction was "physical power."[67] Holmes frequently explained that by truth, he meant no more than that which he could not help thinking was true; significantly, however, he asserted that he had no way of ascertaining whether his "can't helps" had any worth as "cosmic" values.[68] As a result of this explicit acceptance of ethical relativism, Holmes made a rough equation between "*isness and oughtness*," and privately admitted that he came "devilish near to believing that might makes right." As far as he was concerned, "truth" was "the majority vote of that nation that could lick all the others."[69]

Entirely consistent with his opinion of the role of force in international politics, Holmes resigned himself to the fact that the political majority would inevitably have its way in domestic matters as well. An American aristocrat with the most impeccable credentials, Holmes personally did not prefer "a world with a hundred million bores in it to one with ten." Comfortably removed from the actual pain and suffering of a considerable part of society, he had "no urgent desire to change their lot." Rejecting the Christian precept of "loving thy neighbor as thyself" as "the test of the meddling missionary," Holmes believed that in the final analysis, every individual rightly prefers his own interest to that of his neighbor. "At bottom of all relations, however tempered by sympathy and all social feeling," Holmes had written in *The Common Law*, "is a justifiable self-preference. If a man is on a plank in the deep sea which will only float one, and a stranger lays hold of it, he will thrust him off if he can."[70]

Unmoved by any particular interest in shaping the future of American society, Holmes was prepared to let "the crowd" decide the most important questions of public policy. "In my epitaph," he quipped, "they ought to say, 'Here lies the supple tool of power.'"[71] Although Holmes personally held the view that his kind knew what was good for society, his skepticism as to the ultimate worth of social ends left him with "no practical criticism except what the crowd wants."[72] Of course, Holmes admitted, "if the crowd knew more it would not want what it wants," but that was "immaterial."[73] Such collective ignorance was unimportant to Holmes precisely because the conformity of the law to the wishes of the dominant power in the community was the fundamental tenet of his legal theory. No optimist, Holmes fully expected that the majority would in time destroy the very way of life he himself valued.[74] But Holmes insisted that it would do no good to attempt to alter the nation's destiny. Convinced that "the rights of a given crowd are what they will fight for," Holmes was certain that his "crowd" could no longer win such a fight. Holmes did not believe that "it is an absolute principle or even a human ultimate that man always is an end in himself—that his dignity must be respected, etc." Recalling the experience of his own youth, he concluded that the nation could "march up a conscript with bayonets behind to die in a cause he doesn't believe in." "I feel no scruples about it," Holmes said," because "morality seems . . . only a check on the ultimate domination of force, just as . . . politeness is a check on the impulse of every pig to put his feet in the trough."[75] Thus, for Holmes, "the ultimate question" in the development of "a *corpus juris*" was what "the dominant forces of the community want," and whether they wanted it "hard enough to disregard whatever inhibitions may stand in the way."[76] Although it was desirable in Holmes's view that "the dominant power be wise," in the final analysis, "wise or not, the proximate test of a good government is that the dominant power have its way."[77]

Holmes's frank acceptance of the "centrality of force" in human affairs found expression in many of his opinions, and as has been noted by others, "shocks the liberal mind into resentful attention."[78] Contemporary sensibilities still chafe under Holmes's early observation that legislation is "necessarily made a means by which a body, having the power, puts burdens which are disagreeable to them on the shoulders of somebody else,"[79] and are repulsed by opinions that today seem needlessly brutal. In a 1909 case that challenged the ten-month detention of the president of the Western Federation of Miners, who was imprisoned without a formal charge or any judicial proceeding, Holmes wrote for the majority that "the ordinary rights of individuals must yield . . . [when] public danger warrants the substitution of executive process for judicial process."[80] Holmes's preference for strict standards of liability based on objective and external standards of proof clearly reflected his acceptance of the harsh realities of life.[81] As he stated in *Commonwealth* v. *Pierce* (1884) and repeated in *Nash* v. *U.S.* (1913), "a man might have to answer with his life for consequences . . . he neither intended nor foresaw."[82] In many cases, Holmes's "reasonable man" standard was simply the vehicle for asserting the priority of the demands of the majority over the interests of individuals.

This aspect of Holmes's jurisprudence was particularly evident in cases involving civil rights. Holmes's opinions leave little doubt that he was not supportive of the claims of black citizens to equal rights. His opinion for the Court in *Giles* v. *Harris* and his especially strident dissent in *Bailey* v. *Alabama* stand in stark contrast to his reputation as a Progressive.

Giles v. *Harris* involved a 1903 challenge by a black citizen of Alabama alleging that the voter registration provisions of the Alabama Constitution of 1901 effectively "let in all whites and [kept] out a large part, if not all, blacks."[83] In an opinion for the Court from which Justices Harlan, Brown, and Brewer dissented, Holmes held that the charge amounted to an allegation that "the whole registration scheme of the Alabama Constitution is a fraud upon the Constitution of the United States." Although this may have been a fair characterization of the facts, Holmes concluded that a court of equity should not take jurisdiction unless it could provide the remedy sought. Accordingly, he held that as the Court lacked "constitutional power to control [Alabama's] action by any direct means," relief from "a great political wrong, if done as alleged, by the people of a state and the state itself, must be given by them or by the legislative and political department of the government of the United States."[84]

In *Bailey* v. *Alabama,* a case that in its day was compared to the Court's *Dred Scott* and *Plessy* v. *Ferguson* decisions, Holmes wrote a dissenting opinion that especially "surprised" Justice Hughes, the author of the Court's majority opinion.[85] The Alabama statute in question operated, as the U.S. attorney for the Western District of Louisiana wrote the attorney general, "to give the large planters of the state absolute dominion over the Negro laborer."[86] Bailey, a poor Negro farm laborer, had been convicted under the Alabama contract-fraud law. He had contracted to work for a year and had been paid $15 in advance; when Bailey left the plantation on which he was to work after only a month without paying off the balance of the unsatisfied advance, he was arrested and imprisoned. At trial, he was subsequently sentenced to 136 days of imprisonment "at hard labor" since he was unable to pay the $76.40 in fines and court costs. Frequently, the state would in turn sell that "labor" to plantation owners in order to raise revenue. What is particularly striking about Holmes's dissent is the extent to which he went out of his way to justify a law that in practice had the effect of enslaving poor southern blacks. "We all agree," wrote Holmes, "that this case is to be considered and decided in the same way as if it arose in Idaho or New York. . . . The fact that in Alabama it mainly concerns blacks does not matter."[87] The reasoning of Holmes's opinion was especially suspect, as it contradicted the arguments concerning the nature of contractual liability set forth in his own previous writings. In *The Common Law,* Holmes had said the following about the obligation of contract:

> If it be proper to state the common-law meaning of promise and contract in this way, it has the advantage of freeing the subject from the

superfluous theory that contract is a qualified subjection of one will
to another, a kind of limited slavery. It might be so regarded if the
law compelled men to perform their contracts, or if it allowed prom-
ises to exercise such compulsion. . . . But this the law never does.[88]

He had been even more explicit in "The Path of the Law": "The duty to
keep a contract at common law means a prediction that you must pay
damages if you do not keep it—and nothing more."[89] Consequently, it
was difficult for many to understand why Holmes had dissented in the
case, and few if any of his opinions have been more violently challenged.
Reviewing the Court's action in the case, a contemporary journal noted
Holmes's "detached logic," and concluded that "those who wish to see
how ingenious reasoning can lead an acute mind to disregard simple facts
of human experience will do well to read [Holmes's] dissenting opinion."[90] A more recent critic has observed that Holmes payed "homage to
forms without going beyond them to social reality," a charge rarely associated with "the father of judicial realism." Holmes's reliance upon the
findings of an all-white southern jury seemed hard to accept in "the
known context of class and race relations in the South," and his apparent
insensitivity to the clear impact of the facts of the case was particularly
troubling to those who tried to square this opinion with Holmes's larger
judicial theory.[91]

Yet another unusual aspect of the dissent was its high moral tone:
"Breach of contract without excuse is wrong conduct, even if the contract is for labor, and if a state adds to civil liability a criminal liability
to fine, it simply intensifies the legal motive for doing right."[92] Reflecting
a "cold Puritan passion for obligation," Holmes was clearly prepared to
accept a practice that returned southern blacks into actual physical bon-
dage, a practice his colleagues held was expressly forbidden by the Thirteenth Amendment.

In a subsequent case from Alabama involving a similar question of
state-sanctioned peonage, Holmes concurred with the Court's decision
striking down the statute in question. In language that today would be
considered offensive, Holmes concluded that "impulsive people with little intelligence or foresight may be expected to lay hold of anything that
affords a relief from a present pain even though it will cause greater trouble by and by."[93] Referring without question to southern blacks, Holmes
was willing to endorse what he considered a paternalistic decision in
order to protect fundamentally stupid and irresponsible people from the
consequences of their own behavior. The fact that Holmes was either

unable or unwilling to challenge the systematic exploitation and victimization of the black minority in the South by the white majority raises serious questions not only about Holmes's jurisprudence but also about his own racist prejudices.[94]

But perhaps the most blatant example of the consequences of Holmes's acceptance of social Darwinism upon his jurisprudence was his 1929 decision for the Court in *Buck v. Bell.* This case involved the authority of the state of Virginia to sterilize a young white woman, Carrie Buck, who was a ward of the state mental hospital. Observing that "more than once" public welfare had called upon "the best citizens for their lives," Holmes argued that "it would be strange if [the state] could not call upon those who already sap the strength of the State for lesser sacrifices . . . in order to prevent our being swamped with incompetence." Holding that "it is better for all the world if instead of waiting to execute degenerate offspring for crime, or to let them starve for their imbecility, society can prevent those who are manifestly unfit from continuing their kind," Holmes concluded that "three generations of imbeciles is enough."[95]

Several aspects of this case are particularly interesting in light of Holmes's general understanding of his role as a judge. First, there is considerable evidence that the case was a "friendly suit" designed specifically to test the constitutionality of the Virginia statute. The accuracy of the facts that Holmes recited in his opinion—namely, that Carrie Buck's mother and infant daughter were both "feeble-minded"—have also been called into question. Finally, the high court of at least one state had held state-imposed sterilization "inhumane" and therefore unconstitutional, and one U.S. Supreme Court decision—*Meyer v. Nebraska*—had upheld the rights of individuals "to marry, establish a home and bring up children."[96]

Whatever else might be in question, it is clear that Holmes "took pleasure" in sustaining the Virginia statute.[97] Only a few years prior to his decision in *Buck v. Bell,* he had written to a friend that social progress depended more on "trying to build a race" than on "tinkering with the institutions of property": "I believe that Malthus was right. . . . Every society is founded on the death of men. . . . I shall think socialism begins to be entitled to serious treatment when and not before it takes life in hand and prevents the continuance of the unfit."[98] One is left to speculate upon the extent to which Holmes's personal predilections influenced his judicial behavior in this case.

If Justice Holmes was not a humanitarian, neither was he a totalitarian, as some of his harshest critics have charged.[99] Although he believed that with a little help, natural selection would ultimately eliminate the unfit from the "universal struggle of life," it was never his project to try to impose his values on society.[100] Unwilling to force men to conform to his notion of "the good life," it was Holmes who became the champion of individuals challenging the views of the majority. In *Schenck* v. *U.S.* (1919) and *Debs* v. *U.S.* (1919), Holmes upheld the convictions of radicals who were found guilty by juries of violating the Espionage Act of 1915. In these cases, Holmes accepted the juries' findings that Schenck and Debs, both prominent socialists, had in fact interfered with the American war effort. But in a series of important First Amendment cases that followed, Holmes departed from the majority, insisting that some actual harm must be proven. In what quickly became his most famous dissents, Holmes argued that the imposition of harsh punishments could not be justified in cases involving the mere advocacy of unpopular political ideas.

The question for Holmes became whether the words were "used in such circumstances" and were of "such a nature" as to create "a clear and present danger" of the type the state had a right to prevent. The issue was primarily one of "proximity and degree," for even "the most stringent protection of free speech would not protect a man in falsely shouting fire in a theatre and causing a panic." It was clear to Holmes that when "a nation is at war," things that might be said in time of peace become "such a hindrance to its efforts that their utterance will not be endured so long as men fight"; but surely, Congress could not "forbid all effort to change the mind of the country" on so important an issue of public policy as American involvement in World War I.[101] Holmes's powerful dissent in *Abrams* v. *U.S.* (1919) was perhaps his most important one:

> But when men have realized that time has upset many fighting faiths, they may come to believe even more than they believe the very foundations of their own conduct that the ultimate good desired is better reached by free trade in ideas—that the best test of truth is the power of the thought to get itself accepted in the competition of the market, and that truth is the only ground upon which their wishes safely may be carried out. That at any rate is the theory of our Constitution. It is an experiment, as all life is an experiment. Every year if not every day we have to wager our salvation upon some prophecy based upon imperfect knowledge. . . . While that experiment is part of our system, I think that we should be externally vigilant against attempts

to check the expression of opinions that we loathe and believe to be fraught with death.[102]

Although written in a case involving a question of free speech, these words explain as well as any Holmes's overall view of the Constitution and the role of the Court in interpreting it. Disturbed by what he considered the subversive character of this opinion, an outraged Dean Wigmore published a slashing critique of Holmes's argument that emphasized the necessities of war. Mildly annoyed at the behavior of someone who should have known better, Holmes wrote to a mutual friend that "doubtless" Dean Wigmore knew more about the law than he did; "but I think," Holmes continued, "I know a little bit more about war."[103]

In *Gitlow v. N.Y.* (1925), Holmes again dissented, arguing that "every idea is an incitement," and that "the only difference between the expression of opinion and an incitement in the narrower sense is the speaker's enthusiasm for the result. Eloquence may set fire to reason." In a statement typical of him, he added, "If in the long run, the beliefs expressed in proletarian dictatorship are destined to be accepted by the dominant forces of the community, the only meaning of free speech is that they should be given their chance and have their way."[104] "If there is any principle of the Constitution that more imperatively calls for attachment than any other," Holmes said in another opinion, "it is the principle of free thought—not free thought for those who agree with us but freedom for the thought that we hate."[105]

Of the roughly one thousand opinions Holmes wrote during his tenure on the Supreme Court, only seventy-two were written in dissent. Although ten justices in the history of the Court had dissented more frequently, it was Holmes who gained the reputation as "the great dissenter."[106] Undoubtedly, it was the quality and thrust of Holmes's dissenting opinions that attracted public attention, and not their number. As Theodore Roosevelt had accurately observed, the significance of Holmes's participation on the Court was not that he dissented in a particular case; it was his "general attitude," a new way of looking at the law that distanced even his majority opinions from the traditional jurisprudence of others on the Court. Confident that history would ultimately prove him right, Holmes was prepared to chart his own independent course.

9

THE HOLMESIAN LEGACY

On 8 March 1911, Holmes celebrated his seventieth birthday. The Supreme Court had four new associate justices—Hughes, Lamar, Lurton, and Van Devanter—and a new chief justice, former associate justice Edward Douglass White. Chief Justice Fuller had died in July 1910, and there was some question regarding whom President Taft would nominate as his successor. By the end of the year, it had become clear that for reasons known only to the president, White would receive the appointment. Although Holmes may have entertained some private hope that he himself might complete his already distinguished career as chief justice of the United States, he wrote to a friend that he thought it most likely that his able new colleague on the bench, Charles Evans Hughes, would receive the appointment. Concerning his own chances, he added, "they don't appoint side Judges as a rule, and it would be embarrassing to skip my Seniors, and I am too old."[1] Writing on the same subject to another friend, Holmes observed that he and McKenna were the only two sitting justices who "didn't have booms" going for them.[2] Certain that the appointment would go to someone else, Holmes confided to yet another friend that his own ambitions were "so wholly internal" that Court politics moved him personally "but little."[3]

As one year on the Court followed the next, the pattern of Holmes's life became increasingly solitary and detached. With the exception of his

152

inner circle—his wife, his clerk, his Court messenger, and his household servants, Holmes had few close associates. The death of William James in the summer of 1910 affected him deeply. One of the few close friends of his youth, James was among that small group of people who continued to address Holmes by name rather than by title. His death thus "cut a root" for Holmes that "went far into the past." Compelled to render a final judgment of their relationship, Holmes wrote that James's "reason made him skeptical [but] his wishes led him to turn down the lights so as to give miracle a chance."[4]

Only a few years before James's death, Holmes had written him concerning their philosophical differences. "I have learned," he wrote, "that my *can't helps* are not cosmic can't helps—that the universe may not be subject to my limitation." Perhaps feeling some need to justify his position further, he continued: "The great act of faith is when a man decides that he is not God. . . . It seems to me that the only promising activity is to make *my* universe coherent and livable, not to babble about *the* universe. . . . To act affirms, for the moment at least, the worth of an end."[5] Action, not philosophy, was for Holmes the best test of truth, as history rather than theory would ultimately prove the point.

Several personnel changes on the Court in 1916 marked the end of an important period of Holmes's career and signaled the beginning of a new one. During the period of his presidency, William Howard Taft had appointed five men to the high bench—Associate Justices Lurton (1910), Hughes (1910), Van Devanter (1911), Lamar (1911), and Pitney (1912)—and had made Justice White chief justice in 1910. As fate would have it, Taft's successor in the White House, President Woodrow Wilson, would have the opportunity to replace three of Taft's appointments. Justice Lurton died in July 1914, and his seat was filled by Wilson's attorney general, James C. McReynolds. Not long after, in January 1916, Justice Lamar died. After an extremely bitter and prolonged confirmation fight, Louis D. Brandeis was sworn in to replace him on the Court. In June 1916 Justice Charles Evans Hughes, a former governor of the state of New York and the man many thought President Taft should have made chief justice, resigned from the Court to challenge Wilson as the Republican party's nominee in the upcoming presidential election. The Court would not see another change of this significance until the early 1920s when President Harding would have the opportunity to return the Court to conservative Republican control through the appointments of Chief Justice Taft and Associate Justices Sutherland, Butler, and Sanford.

The departure of Hughes and the appointment of three new justices had a significant impact on Holmes, both as a jurist and as a person. McReynolds was a brilliant lawyer with a first-rate mind; however, he was eccentric and increasingly difficult to get along with on the Court. Holmes had less difficulty with McReynolds than others, but certainly never considered the justice a friend. "Poor McReynolds," Holmes wrote to a friend, "a man of feeling and of more secret kindliness than he would get credit for, but as is so common with Southerners, his own personality governs him without much thought of others when an impulse comes."[6] Concerning Justice Clarke, whose life McReynolds made particularly miserable, Holmes took a gentler view. Although Holmes enjoyed a cordial relationship with Clarke, it was never a close one; Clarke resigned from the Court in 1922, ending what many including Holmes thought had been an unfortunate career.

Holmes's relationship with Louis Dembitz Brandeis, however, was another story altogether. Brandeis had joined the Court after one of the most bitter confirmation fights in the Court's history. There were various arguments raised against Brandeis, but beneath the superficially legitimate objections to his appointment lay the fact that Brandeis was a political liberal sympathetic to the claims of labor and, more important, a Jew. Despite the fact that he had established a record of academic excellence unparalleled in the history of the Harvard Law School as a member of the class of 1877, had clerked for Supreme Court Justice Gray, and had gained a national reputation as a member of the trial bar, Brandeis was violently opposed by the most prominent members of the legal profession. No one was a more outspoken critic than the former president and future chief justice, William Howard Taft. Privately outraged that Wilson would nominate a Jew for a position he considered himself better qualified to hold, Taft did everything in his power to defeat Brandeis's nomination.

During the confirmation fight, Holmes remained above the controversy. Although he thought Brandeis eminently qualified to serve on the Court, he was disturbed that so many of the nation's leading lawyers were so strongly opposed to the appointment. Writing to a friend in May 1916, Holmes noted that the "Brandeis matter" was dragging along and that he wasn't sure what would happen. "He always left on me the impression of a good man," Holmes continued, "and I have never fully fathomed the reasons for the strong prejudice against him shown by other good men."[7] In another letter, Holmes wrote favorably of his "total impression" of Brandeis, but noted that he "respected and admired" Brandeis "subject to the inquiry why it was that other good men were down on him."[8] A few years later, Holmes would observe that it never occurred to him "until after the event" that a man he liked might be "a Jew," adding that it really did not matter to him when he did realize it. Rather interestingly, Holmes stated that if he had to choose, he thought he would rather "see power in the hands of the Jews than in the Catholics," though he really did not "want to be run by either."[9]

Within a very short time, Justices Holmes and Brandeis came to enjoy a very close personal friendship, both in Washington and on Cape Cod during the Court's summer recesses. The closeness of this association led Taft to comment bitterly that Holmes allowed Brandeis to cast two votes, and he referred to the justices as the "dangerous twosome."[10] While it is true that Holmes and Brandeis were on the same side of most decisions, Taft's characterization of their relationship on the bench was not justified. Taft, a "party" man if ever there was one, may have found Holmes's friendship with Brandeis hard to accept; moreover, he may not fully have appreciated the intellectual capacity of these two great minds. In 1912, John Chipman Gray of the Harvard Law School had urged Taft's son, Robert, to accept an appointment as Holmes's clerk for the following term, noting that he knew of "no one whose talk on the law is so illuminating." Taft rejected the idea, explaining that it was more important that his son "get started permanently at once in Cincinnati." The president added somewhat gratuitously that he rather doubted whether spending a year at the Court as Holmes's clerk could add much to what his son had already learned at the Harvard Law School.[11]

Had Taft ever read Holmes's work with discernment, he would have recalled that in 1897, Holmes had written that in the future, the law would be shaped by "the man of statistics and the man of economics" who would devote his energies on "a study of the ends sought to be attained [by the law] and the reasons for desiring them."[12] There can be little doubt that Holmes considered Brandeis just such a man. Although Holmes recognized the importance of facts, he himself was not much interested in knowing them. That Brandeis urged Holmes to adopt a more "scientific" approach is evident, but whether Holmes ever seriously accepted the challenge is less certain. "Brandeis the other day drove a harpoon into my midriff," Holmes wrote in 1919; Brandeis had suggested that Holmes "try something new" and "study some domain of fact" over the Court's summer recess. Holmes's response was typical: "I hate facts. . . . I shrink from the bore—or rather, I hate to give up the chance to read this or that, that a gentleman should have read before he dies. I

155

don't remember that I have ever read Machiavelli's *Prince*—and I think of the Day of Judgment."[13]

Nevertheless, Brandeis was like a breath of fresh air on the Court. More than their common Boston associations or experiences, it was the quality and intensity of their intellectual activity that explained the true nature of their friendship. Holmes respected the younger man; Brandeis's desperately earnest qualities may have reminded Holmes of his own Puritan forebears. When Holmes would see Brandeis and say, "Now there goes a really good man," he was more likely calling attention to his colleague's integrity and commitment to hard work rather than to his intellectual capacity. Both men were driven by a personal animus against mediocrity; in time, each would become the other's most respected critic.[14]

If Brandeis judged Holmes the Court's "best intellectual machine," it is clear that the junior justice had an important effect on Holmes.[15] Although Holmes himself had always been "rather skeptical about reforms," he reported that Brandeis had "catpawed" him to do "another dissent on burning themes." In other correspondence, he noted that "the ever-active Brandeis had again "put upon [his] conscience the responsibility of another dissent."[16] Holmes reported to a friend that he found "great comfort" in Brandeis's "companionship," and wrote the following to Brandeis the day prior to his sixtieth birthday:

> You turn the third corner tomorrow. You have done big things with high motives—have swept over great hedges and across wide ditches, and always with the same courage, the same keen eye, the same steady hand. As you take the home stretch the onlookers begin to realize how you have ridden and what you have achieved. I am glad that I am still here to say: Nobly Done."[17]

To be judged by the standards Holmes applied to himself and not to have been found wanting was high praise indeed from a man not known to consider many his equal.

Holmes continued to be driven by his work. During the bleak days of World War I, he wrote: "It is lucky for me that most of the time I have too much work to do to realize my own sadness, not to speak of the world's."[18] Living "in the main" a "happy *solitude a deux*," Justice Holmes and his wife spent evenings together reading to each other.[19] As his eightieth birthday approached, there were few left to call him by his first

156

name. The friends of his youth were gone, and in Washington everyone called him "Mr. Justice Holmes." As he wrote to a friend about student comments in law reviews—and perhaps about the younger generation in general—"I don't mind when the lads say I was wrong [in a decision]; it is when they say 'Mr. Justice Holmes was correct' that I find them insufferable."[20] With no children to fill the house with stories of new experiences, the couple relied on old memories to give their lives meaning, and special occasions like anniversaries and birthdays took on added significance.

During the summer of 1922, Holmes was hospitalized for major surgery, but recovered quickly, largely as a result of his strong constitution and general good health. With his pace slowed only slightly, his clerks continued to marvel at his incredible stamina. As Charles Evans Hughes observed in 1928, Holmes in his eighties was attending to his court work with "the same energy and brilliance that he showed twenty years ago."[21] The first serious change in his familiar routine occurred in the spring of 1929 when Fanny Holmes fell and broke her hip. After a period of declining health brought on by the initial injury, she died several weeks later on 30 April. Having become a virtual recluse during the final years of her life and without intimate friends of her own, Fanny had devoted herself entirely to caring for the needs of her husband. The winter evenings spent reading together and the summers at their "cottage" at Beverly Farms were among Holmes's fondest memories. Those who knew the justice best were fully aware of the impact Fanny's death would have on him; as one close friend wrote: "Her quick and vivid perception, her keen wit and vigorous judgment, and the originality and charm of her character cannot be forgotten by anyone who knew her. It is impossible to think of Justice Holmes without thinking of her also; her effect on his life and career can neither be omitted nor measured in any account of him."[22] Holmes was lost without his constant companion of sixty years, a woman who many thought to be as extraordinary a personality as the justice himself. As Holmes wrote to a friend informing him of his wife's passing, he recalled the "real warmth of her spirit which she did her best to hide," and the "true generosity in her sympathy for those who needed it." In a letter to Frederick Pollock, Holmes noted that "we have had our share," adding that "for sixty years she made life poetry for me." In another letter Holmes acknowledged that Fanny's death not only took away "a half" of his own life but gave "notice" that his own time was drawing to a close.[23] Unable to think about the practical consequences of his wife's death, Holmes accepted Chief Justice Taft's help in arranging a brief Unitarian funeral service and burial in a plot at Arlington National Cemetery.[24]

The following winter, Taft himself became ill, requiring that Holmes as senior associate justice assume more of the Court's administrative responsibilities. The pressure of presiding at oral argument and supervising the Court's weekly conference soon began to take its toll on the eighty-nine-year-old justice. By the time Charles Evans Hughes joined the Court as chief justice following Taft's retirement in February 1930, Holmes had begun to fail noticeably. A year later, in March 1931, the Court and the nation celebrated Justice Holmes's ninetieth birthday. Considered by many to be a great national treasure, Holmes was also honored by his English friends, who made him a member of the Honorable Society of Lincoln's Inn, the only American ever so honored.[25] Holmes was overwhelmed; as he had written to Pollock some time earlier, "They have said what I longed to hear said and would almost willingly have died to hear twenty years ago."[26] In an unprecedented gesture, Holmes agreed to participate in a special national radio address commemorating his birthday. Reminiscent of his birthday greeting to Brandeis and sounding an old theme that William James would surely have recognized, Justice Holmes contributed his own brief but moving remarks: "The riders in a race do not stop short when they reach the goal. . . . The race is over, but the work is never done while the power to work remains. . . . It cannot be while you still live. For to live is to function. That is all there is in living." Holmes concluded the radio address with "a line from a Latin poet": "Death plucks my ear and says, 'Live, I am coming.'"[27]

Few in the nation doubted that here truly was "a Yankee strayed from Olympus."[28] Could anyone question that Holmes's was a life fully lived or that anyone had ever brought to his work a mightier heart? The dignity of Holmes's life inspired reflection and suggested itself naturally for emulation. The sentiments of the nation were aptly expressed by the chief justice who saw beneath the "judicial robe the chivalry of a knight": "The most beautiful and rarest thing in the world is a complete human life, unmarred, unified by intelligent purpose and uninterrupted accomplishment, blessed by great talent employed in the worthiest activities, with a deserved fame never dimmed and always growing."[29]

Holmes continued his work, amazing those who doubted that a man his age could still manage the Court's demanding regimen. During the following summer, however, he began to have difficulty maintaining his traditional routine. When he returned to Washington from Beverly Farms in the fall of 1931, his associates noticed that the legendary zest with which Mr. Justice Holmes attacked his work was gone. For the first time, he seemed an old man. During the Court's fall term, Holmes's health began to fail, and on 11 January 1932, he informed his staff with understated reticence of his decision to retire by announcing simply, "I won't be in tomorrow."[30] In his brief letter of resignation submitted to President Hoover on 12 January 1932, Holmes observed that "the time has come and I bow to the inevitable."[31] His gracious retirement and memorable note of gratitude to his colleagues on the bench further enhanced his public image. Quietly and without fanfare, Holmes had become a legend in his own time.

Following his retirement, Holmes continued to read and write, maintaining his correspondence with old friends. Soon after Franklin Roosevelt's first inauguration on 4 March 1933, the president called on Justice Holmes and found the old man engrossed in his reading, aided in the task by one of his former clerks, Thomas G. Corcoran. "Why do you read Plato, Mr. Justice?" inquired the president. "To improve my mind" was Holmes's matter-of-fact reply.[32] Even at ninety-two, Holmes never doubted that "self-improvement" was "a better aim than the improvement of one's neighbor."[33] Following a short discussion on the state of the nation, Roosevelt departed. Turning to Corcoran, Holmes said, "You know, his Uncle Ted appointed me to the Supreme Court," adding after a short pause, "a second-class intellect, but a first-class temperament."[34] As told by Corcoran, the story of Holmes's judgment of Franklin Roosevelt was repeated by everyone and quickly became well known. It is unfortunate, however, that Holmes's comment had not been more specific. Which Roosevelt did he actually mean—Theodore Roosevelt who had appointed him or Franklin Roosevelt who had just departed? In retrospect, it is very likely that Corcoran misunderstood Holmes's comment. Justice Holmes knew very little about FDR in comparison to Teddy Roosevelt, and although Corcoran was likely unaware of it, Holmes had made a similar comment about Theodore Roosevelt some years earlier. Writing to a friend after TR's death, Holmes had noted that "he was very likeable, a big figure, a rather ordinary intellect, with extraordinary gifts, a shrewd and I think rather unscrupulous politician. He played all his cards—if not more. R.i.p."[35]

The tranquil decline of Holmes's remaining years ended on 6 March 1935, two days before his ninety-fourth birthday, when he died of pneumonia. Upon being informed of the death of his dear friend, Justice

Brandeis reflected quietly, "and so the great man is gone."[36] A Unitarian funeral service held at All Souls Church in Washington was attended by the justice's nephew, Edward Jackson Holmes of Boston, and by President Roosevelt, Chief Justice Hughes, and other members of the Court. Holmes was buried next to his wife in Arlington National Cemetery with full military honors. In accordance with the justice's wishes, the following was inscribed on his gravestone:[37]

OLIVER WENDELL HOLMES
Captain and Brevet Colonel
20th Massachusetts Volunteer Infantry, Civil War
Justice Supreme Court of the United States
March 1841–March 1935

Soon after the justice's death, his executor, John G. Palfrey, informed government officials that without accompanying explanation, Justice Holmes had bequeathed the bulk of his estate, estimated at $270,000, to the United States. The largest gift of its kind ever made, Holmes's legacy gave rise to considerable comment and speculation. Although not an insignificant sum of money, Holmes's estate was quite small in comparison to the multimillion-dollar fortunes of men like Carnegie, Roosevelt, Harriman, and others. Although some scoffed at the gesture, dismissing it as the act of a feeble-minded old man out of touch with the contemporary world, others saw it as the final contribution of a man who had devoted virtually his entire life to public service. Still other explanations were offered by those who knew Holmes better. "Indifferent to the improvement of others while preoccupied with the improvement of himself," Holmes was not known to have contributed much to any charity during his life. When it came to giving money away, this old Yankee may simply have experienced a "lack of imagination."[38] With no children and no relatives save his nephew, who was already relatively well-off, Holmes may have believed that the government was the most logical beneficiary of his estate. It was Holmes who had reminded the country in one of his less famous dissenting opinions that "taxes are what we pay for civilized society," and who had informed his clerks that he rather "liked to pay taxes," because with them he was "buying civilization."[39]

It is also possible, however, that Holmes was trying to justify his life through this final act. Holmes had survived the Civil War, knowing in his heart that he, like most of his closest friends and thousands of other

160

brave young men, should have died. At least in part, Holmes had devoted himself to a life of duty out a sense of loyalty and obligation to those who had not returned from battle. Through his unexplained legacy, Holmes provided clear evidence that, unlike many of his generation, he had not escaped death and survived the war only to get rich in the following decades. By returning the profit of all his labor, he thus made it clear that he had sacrificed himself to his work in pursuit of an ideal. In a letter to Pollock concerning an "innuendo even if disclaimed" that Charles Beard had made in his *An Economic Interpretation of the Constitution*—namely, that "the Constitution primarily represents the triumph of the money power over democratic agrarianism and individualism— Holmes noted that "belittling arguments always have a force of their own." Offended by Beard's bold claim that the Founding Fathers had acted out of financial self-interest, Holmes stated that he would continue to believe "until compelled to think otherwise" that "they wanted to make a nation and invested (bet) on the belief that they would make one, not that they wanted a powerful government because they had invested." He concluded this revealing complaint against Beard by noting that at least he and Pollock still believed that "high-mindedness" was "not impossible to man."[40]

In any event, whatever Justice Holmes's true motive, his bequest was gratefully accepted by President Roosevelt, who offered his own understanding of the gift and the man: "It is a gift from one who, in war and in peace, devoted his life to [his country's] service. Clearly, he thereby sought, with a generous emphasis, to mark the full measure of his faith in those principles of freedom which the country was founded to preserve."[41]

After his death, Holmes continued in an unusual way to be a figure of contemporary interest. The "ubiquity and endurance of Holmes as a figure of historical interest" quickly began to rival the prominence Holmes had achieved during his lifetime.[42] For those bright young men who came to dominate Washington during Roosevelt's "New Deal," Holmes was nothing less than a hero. His reputation and the influence of his ideas were carefully cultivated by those who recognized the important role Holmes could play—even after death—in legitimating the administration's new political agenda. Perhaps the most significant caretaker of Holmes's emerging image as an "ancestral" New Dealer was Felix Frankfurter, a Harvard Law School professor and close friend of both Justice Holmes and Justice Brandeis, who himself became an associate justice of the Supreme Court in January 1939. In a well-orchestrated if subtle campaign, Frankfurter emphasized Holmes's commitment to the use of legislative power to reorganize society. He also made the most of existing commentary that stressed the "progressive" and "realist" nature of Holmes's jurisprudence.[43]

Other voices joined to swell the chorus of praise for Holmes and for what most now agreed was his new way of looking at the law. What mattered most was not what judges might *say* about the law in their opinions, but what judges actually *do* about the law. Holmes's acceptance of the fact that judges actually make law, even if only interstitially, was seized as justification for a new kind of judicial activism. Viewed from this perspective, Holmes had abandoned once and for all, it was argued, "the fantasy of a perfect, consistent, legal uniformity"; his "remarkable tolerance" was deemed "a mark of high maturity," and he was character-ized by one writer as "the completely adult jurist"—"clear, sane, vital, progressive."[44]

If before his death Holmes had worn authority as the crown of old age, after his death the authority of Holmes's opinions became even greater. In the words of one author writing in 1941, Holmes became "a deity," an "Olympian" who in judgment could do no wrong: "The neat phrase, the quotable line, were ultimates, and beauty of form was com-mitted into wisdom of utterance. For the Court, but especially in dissent, thus spoke Holmes and the subject was closed."[45] No less an authority than his successor on the bench, Justice Benjamin Cardozo, judged Holmes as "probably the greatest legal intellect in the history of the English-speaking world."[46] Regarded by many as "a significant figure in the history of civilization and not merely a commanding American fig-ure," it was said that to have known Holmes was to have "had a revela-tion of the possibilities . . . of human personality."[47] It was not surprising that Holmes would gain a posthumous reputation as "the chief liberal of [the nation's] supreme court" and that in time, the nation would come to believe the "cherished American myth" that Justice Holmes had been a great "liberal" and believer in "democratic ideas."[48]

But even as the myth was taking root, some dared to challenge its historical accuracy. In an unusually direct commentary, no less a social critic than H. L. Mencken wrote that what moved Holmes "was far less a positive love of liberty than an amiable and half-contemptuous feeling that those who longed for it ought to get a horse-doctor's dose of it, and so suffer a really first-rate belly ache." From Mencken's vantage point, Holmes evidenced no "genuine belief in democracy"; possessing "a con-siderable talent for epigrams," Holmes wrote opinions of "widespread and beautiful inconsistency," opinions distinguished "more [as] literature than law."[49]

The harshest criticism of Holmes, both as a legal theorist and as a man, came from a group of Catholic lawyers who believed as a matter of personal faith in the existence of "natural law," the fundamental law ordained by God. Corresponding with the rise of fascism in Europe, their attack on Holmes focused on his open acceptance of ethical relativism and his personal conclusion that in the end, one's values were simply a matter of personal taste. For Holmes, in "the universal struggle of life," force settled everything. Fascinated by the role of power in history, Holmes had rejected moral sensibility as a fundamental weakness. Experience had taught him that moral preferences, like all others, were "more or less arbitrary. . . . Do you like sugar in your coffee or don't you? . . . So as to truth."[50]

It was precisely this heresy that the Catholics zealously attacked. In a series of articles published between 1941 and 1945, they called attention to Holmes's rejection of higher law principles in favor of a jurisprudence that explicitly accepted the right of the dominant power in the community to make the law. Such legal pragmatism had paved the way for Hitler and other forms of totalitarianism in Europe, they argued, and if Holmes's teaching were actually followed, "might" would likely replace "right" in America as well.[51]

Despite the rancor between Holmes's supporters and his critics which resulted from the Catholics' obvious attempt to destroy Holmes's reputation, his influence on a generation of lawyers continued intact. "Nobody who sat on [the Supreme Judicial Court of Massachusetts] in my time," observed Judge James M. Morton, Jr., "had quite such a daunting personality—to a young lawyer. . . . his mind was so extraordinarily quick and incisive . . . that it was rather an ordeal to appear before him. . . . Before the argument was a third finished . . . he had seen the whole course of reasoning and was wondering whether it was sound."[52] Such was the memory of Justice Holmes among those young men who had come of age during the early years of the twentieth century.

During the decade following World War II, however, a serious reappraisal of Holmes took place, one that would ultimately change the way he would be remembered by future generations. Often taking the form of "revisionist debunking," the new scholarship found Holmes to have been "a man arrogant beyond the ordinary, a man of narrow and oligarchical sympathies" whose "indulgence of the legislature . . . rested at least as much on contempt as tolerance.[53] Perhaps more important, critics charged that a serious examination of Holmes's opinions could not support the conclusion that he had ever been a champion of individual rights.[54] Characteristic of this type of criticism was the opinion of a prominent law school professor, Grant Gilmore of Yale:

> Put out of your mind the picture of the tolerant aristocrat, the great liberal, the eloquent defender of our liberties, the "Yankee from Olympus." All that was a myth, concocted principally by Harold Laski and Felix Frankfurter about the time of World War I. The real Holmes was savage, harsh, and cruel, a bitter and lifelong pessimist who saw in the course of human life nothing but the continuing struggle in which the rich and powerful impose their will on the poor and weak.[55]

Such a view of Holmes saw "a profoundly injured spirit," a man who suppressed his own feelings and isolated himself from most of those things believed to give life meaning. Although Holmes may have contributed to "the subversion of an untenable orthodoxy," this emotionally impoverished man "gave no help to the succeeding effort at [society's] reconstruction."[56]

Despite conflicting interpretations of the historical record, the significant fact remains that the life and work of Justice Oliver Wendell Holmes, Jr., continues to stimulate serious research and debate more than a half-century after his death.[57] Holmes himself would no doubt have found such interest in his life foolish. Writing of the relative impotence of judges, he recalled the words of a very successful stockbroker: "They talk about our leading the procession—we only follow it a little ahead like little boys. If we turn down a side street, it doesn't follow."[58]

Holmes once commented that he "used to dream of a final calm under old trees," but had grown to accept the fact that his life had begun "and seems likely to end in war."[59] The experiences of his years, most notably those spent in uniform, convinced him that "life, not the parson, teaches conduct."[60] For Holmes, a man full of "cold, puritan passion," life itself was more like "painting a picture" than "doing a sum."[61] Convinced that it was the pursuit of an ideal that could never be achieved that made life worth living, Holmes noted after Lindbergh's famous flight that "people may envy and belittle talents, but they are called to admire a man who quietly bets his life on his own courage and skill."[62] That Holmes applied such a standard to his own life is beyond question.

In a sense, the character of Holmes's life has had as enduring an impact on his reputation as his judicial opinions or his most important scholarly articles. The last of a long line of Puritans, Holmes, like his father before him, could not get "the iron of Calvinism" out of his soul.[63] "Life is war," he wrote in 1898, and "the part of man in it is to be strong."[64] "The mode in which the inevitable comes to pass is through effort," and for him, "devotion to truth" meant "hard obscure work, not wrapping oneself in a toga and talking tall."[65] Throughout his long life, Holmes accepted the conclusion that "every good costs something," that "the real path is the path of most resistance," and that "eternal hard work is the price of living."[66] Holmes's prescription for success and his advice to those who cared to listen was always the same: "The important thing is how you do your job and not how you think or feel about it afterwards"; "Stop whining—stop thinking you can have something for nothing"; "Have faith and pursue the unknown end."[67] In his farewell to the Washington Bar Association in February 1932, Holmes spoke of the "fire in his heart" which his companions had helped to keep alive:

> Life seems to me like a Japanese picture which our imagination does not allow to end with the margin. We aim at the infinite and when our arrow falls to earth it is in flames. . . . If I could think that I have sent a spark to those who come after I should be ready to say Goodbye.[68]

In the end, the nature of Holmes's legacy will depend upon the judgments men make about the quality of his life. In a world that remembers Auschwitz and Hiroshima, Holmes's acceptance of the role of physical power in history is sobering. His jurisprudence undoubtedly sounds different to the ears of a late twentieth-century listener than it did a century ago, but his willingness to defer to the authority of the political majority remains the most troubling aspect of his legal theory. If contemporary Americans have come to accept Holmes's assertion that judges must exercise "the sovereign prerogative of choice," have they also come to accept his conclusion that all values are relative and that "the best test of truth is the power of the thought to get itself accepted in the competition of the market"?

Dr. Holmes once wrote that "a faith which breeds heroes is better than an unbelief which leaves nothing worth being a hero for."[69] Ironically, it is by this very standard that his son's life and work must ultimately be judged. Oliver Wendell Holmes, Jr., devoted his life to proving that "high and dangerous action teaches us to believe as right beyond dispute things for which our doubting minds are slow to find words of proof," and that "out of heroism grows faith in the worth of heroism."[70] Like the Roman Stoic, Holmes steadfastly set his face against a slack universe and waged war against every form of intellectual hypocrisy and philosophical conceit. But he could not find within his own soul the kind of faith of which his father had spoken. In 1895, Holmes had made an observation concerning the tendency of modern science to undermine "established religion in the minds of very many." Today, his own words could be spoken concerning the influence of his life and work:

> It has pursued analysis until at last this thrilling world of colors and sounds and passions has seemed fatally to resolve itself into one vast network of vibrations endlessly weaving an aimless web, and the rainbow flush of cathedral windows, which once to enraptured eyes appeared the very smile of God, fades slowly out into the pale irony of the void.[71]

"And so beyond the vision of battling races and an impoverished earth," Holmes wrote, "I catch a dreaming glimpse of peace."[72] His vision was of a cosmos not of man's making and a universe measured neither by men's hopes nor by their fears. Like the Puritan of old, it was enough for Holmes that God was working his purpose out—man's place in that eternal plan was not his concern. As Holmes correctly observed, "time has upset many fighting faiths." The question remains, however, whether Americans ever shared the faith of Oliver Wendell Holmes, Jr.

CHRONOLOGY

8 March 1841	Oliver Wendell Holmes, Jr., born in Boston, Massachusetts, the first child of Dr. Oliver Wendell Holmes.
1847–1851	Attends Mr. Sullivan's Park Street School.
September 1851	Enters Epes Dixwell's private Latin school to prepare for Harvard College.
August 1857	Moves with his family from 8 Montgomery Place to 21 Charles Street.
September 1857	Matriculates at Harvard College.
June 1860	Is invited to become a member of Phi Beta Kappa.
October 1860	Harvard's *University Quarterly* publishes Holmes's article on Plato; selected as the best essay submitted by an undergraduate. Article on Albert Dürer published by *Harvard Magazine,* of which Holmes is an editor.
25 April 1861	Ten days after the fall of Fort Sumter, leaves Harvard and reports for military duty in the New England Guard; sent to drill with the Fourth Battalion on Castle Island in Boston Harbor.
21 June 1861	Participates in Class Day exercises as class poet and takes degree from Harvard College.
10 July 1861	Receives commission from Governor John Andrew as first lieutenant in the Twentieth Massachusetts Volunteers.
22 August 1861	Joins regiment at Camp Massasoit, near Readville, Massachusetts.

September 1861	Moves south with unit and camps near Poolesville, Maryland.
21 October 1861	Seriously wounded at the Battle of Ball's Bluff, Virginia.
8 March 1862	Celebrates twenty-first birthday in Boston on medical leave; two weeks later, returns to unit with rank of captain.
17 September 1862	Wounded leading a charge at Antietam; "found" by Dr. Holmes, and taken home to convalesce.
3 May 1863	Receives serious shrapnel wound in his heel at Marye's Heights near Fredericksburg, Virginia.
29 January 1864	Joins Gen. Horatio Wright's command as his aide-de-camp.
17 July 1864	Receives final discharge orders, having achieved the rank of brevet lieutenant colonel.
September 1864	After a period of indecision, enrolls in Harvard Law School.
December 1865	Withdraws from Harvard Law School and reads law in the office of Robert Morse, a prominent Boston attorney.
April 1866	Sails for a "grand tour" of Britain and the Continent.
30 June 1866	Harvard Law School awards Holmes degree; satisfies requirements prior to departure for England, and is not present at commencement.
October 1866	Prepares for bar exam as law clerk for George Otis Shattuck.
January 1867	First of several articles for *American Law Review* is published.
4 March 1867	Is admitted to the bar and commences the practice of law.
14 November 1867	Argues first case before the Supreme Judicial Court of Massachusetts.
January 1870	Invited to lecture on constitutional law at Harvard College.
November 1870	Moves with family to 296 Beacon Street. Leaves Chandler, Shattuck, and Thayer to open law office with brother and Issac Hogue. Accepts position of coeditor of *American Law Review.*

13 March 1872	Announces engagement to Fanny Dixwell.
17 June 1872	Marries Fanny Dixwell at Christ Church in Cambridge, Massachusetts.
March 1873	Joins old mentor by becoming a partner in Shattuck, Holmes, and Munroe.
December 1873	Publishes new edition of *Kent's Commentaries*. Purchases summer home on Buzzard's Bay.
Summer 1874	Travels with wife to England; commences lifelong friendship with Frederick Pollock.
September 1874	Returns from England and moves to 10 Beacon Street.
August 1877	Engrossed in practice of law, argues the case of *New Orleans Mutual Insurance Company* before Justice Nathan Clifford.
October 1878	Prepares and successfully argues first case before U.S. Supreme Court, *United States* v. *Ames*.
November 1880	Publishes series of articles in *American Law Review*; invited to deliver Boston's prestigious Lowell Lectures.
March 1881	Publishes Lowell Lectures, *The Common Law*, and celebrates fortieth birthday.
11 February 1882	Largely as a result of the success of *The Common Law*, is invited to join faculty of the Harvard Law School.
3 January 1883	Submits resignation as law professor and is sworn in as associate justice of the Supreme Judicial Court of Massachusetts.
Summer 1883	Moves to 9 Chestnut Street.
30 May 1884	Presents Memorial Day address at Keene, New Hampshire.
Summer 1884	Brother, Edward, dies.
June 1886	Receives honorary degree from Yale University.
February 1888	Mother, Amelia Jackson Holmes, dies.
April 1889	Sister, Amelia Sargent, dies; he and wife return to 269 Beacon Street to live with Dr. Holmes.
7 October 1894	Father, Dr. Holmes, dies.
30 May 1895	Presents Memorial Day address at Harvard College and delivers his "The Soldier's Faith."
1896	Writes famous dissent in *Vegelahn* v. *Guntner*.

8 January 1897	Participates in dedication of Boston University School of Law; delivers important speech, "The Path of the Law."
17 January 1899	Presents important lecture, "Law in Science and Science in Law."
July 1899	Becomes chief justice of Supreme Judicial Court.
1900	Dissents in *Plant* v. *Woods.*
11 August 1902	Nominated by President Theodore Roosevelt to succeed Associate Justice Horace Gray on U.S. Supreme Court.
8 December 1902	Confirmed by Senate; sworn in as associate justice of U.S. Supreme Court.
Spring 1903	Moves to permanent residence at 1720 Eye Street, Washington, D.C.
1903	In opinion for the Court in *Giles* v. *Harris,* holds that racially motivated voting fraud in Alabama presents a "political question" beyond the reach of federal judicial authority.
1904	Dissent in *Northern Securities* case ends cordial relationship with President Roosevelt.
1905	Dissent in *Lochner* v. *N.Y.* attracts attention of Progressives.
December 1910	Edward Douglass White succeeds Melville Fuller as chief justice.
1911	Dissent in *Bailey* v. *Alabama* raises doubts about his support for civil rights.
1916	After prolonged bitter confirmation fight, Louis Brandeis joins the Court, and develops close friendship with Justice Holmes.
1916–1917	The government presses a series of antitrust actions under the Sherman Act, to Holmes's annoyance.
1917	Announces in *Southern Pacific Co.* v. *Jensen* decision that the law is not "a brooding omnipresence in the sky."
1919	In series of famous dissents following his opinion for the Court in *Schneck* v. *U.S.,* acquires reputation as great liberal judge. Among most noted dissents are *Abrams* v. *U.S., Gitlow* v. *N.Y.,* and *U.S.* v. *Schwimmer.*

1921	Sets forth view of the scope of the Fourteenth Amendment in dissent in *Truax v. Corrigan.*
July 1921	William Howard Taft succeeds Edward Douglass White as chief justice.
1923	Presaging the future, dissents in *Adkins v. Children's Hospital.*
1927	Reflecting commitment to principles of social Darwinism, writes majority opinion in *Buck v. Bell.*
30 April 1929	Wife, Fanny, dies and is buried in Arlington National Cemetery.
February 1930	Charles Evans Hughes succeeds William Howard Taft as chief justice.
March 1931	The Court and nation celebrate his ninetieth birthday; Holmes participates in radio address to the nation. In England, is inducted into the Honorable Society of Lincoln's Inn, the only American ever so honored.
12 January 1932	Submits resignation as associate justice of U.S. Supreme Court, having served for thirty years.
March 1933	President Franklin D. Roosevelt visits Holmes and seeks his advice on affairs of state.
6 March 1935	Dies at home, two days before ninety-fourth birthday.
8 March 1935	Following funeral service at All Souls Church in Washington, D.C., is buried with full military honors next to wife at Arlington National Cemetery. He leaves the major portion of his estate to the United States.

NOTES AND REFERENCES

INTRODUCTION

1. Philip Kurland, "Book Review," *University of Chicago Law Review* 25 (1957): 206.

2. Ibid.; Grant Gilmore, *The Ages of American Law* (New Haven: Yale University Press, 1977), 66–67.

3. H. L. Pohlman, *Justice Oliver Wendell Holmes and Utilitarian Jurisprudence* (Cambridge, Mass.: Harvard University Press, 1984), 151–56.

4. G. Edward White, "The Rise and Fall of Justice Holmes," *University of Chicago Law Review* 39:1 (1971): 51–77; republished in White's *Patterns of American Legal Thought* (Charlottesville, Va.: Bobbs-Merrill Co., 1978), 194–226. See also White's more recent review of Holmes's reputation in "Looking at Holmes in the Mirror," *Law and History Review* 4:2 (Fall 1986): 439–65.

5. Max Lerner, "Book Review," *Yale Law Journal* 46 (1937): 904, 908. See also Charles Wyzanski, "The Democracy of Justice Oliver Wendell Holmes," *Vanderbilt Law Review* 7:3 (April 1954): 311–24.

6. White, *Patterns of American Legal Thought*, 194.

7. Yosal Rogat, "The Judge as Spectator," *University of Chicago Law Review* 31:2 (Winter 1964): 213, 230.

8. Ibid., 256.

9. James B. Peabody, ed. *Holmes-Einstein Letters* (London: Macmillan, 1964), 349. Holmes's letter of 30 September 1932 referred to Silas Bent's recently published *Justice Oliver Wendell Holmes.*

10. Mark DeWolfe Howe, *Justice Oliver Wendell Holmes, Jr.: The Shaping Years, 1841–1870* (Cambridge, Mass.: Harvard University Press, Belknap Press, 1957), vi.

11. Oliver Wendell Holmes, Jr., "Walbridge Abner Field," *Speeches* (Boston: Little, Brown & Co., 1913), 79.

12. Dr. Holmes's comment from *The Poet of the Breakfast-Table* is quoted

172

in Mark A. DeWolfe Howe's *Holmes of the Breakfast-Table* (New York: Oxford University Press, 1939), 6.

CHAPTER 1

1. Holmes is quoted in Mark DeWolfe Howe, *Justice Oliver Wendell Holmes: The Shaping Years, 1841–1870* (Cambridge, Mass.: Harvard University Press, Belknap Press 1957), 15–16.

2. Ibid.

3. John T. Morse, *The Life and Letters of Oliver Wendell Holmes* (Boston: Houghton, Mifflin & Co., 1896), 1:322; quoted in Howe, *The Shaping Years*, 1:23. See also Silas Bent, *Justice Oliver Wendell Holmes* (New York: Vanguard Press, 1932), 24; and Catherine Drinker Bowen, *Yankee from Olympus* (Boston: Little, Brown & Co., 1944), 81–82.

4. Francis B. Biddle, *Mr. Justice Holmes* (New York: Scribner's Sons, 1942), 30. See also Bent, *Justice Oliver Wendell Holmes*, 25.

5. Biddle, *Mr. Justice Holmes*, 30. See also Bowen, 126.

6. Bowen, 4–8. For useful geneaological tables dealing with the Holmes family, see Bowen, 6, 80.

7. Mark A Howe, *Holmes of the Breakfast-Table* (New York: Oxford University Press, 1939), 9.

8. Bowen, 8.

9. Ibid., 4, 8–11.

10. Bent, 26–27; Bowen, 15.

11. Bowen, 14.

12. Eleanor M. Tilton, *Amiable Autocrat: A Biography of Dr. Oliver Wendell Holmes* (New York: Henry Schuman, 1947), 14–15; Bowen, 17–18.

13. Bowen, 21. See also Tilton, 4–5.

14. Howe, *Holmes of the Breakfast-Table*, 8; Bowen, 25.

15. Abiel Holmes's correspondence is quoted in Bowen, 44.

16. Oliver Wendell Holmes's correspondence is quoted in Howe, *Holmes of the Breakfast-Table*, 20. See also Bowen, 52–53, and Tilton, 34–68.

17. Bowen, 32–33.

18. Abiel Holmes's comment is quoted in Bowen, 54. See Bowen, 53–54, and Tilton, 43–49.

19. Holmes's correspondence is quoted in Howe, *Holmes of the Breakfast-Table*, 21.

20. Quoted from the Riverside Edition of *The Writings of Oliver Wendell Holmes* (Boston: Houghton Co., 1891), 11:2. See also Howe, *Holmes of the Breakfast-Table*, 24.

21. Holmes's correspondence is quoted in Howe, *Holmes of the Breakfast-Table*, 21.

22. Howe, *Holmes of the Breakfast-Table*, 32–33; Bowen, 59–62; and Tilton, 69–80.

23. Howe, *Holmes of the Breakfast-Table*, 34–35; Bowen, 65–66; and Tilton, 81–95.

24. Holmes's correspondence is quoted in Bent, 31, and Tilton, 97, 100.

25. Holmes's correspondence is quoted in Howe, *Holmes of the Breakfast-Table*, 36–37. See also Tilton, 116–17.

26. Holmes's correspondence is quoted in Howe, *Holmes of the Breakfast-Table*, 37, and Bowen, 66.

27. Holmes's correspondence is quoted in Howe, *Holmes of the Breakfast-Table*, 39.

28. See Bowen, 67, 139.

29. Howe, *Holmes of the Breakfast-Table*, 50–52; Bowen, 69–70; Tilton, 135–42.

30. Howe, *Holmes of the Breakfast-Table*, 53; Bowen, 73–74; Tilton, 146–48.

31. Emerson's address is quoted in Bowen, 76.

32. Tilton, 148–49, 152–54; Bowen, 77.

33. Mark DeWolfe Howe's characterization of the couple is from *The Shaping Years*, 32. See also Bowen, 79–81, and Tilton, 161–62.

34. Howe, *Holmes of the Breakfast-Table*, 55.

35. Ibid., 55–57. See also Bowen, 81–82, and Tilton, 162–63.

36. Howe, *Holmes of the Breakfast-Table*, 59–62; Bowen, 107–8; Tilton, 165–76.

37. Howe, *Holmes of the Breakfast-Table*, 65–71; Tilton, 190, 203–18.

38. Brooks is quoted in Howe, *Holmes of the Breakfast-Table*, 92.

39. Dr. Holmes's description from *The Professor* is quoted in Howe, *Holmes of the Breakfast-Table*, 120.

40. Howe, *Holmes of the Breakfast-Table*, 92–93, 96–98; Bowen, 121–22; Tilton, 233–46.

41. Holmes's description from *Elsie Venner* is quoted in Howe, *Holmes of the Breakfast-Table*, 12.

42. Howe, *Holmes of the Breakfast-Table*, 120–29; Tilton, 248–62.

43. Holmes's comment is quoted in Francis B. Biddle, *Mr. Justice Holmes* (New York: Scribner's Sons, 1942), 24. See also Bowen, 199.

44. Quoted in Howe, *The Shaping Years*, 18, 11–12.

45. Ibid., 19.

CHAPTER 2

1. The actual quotation is from Dr. Holmes's *The Autocrat of the Breakfast-Table*, chap. 6 (1858): "The Boston State House is the hub of the solar system." See also Bent, 37.

2. See Howe, *The Shaping Years*, 13.

3. Quoted from Mrs. Holmes's correspondence to her eldest son in Howe, *The Shaping Years*, 28.

4. Quoted from Oliver Wendell Holmes's correspondence in Howe, *The Shaping Years*, 21.

5. Bowen, 109–10.

6. "Report of Recitations and Deportment," quoted in Howe, *The Shaping Years*, 2.

7. Howe, *The Shaping Years*, 2–4.

8. Ibid., 5–6. See also Bent, 56; and Bowen, 99.

9. Correspondence from Sullivan to Dixwell quoted in Howe, *The Shaping Years*, 5.

10. Bowen, 97. See also Howe, *The Shaping Years*, 6–7.

11. Bowen, 100; Howe, *The Shaping Years*, 10.

12. Frederick C. Fiechter, Jr., "The Preparation of an American Aristocrat," *New England Quarterly* 6:1 (March 1933): 7–8 quoted in Howe, *The Shaping Years*, 9–10.

13. Bowen, 97.

14. Ibid., 103. See also Bent, 47–48; and Howe, *Holmes of the Breakfast-Table*, 79.

15. Howe, *The Shaping Years*, 6, 32.

16. Bowen, 110. See also Howe, *The Shaping Years*, 12, 22–26; and more generally, Arnold L. Goldsmith, "Oliver Wendell Holmes, Father and Son," *Journal of Criminal Law, Criminology and Political Science* 48:4 (November-December 1957): 394–98, for a provocative view of the father-son relationship.

17. Quoted in Howe, *The Shaping Years*, 34.

18. Quoted in Howe, *The Shaping Years*, 32.

19. Bowen, 92.

20. Ibid., 132.

21. Ibid., 124. After 1865, 21 Charles Street was renumbered 164 Charles Street.

22. Elihu Root's characterization, quoted in Bent, 49.

23. Francis Bowen, quoted in Howe, *The Shaping Years*, 35.

24. Charles Francis Adams, quoted in Howe, *The Shaping Years*, 36.

25. Oliver Wendell Holmes, Jr., *Speeches* (Boston: Little, Brown & Co., 1913, 1934), 14, quoted in Bent, 64; Henry Adams, *The Education of Henry Adams* (Boston: Houghton Mifflin Co., 1918), 55, quoted in Howe, *The Shaping Years*, 36.

26. Howe, *The Shaping Years*, 37–41. See also Bowen, 116–18.

27. Bowen, 118.

28. Bent, 36. See also Howe, *The Shaping Years*, 39.

29. Bent, 56, 68; Bowen, 116, 121; Howe, *The Shaping Years*, 40.

30. Howe, *The Shaping Years*, 45.

31. Ibid.
32. Quoted in Bowen, 127; and Howe, *The Shaping Years*, 43.
33. Quoted in Howe, *The Shaping Years*, 50.
34. Ibid., 53.
35. Bowen, 127.
36. Quoted in Howe, *The Shaping Years*, 54.
37. Ibid. See also Bent, 42–44.
38. Howe, *The Shaping Years*, 46–51.
39. Bowen, 129.
40. Howe, *The Shaping Years*, 54.
41. Quoted in Howe, *The Shaping Years*, 57.
42. Ibid., 58.
43. Ibid., 55.
44. Ibid., 58
45. Ibid., 59.
46. Ibid., 60.
47. Ibid., 61–62.
48. Bowen, 134.
49. Quoted in Howe, *The Shaping Years*, 65.
50. Holmes's correspondence quoted in Howe, *The Shaping Years*, 49.
51. Bowen, 98.
52. Ibid., 105.
53. Quoted in Howe, *Holmes of the Breakfast-Table*, 89.
54. Ibid., 86, 88.
55. Howe, *The Shaping Years*, 65–67.
56. Quoted in Howe, *The Shaping Years*, 65.
57. Howe, *The Shaping Years*, 67.
58. Quoted in Howe, *The Shaping Years*, 50–51.
59. Bowen, 137–39.
60. Ibid., 139.
61. Quoted in Howe, *The Shaping Years*, 68–69.
62. Bowen, 140; Howe, *The Shaping Years*, 73–74.
63. Dr. Fenton's correspondence to Dr. Holmes quoted in Howe, *Holmes of the Breakfast-Table*, 101.
64. Dr. Holmes's correspondence to Dr. Felton quoted in Howe, *The Shaping Years*, 77–78.
65. Howe, *The Shaping Years*, 72.
66. Holmes's correspondence quoted in Howe, *The Shaping Years*, 71.
67. Howe, *The Shaping Years*, 74.
68. Holmes's address quoted in Howe, *The Shaping Years*, 75.
69. Holmes's autobiographical sketch quoted in Howe, *The Shaping Years*, 76.

70. Howe, *The Shaping Years*, 77.

71. Biddle, 22.

CHAPTER 3

1. Howe, *The Shaping Years*, 86: Bent, 77.

2. Bent, 70.

3. Oliver Wendell Holmes, *Speeches*, 1, quoted in Bent, 81; Holmes's correspondence quoted in Howe, *The Shaping Years*, 70–71.

4. Holmes's correspondence quoted in James B. Peabody, ed., *Holmes-Einstein Letters* (London: Macmillan, 1964), 90.

5. Bent, 77.

6. Howe, *The Shaping Years*, 81–82.

7. Ibid., 80. See also Bent, 75.

8. Howe, *The Shaping Years*, 82.

9. Dreher's correspondence quoted in Howe, *The Shaping Years*, 84.

10. Governor Andrew's correspondence quoted in Howe, *The Shaping Years*, 84.

11. General Charles Devens's correspondence quoted in Howe, *The Shaping Years*, 84.

12. Howe, *The Shaping Years*, 83–84.

13. Bowen, 152; Howe, *The Shaping Years*, 86.

14. Howe, *The Shaping Years*, 88.

15. Holmes's correspondence quoted in Mark DeWolfe Howe, ed., *Touched with Fire* (Cambridge, Mass.: Harvard University Press, 1947), 4–6.

16. Ibid., 6–8.

17. Bent, 78–79; Howe, *The Shaping Years*, 90–91.

18. Howe, *Touched with Fire*, 6–12.

19. Bent, 79–82.

20. Howe, *The Shaping Years*, 95.

21. Captain Bartlett's account quoted in Howe, *The Shaping Years*, 96–97.

22. Bent, 97.

23. Ibid., 84–85; Howe, *The Shaping Years*, 97–98.

24. Bent, 85; Howe, *The Shaping Years*, 98.

25. Howe, *Touched with Fire*, 14–17.

26. Howe, *The Shaping Years*, 100; Bent, 85–86.

27. Correspondence quoted in Howe, *The Shaping Years*, 100.

28. Dr. Holmes's correspondence quoted in Howe, *The Shaping Years*, 101.

29. Dr. Holmes's correspondence quoted in Bent, *Justice Oliver Wendell Holmes*, 74. See also Howe, *The Shaping Years*, 111–12, and Bowen, 157.

30. Bent, 86.

31. Holmes's "Diary" is printed in Howe, *Touched with Fire*, 23–33.

32. Ibid.

33. Learned Hand's observation of Holmes, quoted in Bent, 18.

34. Howe, *Touched with Fire*, 38.

35. Ibid.

36. Ropes's correspondence quoted in Howe, *The Shaping Years*, 114–15.

37. Holmes's correspondence quoted in Howe, *The Shaping Years*, 114, n. 82.

38. Abbott's correspondence quoted in Howe, *The Shaping Years*, 115, n. 84.

39. Ibid., n. 85.

40. Howe, *Touched with Fire*, 38.

41. Howe, *The Shaping Years*, 116.

42. Bowen, 164; Howe, *The Shaping Years*, 117.

43. Howe, *Touched with Fire*, 49–51.

44. Ibid.

45. Ibid., 51–52.

46. Quoted from Holmes's correspondence in Mark DeWolfe Howe, ed., *Holmes-Laski Letters*, 2 vols. (Cambridge, Mass.: Harvard University Press, 1953), 1:781.

47. Howe, *Touched with Fire*, 56.

48. Ibid., 58.

49. Bowen, 165.

50. Howe, *Touched with Fire*, 62.

51. Quoted in Howe, *The Shaping Years*, 125.

52. Bent, 99; Howe, *The Shaping Years*, 125–26.

53. Howe, *Touched with Fire*, 64.

54. Holmes's account quoted in Howe, *The Shaping Years*, 128.

55. Howe, *Touched with Fire*, 65–66; Howe, *The Shaping Years*, 129. See also Alice Sumner LeDuc, "The Man Who Rescued 'The Captain,'" *Atlantic Monthly* 180:80 (August 1947).

56. Howe, *Touched with Fire*, 67; See also Anna Howard Kennedy Findlay, "Where the Captain Was Found," *Maryland Historical Magazine* 33:109 (June 1938).

57. Howe, *The Shaping Years*, 130–32; Bowen, 173; Bent, 100–4. See also Oliver Wendell Holmes, "My Hunt after 'The Captain,'" *Works*, 8:67.

CHAPTER 4

1. Howe, *The Shaping Years*, 135.

2. Howe, *Touched with Fire*, 63, 80; Howe, *The Shaping Years*, 135.

3. Howe, *Touched with Fire*, 70–71.

4. Ibid., 74; Howe, *The Shaping Years*, 140.

5. Howe, *Touched with Fire*, 70.

6. Ibid., 79–80.

7. Ibid., 74–78.

8. Bent, 106; Howe, *The Shaping Years*, 144.

9. Howe, *Touched with Fire*, 74–78.

10. Ibid., 78.

11. Oliver Wendell Holmes, Jr., *Speeches*, 58, quoted in Bent, 121.

12. Oliver Wendell Holmes, Jr., *Speeches*, 59, quoted in Howe, *The Shaping Years*, 145.

13. Howe, *Touched with Fire*, 79–80.

14. Howe, *The Shaping Years*, 149.

15. Ibid., 151–53.

16. Howe, *Touched with Fire*, 92.

17. Ibid., 93.

18. Whittier's correspondence quoted in Howe, *The Shaping Years*, 155.

19. Quoted by Howe, *The Shaping Years*, 155.

20. Quoted in Mark DeWolfe Howe, ed., *The Holmes-Pollock Letters*, 2 vols. (Cambridge, Mass.: Harvard University Press, 1941), 1:58; Howe, *The Shaping Years*, 156.

21. Howe, *The Shaping Years*, 156.

22. John Ropes's correspondence quoted in Howe, *The Shaping Years*, 157.

23. Howe, *The Shaping Years*, 157–59.

24. Howe, *The Shaping Years*, 159.

25. Ibid.

26. Abbott's correspondence quoted in Howe, *The Shaping Years*, 159.

27. Bent, *Justice Oliver Wendell Holmes*, 115; Howe, *The Shaping Years*, 159–61.

28. Howe, *Touched with Fire*, 106.

29. Oliver Wendell Holmes, Jr., *Speeches*, 100.

30. Howe, *Touched with Fire*, 117.

31. Oliver Wendell Holmes, Jr., *Speeches*, 8, quoted in Howe, *The Shaping Years*, 164.

32. Bowen, 194; Howe, *The Shaping Years*, 167–68.

33. Howe, *Touched with Fire*, 122.

34. Ibid., 135.

35. Ibid., 141–43.

36. Quoted in Howe, *The Shaping Years*, 175.

CHAPTER 5

1. Howe, *Touched with Fire*, vii; Howe, *The Proving Years*, 256.

2. Holmes, *Speeches*, 11, 3.

3. Howe, *The Shaping Years*, 174.

4. Peabody, *Holmes-Einstein Letters*, xvi–xvii.

5. Holmes, *Speeches*, 59.

6. Ibid., 6.

7. See Saul Touster, "In Search of Holmes from Within," *Vanderbilt Law Review* 19 (1964–65): 438–72; and Yosal Rogat, "The Judge as Spectator," *University of Chicago Law Review*, 31:2 (Winter 1964): 213–56.

8. Rogat, 238–39, n. 131. See also Edmund Wilson, *Patriotic Gore: Studies in the Literature of the American Civil War* (New York: Oxford University Press, 1962), 665.

9. Peabody, xix.

10. Holmes, *Speeches*, 6.

11. Howe, *Holmes-Pollock Letters*, 1:29.

12. Holmes, "Autobiographical Sketch," in Max Lerner, *The Mind and Faith of Justice Holmes* (Boston: Little, Brown & Co., 1943), 6, 8.

13. Motley's correspondence quoted in Howe, *The Shaping Years*, 103, n. c.

14. Thomas Hughes's observation quoted in Howe, *The Shaping Years*, 176.

15. Biddle, *Mr. Justice Holmes*, 35.

16. Howe, *The Shaping Years*, 177.

17. Ibid., 178.

18. Holmes's comments to Felix Frankfurter and Mrs. John C. Gray quoted in Howe, *The Shaping Years*, 176.

19. Howe, *The Shaping Years*, 184–85.

20. John Chipman Gray's characterization of Story is quoted in Howe, *The Shaping Years*, 184.

21. Henry James's observation is quoted in Howe, *The Shaping Years*, 184.

22. The observations of Holmes, Henry James, and George W. Smalley— all students of Parker's—are quoted in Howe, *The Shaping Years*, 185.

23. John Fiske's comments are quoted in Howe, *The Shaping Years*, 187.

24. Holmes's and James's observations are quoted in Howe, *The Shaping Years*, 188.

25. Ibid., 187.

26. Ibid., 188–89.

27. Ibid., 190.

28. Ibid., 189–90.

29. John Fiske's comments quoted in Howe, *The Shaping Years*, 193.

30. Holmes's correspondence quoted in Howe, *The Shaping Years*, 196.

31. Bishop William Lawrence's observations quoted in Bent, 139.

32. Howe, *The Shaping Years*, 86, 100.

33. Bowen, 224, 210.

34. Howe, *The Shaping Years*, 199.

35. James's correspondence quoted in Bent, 140; Biddle, 39; Bowen, 223; and Howe, *The Shaping Years*, 198–99.

36. Ropes's correspondence quoted in Howe, *The Shaping Years*, 196.

37. Henry James's remembrance quoted in Howe, *The Shaping Years*, 201.

38. Howe, *Holmes-Laski Letters*, 1:692–93.

39. Holmes's correspondence quoted in Howe, *The Shaping Years*, 203.

40. Ibid., 195.

41. Ibid., 203

42. Biddle, 37.

43. Holmes's correspondence quoted in Howe, *Holmes of the Breakfast-Table*, 36.

44. Holmes's correspondence to Motley is quoted in Bent, 134; Bowen, 227.

45. Motley's correspondence quoted in Howe, *The Shaping Years*, 224.

46. Howe, *The Shaping Years*, 208.

47. Ibid., 223.

48. Holmes's essay on Plato, published in the *University Quarterly* 2:215 (October 1860) is cited in Howe, *The Shaping Years*, 209.

49. Holmes, "The Path of the Law," in *Collected Legal Papers* (New York: Harcourt, Brace & Howe, 1920), 167, 180.

50. Spencer, *First Principles* (London, 1862), 108, quoted in Howe, *The Shaping Years*, 211.

51. Howe, *The Shaping Years*, 212.

52. Ibid., 212–14.

53. Holmes, *New York Trust Co. v. Eisner*, 256 U.S. 345, 349 (1921).

54. Dr. Holmes's article in the *Atlantic Monthly* (June 1859) is quoted in Howe, *Holmes of the Breakfast-Table*, 117.

55. Holmes's diary quoted in Howe, *The Shaping Years*, 224.

56. Ibid.

57. The exchange is quoted in Bowen, 227–28.

58. Holmes's observation is quoted in Howe, *The Shaping Years*, 225.

59. Ibid., 226.

60. Holmes's correspondence quoted in Howe, *The Shaping Years*, 229–30.

61. Howe, *The Shaping Years*, 233.

62. Holmes's note is quoted in Howe, *The Shaping Years*, 232.

63. Barry Cornwall's correspondence to James T. Fields of Boston is quoted in Howe, *The Shaping Years*, 229.

64. Holmes's diary entry is quoted in Howe, *The Shaping Years*, 227.

65. Stephen's comment is quoted in Howe, *The Shaping Years*, 213.

66. Howe, *Holmes-Pollock Letters*, 1:105.

67. Howe, *Holmes-Laski Letters*, 2:862.

68. Russell, *Religion and Science* (London, 1935), 250, quoted in Howe, *The Shaping Years*, 214.

69. Howe, *The Shaping Years*, 228–29.

70. Ibid., 233–34.

71. Ibid., 234–35.

72. Holmes's diary entry is quoted in Howe, *The Shaping Years*, 236.

73. Ibid., 238.

74. Ibid., 237.

75. Stephen's correspondence is quoted in Howe, *The Shaping Years*, 238.

76. Holmes's correspondence is quoted in Howe, *Touched with Fire*, 122, n. 1.

77. Ibid., 135.

78. Peabody, *Holmes-Einstein Letters*, 36.

79. Holmes's diary entry is quoted in Howe, *The Shaping Years*, 240.

80. Ibid.

81. Howe, *Holmes-Laski Letters*, 2:905.

82. Holmes, *Speeches*, 20.

83. Holmes's diary entry is quoted in Howe, *The Shaping Years*, 240.

84. Ibid., 241.

85. Ibid., 243

86. Ibid., 241.

87. Howe, *The Shaping Years*, 243.

CHAPTER 6

1. Holmes's diary entry quoted in Howe, *The Shaping Years*, 245.

2. C. T. Russell's comment is quoted in Howe, *The Shaping Years*, 245.

3. Howe, *The Shaping Years*, 248.

4. Holmes, *Proc. Mass. Hist. Soc.*, 2d ser., 14:361, 368 (1900), quoted in Howe, *The Shaping Years*, 250.

5. Ibid.

6. Holmes, *Speeches*, 73.

7. Howe, *The Shaping Years*, 246.

8. Ibid., 258.

9. Ibid., 262.

10. Holmes's diary entry is quoted in Howe, *The Shaping Years*, 260.

11. Howe, *The Shaping Years*, 260.

12. Ibid., 261.

13. Ibid., 263.

14. Holmes's diary entries are quoted in Howe, *The Shaping Years*, 263–64. See also Bowen, 236.

15. Professor Washburn's comment is quoted in Bowen, 241.

16. Howe, *The Shaping Years*, 265, 277.

17. Holmes, *American Law Review* 1:377 (January 1867), quoted in Howe, *The Shaping Years*, 271.

18. Holmes, "The Path of the Law," in *Collected Legal Papers*, 173; *American Banana Company v. United Fruit Company*, 213 U.S. 347, 366 (1909).

19. Holmes, *American Law Review* 1:554 (April 1867), quoted in Howe, *The Shaping Years*, 273.

20. Holmes, *Southern Pacific Railway Company v. Jensen*, 244 U. S. 205, 22 (1917).

21. Justice Hoar's correspondence and majority opinion are quoted in Howe, *The Shaping Years*, 275.

22. Howe, *The Shaping Years*, 253–54.

23. Arthur D. Hill's comment is quoted in Howe, *The Shaping Years*, 255.

24. Bowen, 210; Howe, *The Shaping Years*, 251.

25. James's correspondence quoted in Howe, *The Shaping Years*, 201.

26. James's correspondence quoted in Biddle, 40.

27. Howe, *The Shaping Years*, 253.

28. Bowen, 241. James's correspondence is quoted in Biddle, 40–41; Bent, 58–59; and Bowen, 241–48.

29. Holmes's correspondence is quoted in Bowen, 247.

30. James's correspondence is quoted in Biddle, 47.

31. Ibid., 48–49.

32. Ibid., 49–50. See also Howe, *The Shaping Years*, 282.

33. James's correspondence quoted in Howe, *The Shaping Years*, 275, n. 92.

34. Mrs. Holmes's comment concerning her son is quoted in Howe, *The Shaping Years*, 280.

35. Holmes's correspondence is quoted in Howe, *The Shaping Years*, 252.

36. Sedgewick's correspondence to Henry James is quoted in Howe, *The Shaping Years*, 273.

37. Ropes's comment to James, and James's response are quoted in Howe, *The Shaping Years*, 273–74.

38. Tilton, 304.

39. Bowen, 254–55.

40. Ibid., 259.

41. Bent, 65. See also Howe, *The Shaping Years*, 269, and *The Proving Years*, 4.

42. Howe, *The Shaping Years*, 201–3.

43. Howe, *The Proving Years*, 27, 61.

44. Holmes's correspondence is quoted in Howe, *The Proving Years*, 31.

45. Howe, *The Proving Years*, 12–13.

46. Thayer's memorandum is quoted in Howe, *The Proving Years*, 13–14.

47. Howe, *The Proving Years*, 21.

48. Mrs. James's correspondence to her son Henry is quoted in Howe, *The Proving Years*, 10.

49. Dr. Holmes's article is quoted in Howe, *The Proving Years*, 5.

50. Ibid., 6.

51. Ibid., 7.

52. Holmes, *Speeches*, 73–74.

53. Dr. Holmes's correspondence is quoted in Howe, *The Proving Years*, 22.

54. Dr. Holmes's statement is quoted in Howe, *The Proving Years*, 23; Holmes, *Speeches*, 85.

55. Holmes, *Speeches*, 85.

56. Ibid., 3.

57. Ibid., 96.

58. Holmes, *Collected Legal Papers*, 165.

59. Ibid., 32; Holmes, *Speeches*, 24–25.

60. Howe, *The Proving Years*, 83–84.

61. Ibid., 85.

62. Holmes's correspondence is quoted in Howe, *The Proving Years*, 7; Bowen, 260.

63. Rose Harper's correspondence with Eleanor Shattuck Whiteside is quoted in Howe, *The Proving Years*, 6.

64. Bent, 141; Bowen, 261; Howe, *The Proving Years*, 9.

65. Peabody, *Holmes-Einstein Letters*, 10.

66. Howe, *The Shaping Years*, 200, n. g & h; Peabody, *Holmes-Einstein Letters*, 289; Howe, *The Proving Years*, 8, n. 17.

67. Holmes's correspondence with James Bryce quoted in Howe, *The Proving Years*, 24–25.

68. Gray, *North American Review* 118:387 (April 1874): 388, quoted in Howe, *The Proving Years*, 20.

69. Howe, *The Proving Years*, 23.

70. Holmes's correspondence is quoted in Howe, *The Proving Years*, 100–101.

71. Sir John Pollock's comment is quoted in Howe, *The Proving Years*, 101.

72. Holmes's correspondence is quoted in Howe, *The Proving Years*, 103.

73. Ibid., 94.

CHAPTER 7

1. Bowen, 271.

2. Ibid., 267–69; Howe, *The Proving Years*, 106.

3. Howe, *The Proving Years*, 109.

4. Holmes, *Speeches*, 70; quoted in Howe, *The Shaping Years*, 248.

5. Howe, *Holmes-Laski Letters*, 2:1300, 930.

6. Holmes's correspondence is quoted in Howe, *The Proving Years*, 111.

7. Bowen, 272; Howe, *The Proving Years*, 257.

8. Howe, *The Proving Years*, 125–28.

9. Ibid., 129.

10. Ibid., 253–54; Bowen, 271.

11. Howe, *The Proving Years*, 255.

12. Peabody, *Holmes-Einstein Letters*, 48, 106, 58.

13. Howe, *Holmes-Pollock Letters*, 1:10.

14. Howe, *The Proving Years*, 130–32; Bowen, 273.

15. Holmes's correspondence is quoted in Howe, *The Proving Years*, 8.

16. Holmes, *Collected Legal Papers*, 260.

17. Francis Biddle, *Justice Holmes, Natural Law, and the Supreme Court* (New York: Macmillan, 1961), 20. See also G. Edward White, *Patterns of American Legal Thought* (New York: Bobbs-Merrill, 1978), 195.

18. Howe, *The Occasional Speeches of Justice Oliver Wendell Holmes* (Cambridge, Mass.: Harvard University Press, 1962), 3.

19. Rogat, 230.

20. Howe, *Holmes-Laski Letters*, 1:429–30.

21. Holmes's correspondence with Benjamin Cardozo is quoted in Bent, 313.

22. Holmes's correspondence with John Wu (12 December 1921) is quoted in Lerner, 419.

23. Howe, *The Proving Years*, 136, 157–58.

24. Blackstone, *Commentaries on the Laws of England* (London: Sweet & Milliken, 1821), 1:151.

25. Choate's statement is quoted in Howe, "The Positivism of Mr. Justice Holmes," *Harvard Law Review* 64:4 (February 1951): 529, 537.

26. Howe, *The Proving Years*, 53, 142–43, 146.

27. Felix Cohen, "The Holmes-Cohen Correspondence," *Journal of the History of Ideas* 9:1 (January 1948): 3, 14.

28. James Willard Hurst, *Justice Holmes on Legal History* (New York: Macmillan, 1964), 1, 3. See also Theodore F. T. Plucknett, "Holmes: The Historian," *Harvard Law Review* 44:5 (March 1931): 712–16.

29. Holmes, "Common Carriers and the Common Law," *American Law Review* 13 (July 1879): 608, 630–31; *The Common Law* (Boston: Little, Brown, and Co., 1881), 35–36.

30. Ibid., 631; 36.

31. Holmes, "Review," *American Law Review* 14 (March 1880) 233, 234. See also Howe, *Holmes-Pollock Letters*, 1;17.

32. Howe, *The Proving Years*, 157–58.

33. Holmes, "Review," 233; "Common Carriers," 630–31; *The Common Law,* 1; Biddle, *Justice Holmes, Natural Law, and the Supreme Court,* 75.

34. David J. Burton, *Oliver Wendell Holmes, Jr.: What Manner of Liberal?* (Huntington, N.Y.: Robert E. Krieger, 1979), 3. For a more complete discussion of the content of Holmes's lectures, see David J. Burton, *Oliver Wendell Holmes, Jr.* (Boston: G. K. Hall & Co., 1980), 51–69.

35. John Austin, *Jurisprudence* (London, 1885), 2:634.

36. Holmes, *The Common Law,* 36, 211, 35, 41.

37. G. Edward White, *Patterns of American Legal Thought,* 199.

38. Holmes, *The Common Law,* 44.

39. Ibid., 43.

40. G. Edward White, *Patterns of American Legal Thought,* 223. See also Henry Steele Commager, *The American Mind* (New Haven, Conn.: Yale University Press, 1950), 374; and Morton White, *Social Thought in America: The Revolt against Formalism* (New York: Viking Press, 1949), 14–18.

41. Cohen, "The Holmes-Cohen Correspondence," 14; see also Jan Vetter, "The Evolution of Holmes, Holmes and Evolution," *California Law Review* 72:3 (May 1984): 343, 362–63; Howe, *The Shaping Years,* 220–21, *The Proving Years,* 44.

42. Holmes, "The Arrangement of Law—Privity," *American Law Review* 7 (October 1872): 46, 47; *The Common Law,* 111. See also Howe, *The Proving Years,* 75.

43. Holmes, *The Common Law,* 110. See also Rogat, 220.

44. Biddle, *Justice Holmes, Natural Law, and the Supreme Court,* 39; Holmes, "Codes and the Arrangements of the Law," *American Law Review* 5 (October 1870): 1, 5.

45. Bowen, 284.

46. Frederick Pollock's comments from his *Saturday Review* article are quoted in Pollock, "Mr. Justice Holmes," *Harvard Law Review* 44:5 (March 1931); 693, 694; Biddle, *Justice Holmes, Natural Law and the Supreme Court,* 13; G. Edward White, *Patterns of American Legal Thought,* 199.

47. *Atlantic Monthly* 55 (1885): 302, 307–8.

48. Howe, *The Proving Years,* 260–62.

49. Ibid., 263–64.

50. Bowen, 291.

51. Howe, *The Proving Years,* 261–62.

52. Ibid., 272.

53. Ibid., 266–68.

54. Holmes's correspondence with James Bryce is quoted in Howe, *The Proving Years,* 280.

55. Holmes's correspondence with Felix Frankfurter is quoted in Howe, *The Shaping Years,* 282.

56. William James's correspondence is quoted in Howe, *The Shaping Years*, 282; *The Proving Years*, 50.

57. Elizabeth Shepley Sergeant, "Justice Touched with Fire," in Frankfurter, ed. *Mr. Justice Holmes* (New York: Coward-McCann, 1931), 183, 201.

58. Howe, *Holmes-Laski Letters*, 2:1019. See also Howe, *The Proving Years*, 258.

59. Bowen, 297.

60. Biddle, *Mr. Justice Holmes*, 50; Bent, 139.

61. Adams's note to Holmes is quoted in Rogat, 233.

62. Dr. Holmes's correspondence is quoted in Lerner, xxviii. See also Bowen, 298–306.

63. Howe, *Holmes-Pollock Letters*, 1:26, 20, 22. See Mark Tushnet, "The Logic of Experience: Oliver Wendell Holmes on the Supreme Judicial Court," *Virginia Law Review* 63 (1977): 975, 977–82.

64. Bowen, 304–5.

65. Biddle, *Mr. Justice Holmes*, 70–75.

66. *Cook v. Merrifield,*, 139 Mass. 139, 141 (1885).

67. Bowen, 309.

68. Howe, *Holmes of the Breakfast-Table*, 151.

69. Dr. Holmes's correspondence is quoted in Howe, *Holmes of the Breakfast-Table*, 147–49.

70. Bowen, 315.

71. Ibid., 314; Biddle, *Mr. Justice Holmes*, 72.

72. Biddle, *Mr. Justice Holmes*, 73.

73. Bowen, 317.

74. Howe, *Holmes-Pollock Letters*, 1:34, 42.

75. Holmes, "Daniel S. Richardson," *Speeches*, 46, 47.

76. Holmes, "Anonymity and Achievement," *Occasional Speeches*, 59.

77. Holmes, "Sidney Bartlett," *Speeches*, 41, 42; Wilson, *Patriotic Gore*, 635, 648.

78. Howe, *Holmes-Pollock Letters*, 1:35.

79. *Commonwealth v. Perry*, 155 Mass. 117, 124–25 (1891).

80. *McAuliffe v. New Bedford*, 155 Mass. 216, 216 (1892).

81. *Commonwealth v. Davis*, 162 Mass. 510, 510 (1895).

82. *Vegelahn v. Guntner*, 167 Mass. 92, 97, 108 (1896).

83. Howe, *Holmes of the Breakfast-Table*, 158.

84. Biddle, *Mr. Justice Holmes*, 78.

85. Bowen, 324–27.

86. Ibid., 335.

87. Tushnet, 981.

88. Hiller B. Zobel, "Enlisted for Life," *American Heritage* 37 (June-July 1986): 57, 63.

89. Howe, *The Proving Years*, 257.

90. Zobel, 63–64.

91. Holmes, "The Soldier's Faith," *Speeches*, 56, 62.

92. Ibid., 62–63.

93. Ibid., 59.

94. Ibid., 58–59.

95. Tushnet, 1023–25; 1046–52.

96. Holmes, "The Path of the Law," *Collected Legal Papers*, 167, 173.

97. *American Banana Company v. United Fruit Company*, 213 U.S. 347, 356 (1909).

98. Holmes, "The Path of the Law," 171.

99. Ibid., 181.

100. This observation was made by Mark Howe about Holmes's "The Path of the Law," but it applies as well to "Law in Science and Science in Law." See Howe, "The Positivism of Mr. Justice Holmes," *Harvard Law Review* 64:4 (February 1951): 529, 540.

101. Holmes, "Learning and Science," *Collected Legal Papers*, 138, 138–39.

102. Ibid. See also Holmes's opinion in *Southern Pacific Co. v. Jensen*, 244 U.S. 205, 218, 220 (1917).

103. Holmes, "Law in Science and Science in Law," *Collected Legal Papers*, 210, 225, 239.

104. Bowen, 335.

105. Howe, *Holmes-Pollock Letters*, 1:98.

106. Holmes, "Speech to the Suffolk Bar," *Speeches*, 83.

107. Ibid.

108. Ibid., 85.

109. James's correspondence is quoted in Lerner, 405.

110. Ibid.

111. Tushnet, 986.

112. *Stack v. New York, New Haven & Hartford Railroad*, 177 Mass. 155, 157 (1900).

113. Tushnet, 1023.

114. *Plant v. Woods*, 176 Mass. 492, 504 (1900).

115. Ibid., 505.

116. Holmes, *The Common Law*, 38, 41. See also Holmes's opinion in *Tyler v. Judges of the Court of Registration*, 175 Mass. 71, 94 (1900).

117. Holmes, "Herbert Spencer: Legislation and Empiricism," *American Law Review* 7 (1873): 582; republished in H. C. Shriver, ed. *Justice Oliver Wendell Holmes: His Book Notices and Uncollected Letters and Papers* (New York: Central Book Co., 1936), 98.

118. Ibid., 104, 107.

119. Ibid., 108. See also Howe, *The Proving Years*, 42–47.

120. G. Edward White, *Patterns of American Legal Thought*, 200.

121. Alexander M. Bickel, "The Judiciary and Responsible Government, 1910–21," *History of the Supreme Court of the United States [Holmes Devise]* (New York: Macmillan, 1984), 9:71.

122. John A. Garraty, "Holmes's Appointment to the U.S. Supreme Court," *New England Quarterly* 22:3 (September 1949): 291, 292.

123. Draper's correspondence is quoted in Garraty, 293–94.

124. Lodge's correspondence is quoted in Garraty, 295. See also Holmes's recollections in Howe, *Holmes-Pollock Letters*, 2:161.

125. Roosevelt's correspondence is quoted in Bowen, 344; Garraty, 296; and Lerner, xxxii.

126. Lodge's comment is quoted in Garraty, 297.

127. Holmes's statement to Lady Pollock in a letter of 6 September 1902, is quoted in Howe, *Holmes-Pollock Letters*, 1:105.

128. Hoar's correspondence is quoted in Garraty, 297–99.

129. Ibid., 299.

130. Press accounts are summarized in Garraty, 300.

131. Howe, *Holmes-Pollock Letters*, 1:106.

132. Ibid.

133. This exchange is quoted in Bowen, 342.

134. Holmes, "Despondency and Hope," *Occasional Speeches*, 146, 147–49.

CHAPTER 8

1. Bowen, 354–55; Biddle, *Mr. Justice Holmes*, 106.

2. Howe, *Holmes-Pollock Letters*, 2:7, See also Biddle, *Mr. Justice Holmes*, 109, and Lerner, xxxvii.

3. Howe, *Holmes-Pollock Letters*, 1:170.

4. Howe, *Holmes-Laski Letters*, 2:896; 1:693.

5. Howe, *Holmes-Pollock Letters*, 2:175; Holmes's correspondence with Felix Frankfurter (20 April 1911) is quoted in P. Freund and S. Katz, eds., *History of the Supreme Court of the United States [Holmes Devise]* (New York: Macmillan 1984), 9:239, n. 112.

6. Biddle, *Mr. Justice Holmes*, 109.

7. Tushnet, 1010–17; 1045.

8. *American Waltham Watch Co. v. United States Watch Co.*, 173 Mass. 85, 86–87 (1899).

9. *Danforth v. Groton Water Co.*, 178 Mass. 472, 477 (1901).

10. *Otis v. Parker*, 187 U.S. 606 (1903); *Noble State Bank v. Haskell*, 219 U.S. 104, 110 (1911).

11. Howe, *Holmes-Laski Letters*, 1:331.

12. *Missouri, Kansas and Texas Railway Company v. May*, 194 U.S. 267, 270 (1904).

13. *Blinn v. Nelson*, 222 U.S. 1, 7 (1911).

14. *Le Roy Fibre Company v. Chicago, Milwaukee & St. Paul Railway*, 232 U.S. 340, 354 (1914).

15. Bowen, 345, 355, 380; Peabody, *Holmes-Einstein Letters*, 7.

16. Peabody, *Holmes-Einstein Letters*, xxii; Fanny Holmes's observation is quoted in Bowen, 362.

17. Lerner, xxxiii; Bowen, 366.

18. Henry J. Abraham, *Justices and Presidents*, 2d ed. (New York: Oxford University Press, 1985), 69.

19. Roosevelt's correspondence is quoted in Garraty, 301, and Abraham, 156.

20. Howe, *Holmes-Pollock Letters*, 2:63–64.

21. Holmes, "Law and the Court," *Speeches*, 101, 102.

22. Howe, *Holmes-Pollock Letters*, 1:103.

23. The incident is reported in Abraham, 69. See also Holmes's reference to the same incident in "Law and the Court," *Speeches*, 101. Holmes's correspondence with Felix Frankfurter (1 April 1928) is quoted in Frankfurter's "Oliver Wendell Holmes," in *Dictionary of American Biography* (New York: Charles Scribner's Sons, 1944), reprinted as pages 1–35 of Frankfurter's *Mr. Justice Holmes and the Supreme Court* (Cambridge, Mass.: Belknap Press, Harvard University Press, 1961), at 18.

24. *Northern Securities Company v. United States*, 193 U.S. 197, 400 (1904).

25. Howe, *Holmes-Pollock Letters*, 1:156.

26. See Justice Cardozo's assessment of Holmes's style in "Mr. Justice Holmes," *Harvard Law Review* 44:5 (March 1931): 682, 689, and Edmund Wilson's in *Patriotic Gore*, 784. Holmes's complaint was made to Pollock; see Howe, *Holmes-Pollock Letters*, 2:132.

27. Holmes's views are quoted in Frankfurter, *Mr. Justice Holmes and the Supreme Court*, 25.

28. Holmes's comment is quoted in Howe, *The Proving Years*, 108.

29. *Southern Pacific Company v. Jensen*, 244 U.S. 205, 221 (1917).

30. Howe, *Holmes-Pollock Letters*, 2:173.

31. 234 U.S. 548 (1914).

32. Holmes's correspondence to former Justice William H. Moody (30 September 1914) is quoted in *History of the Supreme Court of the United States* [*Holmes Devise*], 9:234.

33. Bowen, 379; Biddle, *Mr. Justice Holmes*, 11.

34. Biddle, *Justice Holmes, Natural Law, and the Supreme Court*, 12.

35. The story of Holmes's conversation with a stranger at a Washington

burlesque house is quoted in Bent, 19. See also Edmund Wilson's comments in *Patriotic Gore,* 774–75.

36. Holmes's correspondence is quoted in Bent, 17. See also Howe, *Holmes-Pollock Letters,* 2:227.

37. Peabody, *Holmes-Einstein Letters,* 94–95, 97.

38. Howe, *Holmes-Pollock Letters,* 1:122.

39. This famous exchange is reported in Sergeant's "Justice Touched with Fire," 206, and Biddle's *Justice Holmes, Natural Law, and the Supreme Court,* 71.

40. Howe, *Holmes-Pollock Letters,* 1:123.

41. Biddle, *Justice Holmes, Natural Law, and the Supreme Court,* 9. See also Howe, *Holmes-Laski Letters,* 1:249.

42. See Holmes's opinion in *Otis v. Parker,* 187 U.S. 606 (1903).

43. *Lochner v. New York,* 198 U.S. 45, 74 (1905).

44. *Tyson & Brother v. Banton,* 273 U.S. 418, 445 (1927).

45. *Southern Pacific Co. v. Jensen,* 244 U.S. 205, 218 (1917).

46. *Gompers v. United States,* 233 U.S. 604, 610 (1914).

47. Holmes, "The Path of the Law," *Speeches,* 167, 187.

48. *Noble State Bank v. Haskell,* 219 U.S. 575 (1911).

49. *Missouri v. Holland,* 252 U.S. 416 (1920).

50. *Coppage v. Kansas,* 236 U.S. 1, 28 (1915).

51. *Hammer v. Dagenhart,* 247 U.S. 251, 277 (1918).

52. *Truax v. Corrigan,* 257 U.S. 312, 344 (1921).

53. *Adkins v. Children's Hospital,* 261 U.S. 525, 568 (1923).

54. *Louisville Gas Co. v. Coleman,* 277 U.S. 32, 41 (1927).

55. James Tufts, "The Legal and Social Philosophy of Mr. Justice Holmes," *American Bar Association Journal* 7 (1921): 359. See also White, *Patterns of American Legal Thought,* 202–5.

56. John Dewey, "Justice Holmes and the Liberal Mind," *New Republic* 53 (1928): 210, 211.

57. Holmes's correspondence with John Wigmore (19 November 1915) is quoted in Howe, *The Shaping Years,* 25.

58. Peabody, *Holmes-Einstein Letters,* 50. See also Howe, *Holmes-Laski Letters,* 1:351.

59. Howe, *Holmes-Laski Letters,* 2:946; Howe, "The Positivism of Mr. Justice Holmes," 529, 545.

60. Howe, *Holmes-Pollock Letters,* 2:36.

61. Holmes's correspondence with Felix Frankfurter (5 September 1916) is quoted in Howe, *The Shaping Years,* 25 n. j; Holmes, *Speeches,* 56.

62. Peabody, *Holmes-Einstein Letters,* 101.

63. Howe, *Holmes-Pollock Letters,* 2:230; *Holmes-Laski Letters,* 1:116, 431. See also Howe, *Holmes-Laski Letters,* 2:1071.

64. Holmes's correspondence with John Wu (12 December 1921) is quoted in Lerner, 418.

65. Howe, *Holmes-Laski Letters*, 1:122.

66. Rogat, 252.

67. Howe, *Holmes-Laski Letters*, 1:16; *McDonald v. Mabee*, 243 U.S. 90, 91 (1917).

68. Howe, *Holmes-Pollock Letters*, 1:126; See also *Holmes- Pollock Letters*, 1:139, and 2:251.

69. Howe, *Holmes-Laski Letters*, 2:948; Holmes's correspondence with James Bryce (17 September 1919) is quoted in Howe, *The Proving Years*, 46; Holmes's comment to Felix Frankfurter is quoted in Frankfurter's *Mr. Justice Holmes*, 150–51. See also Howe, *Holmes-Laski Letters*, 2:950, and an early article on this point, Bode, "Justice Holmes, Natural Law, and the Moral Ideal," *International Journal of Ethics* 29 (1919): 397.

70. Biddle, *Justice Holmes, Natural Law, and the Supreme Court*, 7; Holmes, *The Common Law*, 44.

71. Holmes's comment to Charles Evans Hughes is quoted in Merlo J. Pusey, *Charles Evans Hughes* (New York: Macmillan, 1951), 287.

72. Howe, *Holmes-Laski Letters*, 1:762; *Holmes-Pollock Letters*, 1:163.

73. Howe, *Holmes-Pollock Letters*, 1:163.

74. Howe, *Holmes-Laski Letters*, 2:1144.

75. Ibid., 2:762; Holmes's correspondence with John Wu (26 August 1926) is quoted in Lerner, 431.

76. Holmes, "Montesquieu," *Collected Legal Papers*, 258.

77. Lerner, 432.

78. Howe, *The Proving Years*, 48.

79. Holmes, "The Gas-Stokers' Strike," *American Law Review* 7 (1873): 582, republished in the *Harvard Law Review* 44 (March 1931): 795.

80. *Mayer v. Peabody*, 212 U.S. 78 (1909).

81. Rogat, 221–22.

82. *Nash v. United States*, 229 U.S. 373, 377 (1913), quoting from *Commonwealth v. Pierce*, 138 Mass. 165, 178 (1884).

83. *Giles v. Harris*, 189 U.S. 475, 483 (1903).

84. 189 U.S. at 486, 488. For a full discussion of this case, see Benno C. Schmidt, Jr., "Part II: The Judiciary and Responsible Government, 1910–21," in *History of the Supreme Court of the United States* [Holmes Devise], 9:923–27.

85. Hughes's comment is quoted in Schmidt, 867.

86. Ibid., 862.

87. *Bailey v. Alabama*, 219 U.S. 219, 245 (1911).

88. Holmes, *The Common Law*, 300.

89. Holmes, "The Path of the Law," *Collected Legal Papers*, 175. See also Howe, *The Proving Years*, 235.

90. "The Case of Alonzo Bailey," *Outlook*, 98:101 (21 January 1911): 103, quoted in Schmidt, 868.

91. Lerner, 338.

92. 219 U.S. at 246.

93. *United States v. Reynolds*, 235 U.S. 133, 146 (1914).

94. See Schmidt's discussion at 884–85, 900–902.

95. *Buck v. Bell*, 274 U.S. 200, 207 (1927).

96. See Walter Berns, "*Buck v. Bell*: Due Process of Law?" *Western Political Quarterly* 6 (1953): 762.

97. Peabody, *Holmes-Einstein Letters*, 267.

98. Holmes's correspondence to John Wu (21 July 1925) is quoted in Lerner, 427.

99. For a full review of this criticism, see Biddle, *Justice Holmes, Natural Law, and the Supreme Court*, 33–49.

100. Rogat, 226.

101. *Schenck v. United States*, 249 U.S. 47, 52 (1919).

102. *Abrams v. United States*, 250, U.S. 616, 624 (1919).

103. Holmes's correspondence is quoted in Paul A. Freund, "Oliver Wendell Holmes," in L. Friedman and F. Israel, eds., *The Justices of the United States Supreme Court, 1789–1978* (New York: Chelsea House Publishers, 1980), 3:1760.

104. *Gitlow v. United States*, 268 U.S. 652, 673 (1925).

105. *United States v. Schwimmer*, 279 U.S. 644, 653 (1929).

106. Abraham, 159.

CHAPTER 9

1. Howe, *Holmes-Pollock Letters*, 1:170.

2. Howe, *Holmes-Laski Letters*, 1:846. See also *Holmes-Laski Letters*, 1:339; 2:1227.

3. Peabody, *Holmes-Einstein Letters*, 57.

4. Howe, *Holmes-Pollock Letters*, 1:167.

5. Holmes's correspondence with William James (24 March 1907) is quoted in Lerner, 415.

6. Howe, *Holmes-Laski Letters*, 2:842, See also *Holmes-Laski Letters*, 2:1254.

7. Holmes's correspondence with Lewis Einstein (14 May 1916) is quoted in *History of the Supreme Court of the United States* [Holmes Devise] 9:386.

8. Ibid.

9. Holmes's correspondence with Frederick Pollock (5 April 1919) is quoted in Lerner, 443.

10. Lerner, xi; Abraham, 184.

11. The correspondence between Gray and Taft is quoted in *History of the Supreme Court of the United States* [*Holmes Devise*], 9:70.

12. Holmes, "The Path of the Law," *Collected Legal Papers*, 167, 187, 195.

13. Howe, *Holmes-Pollock Letters*, 2:13. See also Howe, *Holmes-Pollock Letters*, 1:118.

14. Biddle, *Mr. Justice Holmes*, 52. For a fuller discussion of their "mutually nourishing" relationship, see Samuel J. Konefsky, *The Legacy of Holmes and Brandeis* (New York: Macmillan, 1956).

15. Brandeis's characterization is quoted in *History of the Supreme Court of the United States* [*Holmes Devise*], 9:70.

16. Howe, *Holmes-Pollock Letters*, 1:152; Howe, *Holmes-Laski Letters*, 1:176; 2:1347.

17. Howe, *Holmes-Laski Letters*, 1:810; Holmes's birthday message to Brandeis is quoted in M. Urofsky and D. Levy, eds., *Letters of Louis D. Brandeis* (Albany: State University of New York Press, 1971–78), 5: xvi.

18. Peabody, *Holmes-Einstein Letters*, 140.

19. Ibid., 18.

20. Holmes's comment is quoted in Paul A. Freund, "Oliver Wendell Holmes," in *The Justices of the United States Supreme Court, 1789–1978*, 3:1759.

21. Charles Evans Hughes, *The Supreme Court of the United States* (New York: Columbia University Press, 1928), 75.

22. Arthur D. Hill's tribute from the *Harvard Graduates' Magazine* of March 1931 is quoted in Frankfurter's "Oliver Wendell Holmes," *Dictionary of American Biography* reprinted in *Mr. Justice Holmes and the Supreme Court*, at 15.

23. Peabody, *Holmes-Einstein Letters*, 296; Howe, *Holmes-Pollock Letters*, 2:243; Holmes's correspondence with John Wu (1 July 1919) is quoted in Lerner, 436.

24. Bowen, 403.

25. Ibid., 408; Bent, 315.

26. Howe, *Holmes-Pollock Letters*, 2:92.

27. Holmes's March 1931 radio address is quoted in Bent, 317–18, and Lerner, 451.

28. Sergeant, "Justice Touched with Fire," 183.

29. Charles Evans Hughes, "Mr. Justice Holmes," *Harvard Law Review* 44:5 (March 1931); 679; Hughes's comments are also quoted in Bent, 321.

30. Bent, 21.

31. Holmes's letter of resignation is quoted in Frankfurter, *Mr. Justice Holmes and the Supreme Court*, 32.

32. Bowen, 414.

33. Peabody, *Holmes-Einstein Letters*, 240.

34. Holmes's comment is quoted in James McGregor Burns, *Roosevelt: The Lion and the Fox* (New York: Harcourt, Brace & Co. 1956), 156–57.

35. Howe, *Holmes-Pollock Letters*, 2:63–64.

36. Brandeis's response is quoted in Frankfurter, *Mr. Justice Holmes and the Supreme Court*, 33.

33. Biddle, *Mr. Justice Holmes*, 207; Bowen, 417–18.

38. Biddle, *Justice Holmes, Natural Law, and the Supreme Court*, 20; Wilson, *Patriotic Gore*, 796.

39. *Compania General De Tabacos de Filipinas v. Collector of the Internal Revenue*, 275 U.S. 87, 100 (1927); Holmes's comment about paying taxes is quoted in Frankfurter, *Mr. Justice Holmes and the Supreme Court*, 71.

40. Howe, *Holmes-Pollock Letters*, 2:223.

41. President Roosevelt's tribute is quoted in Frankfurter, *Mr. Justice Holmes and the Supreme Court*, 33.

42. White, "Looking at Holmes in the Mirror," 439, 465.

43. White, *Patterns of American Legal Thought*, 209–10.

44. Ibid., 204–8.

45. Walton H. Hamilton, "On Dating Justice Holmes," *University of California Law Review* 9:1 (December 1941): 1.

46. Benjamin Cardozo, "Mr. Justice Holmes," in Frankfurter, ed., *Mr. Justice Holmes* (New York: Coward-McCann, 1931), 29.

47. Frankfurter, *Mr. Justice Holmes and the Supreme Court*, 3; Morris R. Cohen, *New Republic* 82 (3 April 1935): 206.

48. The characterization of Holmes is from an editorial in the *New York Times*, 6 March 1935, quoted in White, *Patterns of American Legal Thought*, 210; Irving Bernstein, "Patrician Conservatism: Mr. Justice Holmes," in C. Strout, ed., *Intellectual History in America* (New York: Harper & Row, 1968), 2:83; Charles E. Wyzanski, "The Democracy of Justice Holmes," *Vanderbilt Law Review* 7:3 (April 1954): 311.

49. H. L. Mencken, "The Great Holmes Mystery," *American Mercury* 26 (1932): 123–24.

50. Howe, *Holmes-Pollock Letters*, 1:105.

51. See generally Francis E. Lucey, "Natural Law and American Legal Realism," *Georgetown Law Journal* 30:6 (April 1942): 493–533, and "Holmes: Liberal—Humanitarian—Believer in Democracy?" *Georgetown Law Journal* 39:4 (May 1951): 523–662; John C. Ford, "The Fundamentals of Holmes' Juristic Philosophy," *Fordham Law Review* 9:4 (November 1942): 255–78; Ben W. Palmer, "Hobbes, Holmes, Hitler," *American Bar Association Journal* 31 (November 1945): 569–73. See also David H. Burton, "Justice Holmes and the Jesuits," *American Journal of Jurisprudence* 27 (1982): 32.

52. Morton's 1937 recollections of Judge Holmes are quoted in Frankfurter, *Mr. Justice Holmes and the Supreme Court*, 16–17.

53. Martin Hickman, "Mr. Justice Holmes: A Reappraisal," *Western Political Quarterly* 5 (1952): 66, 83.

54. See Henry M. Hart, Jr., "Holmes' Positivism—An Addendum," *Harvard Law Review* 64:4 (February 1951): 929–37.

55. Gilmore, *The Ages of American Law*, 48–49.

56. Saul Touster, "In Search of Holmes from Within," *Vanderbilt Law Review* 19 (1964–65): 437, 470; Jan Vetter, "The Evolution of Holmes, Holmes and Evolution," *California Law Review* 72:3 (May 1984): 343, 349.

57. White, "Looking at Holmes in the Mirror," 465.

58. Holmes's correspondence with Pollock (25 May 1906) is quoted in Lerner, 439.

59. Peabody, *Holmes-Einstein Letters*, 142.

60. Holmes's correspondence with Pollock (2 April 1926) is quoted in Lerner, 447.

61. Sergeant, "Justice Touched with Fire," 211; Holmes, "Fiftieth Anniversary Speech," *Speeches*, 96. See also Peabody, *Holmes-Einstein Letters*, 24.

62. Peabody, *Holmes-Einstein Letters*, 269.

63. Howe, *Holmes of the Breakfast-Table*, 156.

64. Holmes, "Edward Avery and Erastus Worthington," *Occasional Speeches*, 105.

65. John C. H. Wu, ed., *Justice Holmes to Doctor Wu: An Intimate Correspondence, 1921–1932* (New York: Central Book Co. 1947), 51; Peabody, *Holmes-Einstein Letters*, 26.

66. Peabody, *Holmes-Einstein Letters*, 88, 64; Howe, *Holmes-Pollock Letters*, 2:25.

67. Holmes's correspondence with Lady Ellen Askwith (3 March 1915) is quoted in Howe, *The Shaping Years*, 227 n. a; Peabody, *Holmes-Einstein Letters*, 75; Holmes's correspondence with John Wu (10 April 1924) is quoted in Lerner, 423.

68. Holmes's message is quoted in Lerner, 451.

69. Dr. Holmes's correspondence is quoted in Howe, *The Shaping Years*, 26.

70. Holmes, "The Soldier's Faith," *Speeches*, 63.

71. Ibid., 57.

72. Holmes, "Law and the Court," *Speeches*, 98, 103.

BIBLIOGRAPHIC ESSAY

PRIMARY SOURCES

Unlike many public men, Oliver Wendell Holmes, Jr., intentionally left no memoirs. Despite his deliberate attempt to reduce the availability of primary materials, a sizable corpus of such documents nevertheless exists. It comprises essentially four distinct types. First, there are the collections of his papers. The principal one is located at the Harvard Law School Library, in Cambridge, Massachusetts. This extensive collection of some thirty-two thousand items includes his correspondence with various public figures, and biographical and family materials of a more personal nature, including the diaries of Holmes and his wife, Fanny Dixwell Holmes. This material, together with a printed guide, is available on microfilm from the Harvard Law School. The collection of Holmes papers at the Library of Congress contains some two hundred additional items, and Holmes's correspondence with Thomas M. Cooley is included in the Cooley papers in the University of Michigan Historical Collections, Ann Arbor. Concerning the second type of primary materials, Holmes's roughly two thousand published judicial opinions are available in the *Reports* of the Supreme Court of the United States, and the Supreme Judicial Court of Massachusetts. Holmes's opinions are indexed in Linda A. Blanford and Patricia R. Evans, eds., *Supreme Court of the United States, 1789–1980: An Index to Opinions Arranged by Justice*, 2 vols. (Millwood, N.Y.: Kraus International Publications, 1983), and in Harry C. Shriver, *The Judicial Opinions of Oliver Wendell Holmes* (Buffalo, N.Y.: Dennis, 1940), a very helpful guide to Holmes's opinions as a state judge. A handy collection of Holmes's most significant dissenting opinions can be found in Alfred Lief, ed., *The Dissenting Opinions of Mr. Justice Holmes* (New York: Vanguard Press, 1929, 1943), and an equally helpful but more general collection is Lief's companion edition, *Representative Opinions of Mr. Justice Holmes* (New York: Vanguard Press, 1931; Greenwood Press, 1976). The third category of material consists of Holmes's own published works. These include his editing of

Kent's Commentaries on American Law, 4 vols., 12th ed. (Boston: Little, Brown & Co., 1873), and his considerably more important *The Common Law* (Boston: Little, Brown & Co., 1881). A subsequent edition of the latter work edited by Mark DeWolfe Howe (Cambridge, Mass.: Harvard University Press, 1962) includes an excellent introductory essay. Howe was also responsible for editing *The Occasional Speeches of Justice Oliver Wendell Holmes* (Cambridge, Mass.: Belknap Press, Harvard University Press, 1962), an assortment of some forty-two short addresses delivered by Holmes between 1880 and 1931. A fuller collection of Holmes's public addresses can be found in his *Speeches* (Boston: Little, Brown & Co., 1913, 1934), which contains Holmes's important speeches from 1884–1913. Holmes's significant extrajudicial legal statements were published in his *Collected Legal Papers* (New York: Harcourt, Brace & Co., 1920), and in a subsequent edition edited by Harold J. Laski (New York: Harcourt, Brace & Co., 1921). Max Lerner, ed., *The Mind and Faith of Justice Holmes* (Boston: Little, Brown & Co., 1943; Random House, 1954), contains a comprehensive selection of Holmes's most important essays, speeches, letters, and judicial opinions, as well as a very insightful introduction by the editor. Another convenient anthology of Holmes's work is Julius Marke, ed., *The Holmes Reader* (Dobbs Ferry, N.Y.: Oceana Publications, 1964). Many of Holmes's most frequently quoted statements, as well as familiar comments and stories told about him, are collected in Edward J. Bander, ed., *Justice Holmes Ex Cathedra* (Charlottesville, Va.: Michie Co., 1966). Finally, miscellaneous fragments of Holmes's written words can be found in Harry C. Shriver, ed., *Justice Oliver Wendell Holmes, His Book Notices and Uncollected Letters and Papers* (New York: Central Book Co., 1936; Da Capo Press, 1973). One important early article that still deserves a serious reading but appears to have escaped publication elsewhere is Holmes's award-winning undergraduate essay, "Plato," originally published in the *University Quarterly* 2:1 (October 1860): 205–17. The fourth category of materials comprises Holmes's published correspondence, which in many ways more than compensates for the lack of a personal set of memoirs. That Holmes took his correspondence seriously is clear from the letters themselves, and as published, they provide a rich and substantially "unedited" record of their author's thoughts and deeds. The earliest Holmes correspondence is found in Mark DeWolfe Howe, ed., *Touched with Fire: Civil War Letters and Diary of Oliver Wendell Holmes, Jr., 1861–1864* (Cambridge, Mass.: Harvard University Press, 1947; Da Capo Press, 1969), which provides important insights into Holmes's development during a very trying period of his life. Perhaps his most important correspondence in terms of legal and philosophical insights is found in Mark DeWolfe Howe, ed., *The Holmes-Pollock Letters: The Correspondence of Mr. Justice Holmes and Sir Frederick Pollock, 1874–1932,* 2 vols. (Cambridge, Mass.: Harvard University Press, 1941; Atheneum, 1963). An equally significant collection of letters that contains Holmes's candid comments and observations about the life of a Supreme Court justice, the business of the Court, and those who served on it is Mark DeWolfe Howe, ed., *The Holmes-Laski Letters: The Correspondence of Mr. Justice Holmes and Harold J. Laski, 1916–1935*, 2 vols. (Cambridge, Mass.: Harvard University Press, 1953; Atheneum, 1963). Less comprehensive but nevertheless revealing is the collection of letters edited by Felix Cohen, "The Holmes-Cohen Correspondence," *Journal of History of Ideas* 9:1 (January 1948): 3–51, which contains an extremely sophisticated exchange marked by both humor and humility. Correspondence with a different tone is found in David H. Burton, ed., *Progressive Masks: Letters of Oliver Wendell Holmes, Jr., and Franklin Ford* (Newark: University of Delaware Press, 1981). Holmes's letters to two of the young men with whom he corresponded more or less regularly over an extended period of time are collected in James B. Peabody, ed., *Holmes-Einstein Letters* (London: Macmillan Co., 1964), an exchange that reveals an older man's attempt to inform and understand the views of a very civilized Lewis Einstein from 1903 to 1935, and John Wu, ed., *Justice Holmes to Dr. Wu: An Intimate Correspondence* (New York: Central Book Co., 1947), a series of letters in which a justice of the U.S. Supreme Court serves as mentor and confidant to an unusually ambitious and perceptive Chinese law student. Perhaps the most unusual collection of Holmes's correspondence, however, is David H. Burton, ed., *Holmes-Sheehan Correspondence* (Port Washington, N.Y.: Kennikat Press, 1977), in which a gentler Holmes is suggested through his letters with Canon Patrick Augustine Sheehan, a kindly Irish parish priest Holmes had the good fortune to meet on one of his trips and with whom he corresponded thereafter. Taken as a whole, Holmes's published letters provide a wealth of material that deserves to be seriously examined.

SECONDARY SOURCES

BIOGRAPHIES

For whatever reason, although much has been written about Justice Holmes, few book-length studies of his life have been published. The earliest, by Silas Bent, *Justice Oliver Wendell Holmes* (New York: Vanguard Press, 1932), is a comprehensive and critical work, but nevertheless one that is seriously limited by its early date. Although the only biography of Justice Holmes published during his lifetime, it is certain that Holmes had nothing whatsoever to do with the work. In another now dated work, Catherine Drinker Bowen, *Yankee from Olympus* (Boston: Little, Brown & Co., 1944), Holmes is examined through a hybrid style which relies on elements of fiction as well as serious scholarship. Perhaps partly justified by the unavailability of reliable primary source materials for major portions of Holmes's life, this still popular account was largely responsible for perpetuating the legend that has overtaken the historical figure. Bowen's account focuses heavily on Holmes's relationship with his father and treats him with more sympathy than an objective examination of the facts supports. Two additional studies—Edith P. Mayer, *That Remarkable Man: Justice Oliver Wendell Holmes* (Boston: Little, Brown & Co., 1967), and David H. Burton, *Oliver Wendell Holmes, Jr.* (Boston: Twayne Publishers, 1980)—provide useful if rather conventional examinations of Holmes's life and contributions; both, however, are limited in their scope and focus. Offering significant insights but again limited to scope is Francis B. Biddle, *Mr. Justice Holmes* (New York: Scribner's Sons, 1942), which is really more a personal memoir and warm personal biographical sketch than a comprehensive study of Holmes's life. Without question, the finest biographical work on Holmes has been done by Mark DeWolfe Howe, whose two-volume study, *Justice Oliver Wendell Holmes: The Shaping Years, 1841–1870* (Cambridge, Mass.: Belknap Press, Harvard University Press, 1957) and *Justice Oliver Wendell Holmes: The Proving Years, 1870–1882* (Cambridge, Mass.: Belknap Press, Harvard University Press, 1963), constitutes the essential starting point for anyone interested in understanding Holmes. Unfortunately, however, the second volume is as much the story of a book—*The Common Law*—as it is of the man. The greater difficulty is that Howe's work examines only the first half of Holmes's life, as Howe's own death terminated the multivolume project. These two majestic volumes have perhaps been unfairly criticized for their lack of distance from the subject, but given Howe's personal association with Holmes, his perspective remained remarkably objective. In connection with Howe's volumes, Philip B. Kurland's review essay, "Portrait of a Jurist as a Young Mind," *University of Chicago Law Review* 25 (1957) 206–25, is particularly helpful.

Fortunately, several excellent biographical articles are available to augment these rather sparse biographical sources. Perhaps the finest is Felix Frankfurter, "Oliver Wendell Holmes, March 8, 1841–March 6, 1935," which originally appeared in the *Dictionary of American Biography* (New York: Charles Scribner's Sons, 1944), and which was subsequently republished in Felix Frankfurter, *Mr. Justice Holmes and the Supreme Court* (Cambridge, Mass.: Belknap Press, Harvard Press, 1961), 1–35. Additional sources of information concerning Holmes's early years include an excellent article by Frederick C. Fiechter, Jr., "The Preparation of an American Aristocrat," *New England Quarterly* 6:1 (March 1933): 3–28, and portions of three book-length works on the life of Dr. Oliver Wendell Holmes—Mark A. DeWolfe Howe, *Holmes of the Breakfast-Table* (New York: Oxford University Press, 1939), Eleanor M. Tilton, *Amiable Autocrat: A Biography of Dr. Oliver Wendell Holmes* (New York: Henry Schuman, 1947), and John T. Morse, Jr., *The Life and Letters of Oliver Wendell Holmes* (Boston: Houghton, Mifflin & Co., 1896). Also, Arnold L. Goldsmith, "Oliver Wendell Holmes, Father and Son," *Journal of Criminal Law, Criminology and Political Science*, 48:4 (November-December 1957): 394–98, explores in some depth the psychological dimension of Holmes's relationship with his famous father and stresses the importance of similarities as well as tensions between the two. Daniel J. Boorstin, "The Elusiveness of Mr. Justice Holmes," *New England Quarterly* 14:3 (September 1941): 478–87, discusses the important contributions of two distinct influences on Holmes's intellectual growth—pragmatism and mysticism. Two important articles that examine the impact of Holmes's psyche on his subsequent behavior as a judge are Yosal Rogat, "The Judge as Spectator," *University of Chicago Law Review* 31:2 (Winter 1964): 213–56, which probes Holmes's personal development and succeeds in placing him in a larger intellectual environment that includes his close personal associates, Henry Adams and William James, and Saul Touster, "In Search of Holmes from Within," *Vanderbilt Law Review* 19 (1964–65): 437–72, which examines in considerable detail the impact of Holmes's Civil War experiences, concluding that his understanding of the role of physical force and his underlying worldview were directly attributable to his wartime experiences. This question is also explored with considerable insight in a chapter devoted to Holmes in Edmund Wilson, *Patriotic Gore: Studies in the Literature of the American Civil War* (New York: Oxford University Press, 1962), 743–96. Like Touster, Wilson finds in Holmes's Civil War experience the foundations for much of his philosophical and literary evolution. For works that also help place Holmes's development in a larger context, see Arthur F. Beringause, *Brooks Adams: A Biography* (New York: Alfred A. Knopf, 1955), which discusses the influence of a fellow Brahmin, and Ralph Barton Perry, *The Thought and Character of William James,* 2 vols. (Boston: Little, Brown & Co., 1935). Two other articles that deal extensively with biographical aspects of Holmes's life are Mark Tushnet, "The Logic of Experience: Oliver Wendell Holmes on the Supreme Judicial Court," *Virginia Law Review* 63 (1977): 975–1052, which provides the most significant study of Holmes's state court service and stresses the extent to which his judicial behavior deviated from his legal theory, and John Garraty, "Holmes's Appointment to the Supreme Court," *New England Quarterly* 22:3 (September 1949): 291–303, which presents a detailed account of Holmes's appointment to the U.S. Supreme Court. Alexander M. Bickel, "The Judiciary and Responsible Government, 1910–21, Part One," and Benno C. Schmidt, Jr., "The Judiciary and Responsible Government, 1910–21, Part Two," in volume 9 of the Oliver Wendell Holmes Devise *History of the Supreme Court of the United States* (New York: Macmillan Co., 1984), provide the most detailed and comprehensive accounts of Holmes's activity as an associate justice of the U.S. Supreme Court during the period 1910–21.

OTHER STUDIES

Other book-length studies on Holmes are also limited. One early work, Felix Frankfurter, ed., *Mr. Justice Holmes* (New York: Coward-McCann, 1931), is a republication of a group of articles, several of which were initially published in the March 1931 issue of the *Harvard Law Review*, an issue devoted entirely to Holmes. Among articles by Benjamin N. Cardozo, Morris R. Cohen, John Dewey, Harold J. Laski, Walter Lippmann, and others is a beautifully written tribute by Elizabeth Shepley Sergeant, "Justice Touched with Fire," at pages 183–211. An article that had originally appeared in the *Harvard Law Review* and was not republished in *Mr. Justice Holmes* is Theodore F. T. Plucknett, "Holmes, the Historian," *Harvard Law Review* 44:5 (March 1931): 820–27, which presents an excellent brief account of Holmes's uses of history. A much fuller and more comprehensive study of Holmes the historian is James W. Hurst, *Justice Holmes on Legal History* (New York: Macmillan Co., 1964). A quite recent work that examines the development of Holmes's jurisprudence in considerable detail is H. J. Pohlman, *Justice Oliver Wendell Holmes and Utilitarian Jurisprudence* (Cambridge, Mass.: Harvard University Press, 1984). Two additional works address the controversy that developed between Holmes's critics and defenders. Francis B. Biddle, *Justice Holmes, Natural Law, and the Supreme Court* (New York: Macmillan Co., 1961), is largely a defense of Holmes's positive contributions to American law and culture by one of his former clerks; David H. Burton, ed., *Oliver Wendell Holmes, Jr.: What Manner of Liberal?* (Huntington, N.Y.: Krieger Publishing Co., 1979), provides a more balanced investigation of the nature of Holmes's judicial contributions. Holmes also receives important consideration in a number of other books, which though not devoted exclusively to Holmes, provide significant contributions. Two of these are Samuel J. Konefsky, *The Legacy of Holmes and Brandeis: A Study of the Influence of Ideas* (New York: Macmillan Co., 1956; Da Capo, 1974), which explores the important relationship that developed between the two justices, and Alpheus Mason, *Brandeis: A Free Man's Life* (New York: Viking Press, 1946), which also considers Holmes from the perspective of his close friendship with Brandeis. General works that attempt to place Holmes in historical and intellectual context include Paul F. Boller, *American Thought in Transition* (Chicago: Rand McNally, 1969), Henry S. Commager, *The American Mind* (New Haven, Conn.: Yale University Press, 1950), Merle Curti, *The Growth of American Thought* (New York: Harper & Row, 1964), Ralph H. Gabriel, *The Course of American Democratic Thought* (New York: Ronald Press, 1956), and John T. Noonan, *Persons and Masks of the Law* (New York: Farrar, Straus, & Giroux, 1976). A more detailed examination of the origins, evolution and importance of Holmes's jurisprudence is provided in Philip P. Wiener, *Evolution and the Founders of Pragmatism* (Cambridge, Mass.: Harvard University Press, 1949) and Morton White, *Social Thought in America: The Revolt against Formalism* (New York: Viking Press, 1949). Although Wiener's expert exposition of Holmes's contribution to a more scientific approach to the law is still quite valuable, White's attempt to link Holmes's work intellectually to the work of Charles A. Beard, John Dewey, James Harvey Robinson, and Thorstein Veblen has largely been discredited. Two more recent and thorough studies are Wilfred E. Rumble,

Jr., *American Legal Realism: Skepticism, Reform, and the Judicial Process* (Ithaca, N.Y.: Cornell University Press, 1968), and Edward A. Purcell, Jr., *The Crisis of Democratic Theory: Scientific Naturalism and the Problem of Value* (Lexington: University Press of Kentucky, 1973). An important article concerning this critical aspect of Holmes's jurisprudence is Max H. Frisch, "Justice Holmes, the Predictive Theory of Law, and Pragmatism," *Journal of Philosophy* 39:4 (February 1962): 85–97. Two other works include extended considerations of Holmes's legal theory and judicial behavior. G. Edward White, *The American Judicial Tradition* (New York: Oxford University Press, 1976), presents a particularly convincing summary of Holmes's historic significance; Grant Gilmore, *The Ages of American Law* (New Haven, Conn.: Yale University Press, 1977), challenges directly the traditional view of Holmes as a liberal, suggesting instead that he cared little for individual rights. Interestingly, both G. Edward White and Grant Gilmore treated Holmes specifically in their respective studies of two important substantive areas of American law: G. Edward White, *Tort Law in America: An Intellectual History* (New York: Oxford University Press, 1980); and Grant Gilmore, *The Death of Contract* (Columbus: Ohio State University Press, 1974). Articles examining similar aspects of Holmes's legal theory include Harry Kalven, Jr., "Torts," *University of Chicago Law Review* 31:2 (Winter 1964): 263–67; John P. Reid, "Experience or Reason: The Tort Theories of Holmes and Doe," *Vanderbilt Law Review* 18 (1965): 405–36; Patrick J. Kelley, "A Critical Analysis of Holmes's Theory of Torts," *Washington University Law Quarterly* 61 (1983): 681; and Malcolm Sharp, "Contracts," *University of Chicago Law Review* 31:2 (Winter 1964): 268–78. An article dealing in the same way with a related topic is Francis A. Allen, "Criminal Law," *University of Chicago Law Review* 31:2 (Winter 1964): 257–62. Without question, however, the bulk of the periodical literature about Holmes deals with the issue raised by Grant Gilmore in *The Ages of American Law*: put simply, was Holmes a positive or negative influence on the development of American jurisprudence? Two important articles attempt to put that question into proper perspective: G. Edward White, "The Rise and Fall of Justice Holmes," *University of Chicago Law Review* 39:1 (1971–72): 1–77 (republished in *Patterns of American Legal Thought* [New York: Bobbs-Merrill Co., 1978], 194–226), traces the evolution of secondary criticism on Holmes over a period of fifty years; an earlier article, Walton H. Hamilton, "On Dating Mr. Justice Holmes," *University of Chicago Law Review* 9:1 (December 1941): 1–29, suggested in a similar way that Holmes's reputation could not sustain serious critical investigation and that future generations might apply different standards of review to the justice's work than those applicable in the 1920s and 1930s. Among the most tightly argued articles dealing with Holmes's legal theory are Harold J. Laski, "The Political Philosophy of Mr. Justice Holmes," *Yale Law Journal* 40:5 (March 1931): 683–95; Hessel E. Yntema, "Mr. Justice Holmes' View of Legal Science," *Yale Law Journal* 40:5 (March 1931): 696–703; and a significant exchange of articles, Mark DeWolfe Howe, "The Positivism of Mr.

Justice Holmes," *Harvard Law Review* 64:4 (February 1951): 529–46; Henry M. Hart, "Holmes' Positivism—An Addendum," *Harvard Law Review* 64:4 (February 1951): 929–37; and Mark DeWolfe Howe, "Holmes' Positivism—A Brief Rejoinder," *Harvard Law Review* 64:4 (February 1951): 937–39. Whereas these articles present a scholarly debate between two preeminent legal scholars concerning the extent to which Holmes intended his jurisprudence to create a schism between law and morality, others are not as balanced. Among the harshest critics of Holmes's contributions are John C. Ford, "The Fundamentals of Holmes' Juristic Philosophy," *Fordham Law Review* 9:4 (November 1942):255–78; Paul L. Gregg, "The Pragmatism of Mr. Justice Holmes," *Georgetown Law Journal* 31:3 (March 1943): 262–95; Francis E. Lucey, "Natural Law and American Legal Realism," *Georgetown Law Journal* 30:6 (April 1942): 493–533; "Holmes: Liberal—Humanitarian—Believer in Democracy?" *Georgetown Law Journal* 39:4 (May 1951): 523–622; Harold R. McKinnon, "The Secret of Mr. Justice Holmes: An Analysis," *American Bar Association Journal* 36 (April 1950): 261–64, 342–46; and Ben W. Palmer, "Hobbes, Holmes, Hitler," *American Bar Association Journal* 31 (November 1945): 569–73. In varying degrees, each of these authors accused Holmes of being a fascist who encouraged a complete divorce of law and morality in American society. Reflecting primarily the commitment of Roman Catholic legal scholars and lawyers to a traditional understanding of the fundamental importance of natural law, these attacks also called attention to Holmes's denial of the existence of a personal god. In addition to Biddle and Howe, both of whom violently rejected this view of Holmes, others attempted to respond to the Catholic critique. Prepared to discard as untenable Holmes's reputation as a great liberal, Irving Bernstein in "The Conservative Mr. Justice Holmes," *New England Quarterly* 23:4 (December 1950): 435–52, and "Patrician Conservatism: Mr. Justice Holmes," in Cushing Strout, ed., *Intellectual History in America: From Darwin to Niebuhr* (New York: Harper & Row, 1968), 2:83–97, argues rather convincingly that Holmes is better understood as a great American conservative who was committed to representative government and majority rule. Nathan Green, "Mr. Justice Holmes and the Age of Man," *Wayne Law Review* 6:3 (Summer 1960): 394–412, also presents a more balanced view of the liberal and conservative elements in Holmes's jurisprudence. Perhaps the most compelling defense of Holmes's dedication to popular government, civil liberties, and the basic dignity of man is Charles E. Wyzanski, "The Democracy of Justice Holmes," *Vanderbilt Law Review* 7:3 (April 1954): 311–24. Addressing these periodic shifts in Holmes's reputation is Samuel Krislow, "O. W. Holmes: The Ebb and Flow of Judicial Legendry," *Northwestern University Law Review* 52 (September-October 1957): 514–25. More recent scholarship continues to view Holmes as having exerted a critical influence on the development of twentieth-century American jurisprudence, even if scholars cannot agree precisely on the nature of that influence. G. Edward White, "The Integrity of Holmes' Jurisprudence," *Hofstra Law Review* 10 (Spring 1982): 633–

72, considers the lasting worth of Holmes's work. Included in the same journal are Saul Touster, "Holmes a Hundred Years Ago," at 673, and Robert Gordon, "Holmes's *Common Law* as Legal Science," at 719. David H. Burton, "Justice Holmes and the Jesuits," *American Journal of Jurisprudence* 27 (1982): 32, takes yet another look at the sources of disagreement between Holmes and proponents of natural law. Yosal Rogat, "Mr. Justice Holmes: A Dissenting Opinion," *Stanford Law Review* 15:3 (1983): 254–89, presents an updated version of Rogat's earlier analysis of Holmes's distanced perspective on human society. Two articles that examine the influence of theories of evolution on Holmes's jurisprudence are E. Donald Elliot, "Holmes and Evolution," *Journal of Legal Studies* 13 (1984): 113, and Jan Vetter, "The Evolution of Holmes, Holmes and Evolution," *California Law Review* 72:3 (May 1984): 343–68. A collection of recent articles on Holmes was published as *Holmes and the Common Law: A Century Later*, Occasional Pamphlet no. 10 (Cambridge, Mass., Harvard Law School, 1983). Included are Benjamin Kaplan, "Encounters with O. W. Holmes, Jr.," Patrick Atiyah, "The Legacy of Holmes through English Eyes," as well as Vetter's "The Evolution of Holmes, Holmes and Evolution." Joan I. Schwartz, "Oliver Wendell Holmes's 'The Path of the Law': Conflicting Views of the Legal World," *American Journal of Legal History* 29 (1985): 235, presents a critical reexamination of one of the most important statements of Holmes's legal theory. A final article of recent date, G. Edward White, "Looking at Holmes in the Mirror," *Law and History Review* 4:2 (Fall 1986): 439–65, argues persuasively that the continuing attention paid to Holmes by contemporary scholars is one clear indication of his ongoing significance as an American jurist and legal theorist.

INDEX

ABOUT THE AUTHOR

Gary J. Aichele teaches public law and political philosophy at Juniata College in Huntingdon, Pennsylvania. In 1973 he received his B.A. with honors from the University of Virginia, continuing there to do his graduate study and to earn his J.D. in 1976 and Ph.D. in political science in 1983. After a year as a judicial fellow at the U.S. Supreme Court, Aichele served as executive director of the Supreme Court Historical Society from 1980 to 1984. He was assistant professor of political science at Norwich University in Northfield, Vermont, from 1984 to 1988 and has lectured widely on constitutionalism, the American founding, and judicial politics. He currently lives in Huntingdon with his wife, Wendy, and daughters Anne and Molly.